Conflict & Prosperity
Geopolitics and Energy in the Eastern Mediterranean

Edited by

Andreas Stergiou, Kivanç Ulusoy and Menahem Blondheim

2017

Conflict & Prosperity
Geopolitics and Energy in the Eastern Mediterranean

Edited by
Andreas Stergiou, Kivanç Ulusoy and Menahem Blondheim

©2017

Konrad-Adenauer-Stiftung/Israel Office

The Harry S. Truman Research Institute for the Advancement of Peace
The Hebrew University of Jerusalem

In cooperation with **Israel Academic Press –**
A subsidiary of MULTIEDUCATOR, INC.
180 E. Prosepect Avenue Mamaroneck, NY 10543

ISBN # 978-1-885881-58-8
© 2017 Andreas Stergiou, Menahem Blondheim, Kivanç Ulusoy
All Rights Reserved

The right of Andreas Stergiou, Kivanç Ulusoy and Menahem Blondheim to be identified as author of this work has been asserted in accordance with the US 1976 Copyright 2007 Act and Israel's תשס״ח, יוצרים זכויות חוק No part of this book may be reproduced or utilized in any form or by any means, electronic or mechanical, or by any information storage and retrieval system without the prior permission of the publisher. The only exception to this prohibition is "fair use" as defined by U.S. copyright law.

Table of Contents

Introduction
Energy in the Eastern Mediterranean:
A Bridge under Troubled Water? 7
Andreas Stergiou, Kivanç Ulusoy, Menahem Blondheim

Section A: Background Analyses

[1] The Strategic Repercussions of the "Arab Spring"
 in the Middle East 16
Moshe Ma'oz

[2] Some Political and Legal Aspects of Hydro-Carbon
 Exploration & Exploitation in the Eastern Mediterranean 32
Rauf Versan

[3] The Eastern and Central Mediterranean Era of Oil & Gas:
 Importance for the European Energy Security 41
Anthony F. Foskolos

[4] A Framework for the Sustainable Development of
 East Med's Hydrocarbons, the Eastern Med's "Triangle
 of Fire" and the Case of South/East China Sea 55
Sotiris Kamenopoulos

[5] Russian Federation's Foreign Policy in the Eastern
 Mediterranean Since the End of Cold War: Geoeconomic
 and Geopolitical Parameters 77
Andreas Stergiou

Section B: Regional Players

[6] THE 'COMFORTABLE' QUASI-ALLIANCE OF ISRAEL, CYPRUS & GREECE 112
Zenonas Tziarras

[7] TURKEY AND THE TURKISH REPUBLIC OF NORTHERN CYPRUS:
A THORNY RELATIONSHIP 139
Kivanç Ulusoy

[8] GREECE–ISRAEL–THE EAST-MEDITERRANEAN:
WILL COMMON DENOMINATORS HELP THE THIRD STAGE? 155
Amikam Nachmani

[9] CAN EGYPT REVERSE ITS DISMAL ENERGY PICTURE? 187
Sohbet Karbuz

Bibliography 213

About the Authors 226

List of Figures and Tables

FIGURES/ Chapter [3]
Figure 1: OECD Europe Gas Scenario 41
Figure 2: North Sea Petroleum declining production 42
Figure 3: Gas shipments by pipelines and LNG 42
Figure 4: Hydrocarbon potential of Nile Delta basin and Levantine Basin, USGS Technical Reports 2010-3014 and 2010-3027 44
Figure 5: Proven reserves of natural gas in Northern America and Western Siberia basin and 50% probable natural gas reserves in Eastern Mediterranean basin 45
Figure 6: Proposed East Med natural gas pipeline to carry 10-15 bcm/year from Israel and Cyprus to Europe. Beyond 2020 the European Union will need 200 bcm/year. 46
Figure 7: TANAP/TAP natural gas pipeline to carry 15 bcm/year. from Shah Deniz, Azerbaijan to European Union 46
Figure 8: Potential of annual natural gas supply from Eastern Mediterranean (Israel and Cyprus) 50-65 bcm/year and Greece 120-130 bcm/year 47
Figure 9: 3,858 offshore active platforms in the Gulf of Mexico producing 1.5 million barrels of oil/day and 46 bcf (billion cubic feet)/day natural gas 50
Figure 10: LNG stations in Europe 50
Figure 11: Total LNG in bcm/year to be delivered www.sigmaline.com/files/download/pdf 51

FIGURES/ Chapter [4]
Figure 1: The Eastern Mediterranean "Triangle of Fire" model 58
Figure 2: Fishbone diagram representing the "effect" of each stakeholder to Eastern Med's "Fire Triangle" 59

Figure 3: Plausible framework for the sustainable development of Eastern Med's Offshore Hydrocarbon Projects 60
Figure 4: Application of the plausible framework in the case of Eastern Med's Offshore Hydrocarbon Projects 61
Figure 5: Michael Klare, The New Geography of Conflict 62
Figure 6: Mark Landler, A new era of gunboat diplomacy 63

FIGURES/ Chapter [9]

Figure 1: Natural Gas Export Infrastructure 195
Figure 2: Location map of Egypt's Mediterranean Sea area showing licensed acreage together with the frontier area west of the Nile Delta 199
Figure 3: BG operations in Egypt 204

TABLES/ Chapter [3]

Table 1: Expected (Possible) Conventional Natural Gas Reserves In Eastern and Central Mediterranean 47
Table 2: Reserves and Exportable amounts of natural gas reserves from Israel and Cyprus 48
Table 3: Proven, highly probable and probable conventional Southern Crete and the Ionian Sea Oil Reserves (Bbo) in Eastern Mediterranean and Offshore 52

TABLES/ Chapter [4]

Table 1: Time and event table for Eastern Mediterranean region 57
Table 2: Framework of the problem 65
Table 3: Potential qualitative variables and comparative comments for the two studied cases 66

Introduction
ENERGY IN THE EASTERN MEDITERRANEAN: A BRIDGE UNDER TROUBLED WATER?

Andreas Stergiou, Kivanç Ulusoy, Menahem Blondheim

The eastern part of the Mediterranean is witnessing some of the most intriguing, worrisome and dangerous events in today's world. It is home to the civil war raging in Syria, the rise of ISIS, the traditionally strained Greek-Turkish relations, the Cyprus conflict, and not to be forgotten, the chronic Palestinian Israeli conflict. The Eastern Mediterranean is also a key route for refugee flows, illegal immigration, drug and human trafficking, let alone ideological and religious movements that are destabilizing adjacent regions. It features weak or collapsed states, direct and proxy wars, and a confluence of great power stakes, all threatening the security of societies and the well-being of individuals and the whole region.

In recent years a new and significant element has been unexpectedly added to the region's troubled search for equilibrium: the discovery of substantial treasures of offshore energy. These new energy resources represent a powerful new economic factor carrying political implications that are affecting the existing delicate, even fragile, balance of power in the region. They raise the dilemma of choosing between competition or cooperation among central players in the troubled region, notably Greece, Cyprus, Israel, Turkey and Egypt, but the play of these nations and the new energy playing field, inevitaby affects the often antagonistic relationship between Russia and the EU-NATO-USA triangle.

The present volume aims to explore the changing patterns of alliances in the Eastern Mediterranean in the context of these energy discoveries, and over the backdrop of the political upheavals of the "Arab Spring". It focuses, through a comparative perspective, on the new geopolitical complexities arising from the conflicts and new alliances that have occurred in the Eastern Mediterranean in recent years. The domestic political changes in the states of the Eastern Mediterranean, coupled with the immense economic stakes raised by the discovery of gas and oil, leave the existing alliance structures under pressure, pushing regional powers to balance each other, seeking new alliances and new strategies.

The recent offshore energy discoveries are widely recognized as a game-changer, in both the global energy arena and in the geopolitics of the region. One of this volume's purposes is to investigate the extent of this change and the range of its implications. In this regard, the volume focuses in particular on the balance of power between Israel, Turkey, Greece Cyprus and Egypt, as well as between the United States and Russia in the wider region. It also considers the potential role of more remote players that previously have not been regarded as particularly relevant. They include the energy producing republics of Central Asia, and China, whose "belt and road" strategy is making it increasingly relevant and present in the Eastern Mediterranean.

Nevertheless, the overall perspective this volume is based on sees the Eastern Mediterranean as a separate "new" region, and not as merely an extension of the Middle East or of southeastern Europe. This analytical conception that stands at the center of the present book responds, we believe, to the needs of the international relations of the 21st century. According to this perspective the region constitutes in geopolitical terms a very specific subsystem for whose analysis different interpretative tools are required. At the crossroads of three continents, Europe, Asia and Africa, the geopolitics of the Eastern Mediterranean does not involve only regional actors but also other actors placed along antagonistic, concentric circles: the United States, the Russian Federation and the European Union. The Eastern Mediterranean has also been a meeting point of east and west, of the economic north and south and of three major world religions: Christianity, Islam and Judaism.

The region also stands at the apex of two important geostrategic triangles: one formed in the north and north-east with the Black Sea and the Caspian Sea, the other in the south and south-east with the Middle East and the Persian Gulf. Crucial to both these triangles is the Bosporus, the cause of conflict going back to at least the Trojan Wars, currently in Turkish territory, but subject to the international regime of the Montreux Convention. This explosive geopolitical complex is well manifested in the numerous conflicts that have occurred historically within the region, provoking fluid and changing patterns of alliances.

The major natural gas reservoirs that have been discovered off the Mediterranean shores in recent years have added to the focusing of international interest on the region. The American Geosciences Institute estimated in 2010 that the Eastern Mediterranean basin, which includes the territorial waters of Israel, the Gaza Strip, Lebanon, Syria, and Cyprus, has 3,450 BCM of natural gas and 1.7 billion barrels of oil. Since that estimate new findings have been added, in particularly gigantic deposits off Egypt's shore. The discovery of these reservoirs in their territory might give countries that were previously dependent on energy imports the opportunity to develop gas fields, achieve energy independence, and even earn money by exporting gas to other countries. But it has also raised challenges, such as competition for new remote markets, attracting strong international business operators, technical difficulties in building the infrastructure for gas exports, as well as key commercial and geopolitical questions alluded to above. One of the most significant among them is compounding the existing disputes and refueling Russia-EU-US energy-competition.

After all, the exploitation of the energy resources has predictably attracted EU interest, given the enormous European demand for the relatively cleaner power of natural gas, as it would allow EU countries to both diversify and secure their gas supply from abroad. This would also coincide with Washington's long-pursued aim of putting an end to Moscow's tactic of using its natural gas exports to exercise economic and political influence in Europe. The monetization of the reserves brings into the game China as well that at the same time has been seeking to pave a new *Silk Road* through the region.

The prospective intra-regional changes in the aftermath of the energy discoveries are no less significant. The most notorious conflict to emerge from the discovery of energy resources in the Eastern Mediterranean is the Turkish-Greek-Cypriot and Israeli crucible affecting the monetization of the findings. Israel, the formerly energy-starved country, is especially noteworthy in this context, as it has come to sudden prominence in the energy arena. However, contentious debates in this country relating to the exploitation of its newly found energy riches, still rages over how much gas Israel will eventually possess, whether it will be able to export it, to whom, and by what means. The possibility of Israel exporting gas to Egypt was considered for a while, but the memoranda of understanding signed between the two countries have not precipitated a final agreement yet. It now appears that using Cyprus is a more realistic channel for exporting gas to Europe, but the new discoveries in Egypt may nevertheless still provide a basis for cooperation in building infrastructure for gas exports to Europe and Asia. Talks with Greece and Cyprus about gas have been going on for several years now, without any real results.[1] It is conceivable in principle to build a pipeline connecting the three countries, but it would be very complicated from a technical standpoint, and would incur considerable cost.[2]

Publicly the three countries have repeatedly announced that they are considering constructing a shared infrastructure for gas export under the EU umbrella; but in fact Cyprus and Israel are competing to export gas to other countries. Furthermore, Israel can prevent Cyprus from exporting its Aphrodite gas to Egypt and Cyprus can prevent Israel from exporting its Leviathan stock to Turkey. This latter arrangement, if not prevented, seems to be from an economic point of view the ideal monetization of Mediterranean gas, especially since Israel and Turkey reached a deal to normalize their fraught relations in June 2016. That option, however, presupposes a settlement of the Cyprus conflict or at least an improvement of bi-communal relations, as the pipeline would pass through the internationally recognized Exclusive Economic Zone of the Republic of Cyprus. Such a unilateral move by Tel Aviv, however, could complicate things further, as it would amount to recognition of the 'Turkish Republic of Northern Cyprus', only recognized by Turkey, torpedoing Israel-Cyprus relations for good.

The Syria War added an additional imponderable variable to the power architecture of the greater Middle East, forcing the great powers to rapidly change their former strategy towards Syria and the adjacent countries and more importantly causing a tremendous humanitarian crisis compelling millions of people to leave their country. The Kremlin decided to undertake, for the first time since WWII, military action in the region. NATO was also called through

Turkey's actions to provide protection to one of its members (Article 4 of the organization's charter). Russia argues that it is acting at the invitation of the State of Syria, represented by the government of Syria led by Bashar Assad. This sounds similar to the US and UK argument that they are undertaking military action in Iraq at the request of the Iraqi government.

Throughout this area, Russia and Turkey have shown their capability and willingness to deploy and use conventional and special forces, often following hybrid warfare doctrine, to achieve limited objectives of long-term strategic importance. The Syrian conflict, however, has turned out to be a war of attrition for both countries. Therefore, Ankara, Moscow and the Syrian government as well as Iran and Syrian rebel groups supported by Turkey felt compelled to negotiate a ceasefire by the end of December 2016, which was adopted unanimously by the UN Security Council on 31 December 2016. Though the deal, which explicitly excludes factions deemed by the United Nations Security Council as "terrorists," is very fragile, it has been the most serious effort undertaken so far to terminate the nearly six years long war.

The Cyprus conflict has also entered a very critical phase, between November 2016 and January 2017, the latest and maybe more promising talks which have been ongoing for the past 18 months aimed at the reunification of the island that has been divided since 1974 reached the final round of negotiations. Though for the first time issues were discussed that had been taboo subjects for decades and maps were exchanged after years again, between the Turkish and Greek-Cypriot sides. The negotiations came at least to an impasse, allegedly because of disagreements on the territorial issue. The general geopolitical environment and the deterioration of Greek-Turkish relations seem to have adversely affected the negotiations. Indeed, after the failed coup d'état in July 2016 an array of incidents have caused serious harm and tension in those countries' bilateral relations. Since September 2016 Turkish officials repeatedly disputed the Treaty of Lausanne, the pact that defined the borders of modern Turkey following the collapse of the Ottoman Empire, prompting response from Athens. In January 2017 the decision by the Greek Supreme Court to reject Turkey's request for the extradition of eight Turkish servicemen seeking asylum in Greece after the July coup also prompted anger in Ankara which organized a maritime operation on the Imia island on the anniversary of the 1996 Imia crisis that had brought the two countries to the verge of war. Though the Greek courts did not examine the acts of the officers during the crucial period surrounding the coup attempt, but whether they would receive a fair trial in Turkey, which also considered the issue of bringing back the death penalty. It is believed that Erdogan appears to have taken personally the Greek justice system's decision. In this context, it is also not surprising that the June-July 2017 UN-backed Cyprus peace talks collapsed, despite hopes of a deal marking the dramatic culmination of a process that lasted more than two years.

The authors of the volume attempt to cover most of the aforementioned aspects, as the book has its origins in a series of conferences and events that were initiated by the Truman Institute in partnership with the Konrad-Adenauer-Stiftung on the Eastern Mediterranean. The inaugural conference in the series (Jerusalem, November 27-28, 2013), titled "A Bridge under Troubled Water? Offshore Energy Discoveries and the Geopolitics of the Eastern, Mediterranean" co-organized by the Harry S. Truman Research Institute for the Advancement of Peace at the Hebrew University of Jerusalem and the Konrad-Adenauer-Stiftung brought together a group of scholars and experts that took pleasure in working together and meeting in subsequent conferences in Israel and abroad.

The book is divided in two sections: A background analysis comprising the chapters by Moshe Maoz, Rauf Versan, Anthony Foskolos, Sotiris Kamenopoulos and Andreas Stergiou and then a section concerning the regional players composed by the essays of Zinonas Tziarras, Kivanç Ulusoy, Amikam Nachmani, and Sohbet Karbuz.

Moshe Ma'oz' chapter concerning the strategic upheavals in Mediterranean and Middle Eastern Countries since the "Arab Spring" touches upon the remarkable strategic changes that have occurred since early 2011 in half a dozen of Arab states along the Mediterranean and in the Middle East, impacting one another and causing crucial domestic, regional and global repercussions. It examines the major domestic and regional changes in the area during these last years, starting with the "Arab Spring" uprisings and their implications, particularly in Syria, and discussing the role of other relevant actors, such as Iraq, Saudi Arabia, Lebanon and Israel.

Rauf Versan analyses the political and legal aspects of Hydrocarbon Exploration and Exploitation in the Eastern Mediterranean. Its contribution is of great importance in order to understand the problems arising from the settlement of Continental Shelf and Exclusive Economic Zone Boundaries, which has been a bone of contention in the relations between the regional countries.

Anthony Foskolos' chapter analyses the importance of the recent energy discoveries for Europe's energy security. On the ground of geological, geophysical and geochemical data, he argues that if exploration and exploitation of the hydrocarbon fields is expedited, Israel, Cyprus and Greece can supply the European Union with at least 188 bcm/year, thus covering the additional European Union gas deficit which is forthcoming after 2020.

Sotiris N. Kamenopoulos' contribution is a comparative analysis of the cases of Eastern Mediterranean and South/East China Seas based on two pillars. The first approaches East Med geopolitics by using a model called "Triangle of Fire" and the second tries by identifying seven potential qualitative variables to check the validation of a model-related hypothesis applied to the two cases.

Russia's foreign policy, analysed by Andreas Stergiou, has been deployed in the framework of the EU-NATO-Russian antagonism surrounding mainly energy and security that has been raging in the wider region since the 1990s. security vacuum opened up every time' should be replaced by the following: 'It is argued that Moscow tried by exploiting the rifts and the conflicts that repeatedly emerged among the regional players in this time to maintain a delicate, low-key, balancing strategy, in order to fill the economic and security vacuum opened up every time'.

Zinonas Tziarras' essay focuses on the axis of cooperation that has gradually emerged between Israel, Cyprus and Greece, mainly since 2011. The chapter has three main goals: (i) to identify the collective and individual reasons behind the formation of the partnership among Israel, Greece and Cyprus; (ii) to examine the challenges and prospects of the partnership, especially in light of developments in Turkish–Israeli relations; and (iii) to suggest that the trilateral co-operation can be characterized as a 'comfortable' quasi-alliance. In so doing, the geostrategic needs of each of the three countries as well as the role of Turkish foreign policy are looked at within the regional security environment and an analytical framework of quasi-alliance formation.

Kıvanç Ulusoy discusses the thorny relationship between Turkey and the Turkish Republic of Northern Cyprus. It seeks to explain the political context that brought Mustafa Akıncı, the ex-mayor of Nicosia between 1976-1990, to power and the possible repercussions of his election as president on the resolution of the Cyprus conflict and to the latest negotiations process for the settlement of the dispute.

Amikam Nachmani gives a comprehensive analysis of the Greek-Israeli relationship from 1948 until today. The author discerns some common denominators in the Greek-Israeli history, culture, politics and societies and endeavours on that ground to explain how the two countries address some daunting challenges they are facing at the moment such as illegal immigration, no effective political leadership etc.

Sohbet Karbuz's contribution is a background analysis of the role Egypt plays in the East Med energy chest. It is argued that the future of Egypt's energy sector will depend on the depth, timing and implementation of government policies. Decisions and choices made today will shape the country's energy future and the ability of the government to convert many challenges it faces into opportunities, as there are plenty of good perspectives for new discoveries.

All the opinions expressed in this volume are the views of the authors and do not necessarily reflect those of the editors who fully respected the freedom of expression of the contributors.

Notes

1 The Aphrodite Reservoir, discovered in Bloc 12 in Cypriot territorial waters, partly extends into Israeli territorial waters. This has been complicating Israel-Cyprus' joint development of the reservoir by delaying the signing of a unitization agreement. Since 2010 the two parties have been disputing the quantity of gas in Israeli territory and Israel's level of involvement in the reservoir's development.

2 A. Mekel, A new geopolitical bloc is born in the Eastern Mediterranean: Israel, Greece and Cyprus, BESA Center Perspectives Paper No. 329, 16 February 2016.

Section A:
Background Analyses

[1]
THE STRATEGIC REPERCUSSIONS OF THE "ARAB SPRING" IN THE MIDDLE EAST[1]

Moshe Ma'oz

People's revolutions, democracy and political Islam

The causes for the Arab Spring's upheavals were similar all over: anger, frustration and antagonism toward authoritarian oppressive and corrupt rulers and regimes. The demands of the rebels were alike: freedom, justice, equal rights, economic opportunities and also significantly democracy.

These demands were made by hundreds of thousands of protestors, men and women, old and young, secular and religious, ignoring harsh governments' measures up to using live fire. Consequently, the autocratic rulers in Tunisia, Egypt and Libya were ousted and democratically elected Islamic governments were established. However, only in Tunisia a moderate Islamic regime has sustained, despite strong opposition from both secular and radical Islamic parties. Its final draft constitution is the most secular liberal amongst Arab countries (except for Lebanon). It is still defined as an Islamic Arab state, but Islam is not the major source of legislation. Women have parity in elected bodies, while non-Muslims are guaranteed with freedom of religion, conscience and expression. In the first coalition, headed by the *Al-Nahda* (revival) Islamic party, secular parties participated and a Jew was appointed Minister of Tourism. In the elections in October and December 2014 secular-liberal party – *al-Nida Tunis* (The Call for Tunisia) came to power.[2]

In Libya and Yemen the tribal and regional conflicts have thwarted the attempts of maintaining functional democratic governments. Libya has been in a state of chaos, while Yemen's government has also been threatened by both Al Qaeda groups and the Shiite Huti tribe. In Egypt the democratically elected

Islamic government (2012) was toppled after only one year in power in late June 2013, following huge demonstrations by mostly secular groups, strongly backed by the army's command. Finally, Syria's brutal dictator, Bashar al Asad, has prevailed in the face of a resistance by religious and secular rebels who partly continue their struggle for a new democratic and pluralistic regime.[3]

It is worth noting that following his ascendency (July 2000) Bashar al Asad proclaimed a new reform program which included "pluralism and democracy," and was labeled "The Damascus Spring." It promised socioeconomic changes, political openness and transparency, and use of internet and cellphones, as well as establishing new universities and newspapers. Consequently, Syrian intellectuals and former politicians created new discussion forums and clubs, while hundreds of citizens signed petitions, calling for freedom of expression and assembly, as well as social and political democracy.[4] Concerned that these democratic activities should undermine his rule, Bashar ordered to close these forums and clubs, and dismissed or arrested many of the activists.

Some ten years later, during the "Arab Spring" events, he crushed with brutal force new calls of Syrian citizens for freedom and democracy. Thus, like other Arab leaders, he has halted the democratization process in this country.

It is true that Arab and Muslim countries have not experienced, by and large, evolutionary processes toward democracy, such as in Western Europe and North America [developing advanced civil societies, human rights, free organizations, press and speech]. Still, even the 1848 revolutions in Western Europe i.e. "The Spring of Nations" and in 1968 the Prague Spring protests did not bring about fully democratic systems in the short run. It is then possible that in various Arab and Muslim countries the seeds of democratic values are gradually spreading, particularly amongst the new generations, bearing better political fruits.[5] Thus, contrary to widespread Western notions that Islam and democracy are incompatible, a growing number of Muslim and Arab countries and communities have adopted various democratic systems during recent decades, for example: Indonesia - the largest Muslim nation, Malaysia, Bangladesh, Pakistan, Turkey, Senegal, Albania, Bosnia, Kosovo, Lebanon and the Palestinian Authority, as well as Muslim communities in India and Israel. To be sure, several of these Muslim democracies have not fully adhered to Western models such as Westminster or Jefferson, and have sustained serious flaws concerning human rights as well as rights for women. Nonetheless, freedom of representation in parliaments and councils as well as better equality and justice have noticeably improved in these countries. And according to Muslim scholars, ideas such as justice, consensus (*ijma*) and counseling are advocated by the Qur'an.[6]

Significantly, the Muslim Brotherhood, one of the oldest Muslim socio-religious movements in the Arab world was founded in 1928 in Egypt, has advocated the adoption of a democratic system in Arab states, but under Islamic supervision.[7] In fact, the Muslim Brotherhood movement in Tunisia and Egypt constituted major revolutionary forces during the Arab Spring upheavals, and were democratically elected in both countries, but survived only in Tunisia.

In Syria the Muslim Brotherhood (MB) joined only at a later stage with the revolution that erupted in March 2011 in nonviolent protests. A major reason for this delay had been the prolonged trauma of the Hama massacre of 1982, when Bashar's father, Hafiz al Asad, then Syria's president, massacred some 30,000 rebellious Muslim Brothers and their families.[8] Another reason for the late participation of the MB was the 2011 rebellion that initially started by thousands of non-partisan and impoverished people, from various villages and small towns in Syria. Only subsequently the MB emerged as important partners in the main stream of Syrian Muslim opposition. They, as well as other rebel groups, have struggled to create a democratic regime for a post-Bashar era, but have been unable to oust the tyrannical rule of Bashar; likewise they could not match the strength and gains of the ultra-militant Islamic groups, notably the Al Qaeda's affiliates, which are definitely anti-democratic.

Militant Islamic groups and their regional implications

Indeed, the emergence or empowerments of militant Islamic groups in the region have constituted another crucial development of the Arab Spring upheavals. They consist of Salafis, not all of whom are violent, belligerent Salafist-Jihadists and particularly Al Qaeda affiliated groups. They have taken advantage of the popular uprisings, of the domestic instability to occupy territories and spread their radical Islamic ideas. Thus the Al Qaeda groups – ISIS and JN – have employed great violence and took control over large areas in the region, such as Southern Yemen, Western Iraq, Northern Syria, parts of Sinai and of Libya as well as along Syria's borders with Iraq, Turkey, Lebanon, Jordan and Israel. Their aim is to establish an Islamic Caliphate and imposing *shari'a* law in the region.[9]

These militant organizations have indeed become in 2014 the most powerful Islamic opposition in Syria and Iraq, overshadowing other opposition groups, such as the secular "Free Syrian Army" (FSA), the two "Islamic Fronts" and other Muslim rebel groups. These organizations did not only contribute to aggravate the Sunni-Shiite conflict in Syria, Iraq and Lebanon. Ironically they have also indirectly helped Bashar to maintain his position as Syria's ruler, amongst a growing number of Arabs, Europeans, Americans and Israelis. They have openly or tacitly adopted Bashar's continuous claim that the alternative to his own pragmatic, secular and stable rule is a fanatic Islamic government in Syria and the region. In an interview with The Sunday Times, London on 5 March 2013, Bashar claimed: "The Arabs had two options, either his regime or Al Qaeda rule...we are the last stronghold for secularism in the region...the entire world must be worried about its stability." Bashar's propaganda strategy notwithstanding Al Qaeda affiliated groups – ISIS and JN – have remained the major challenge and threat to his rule. This, until September 2015 when Russia dispatched dozens of warplanes to Syria and has helped Bashar to sustain his position.

ISIS was created by Al Qaeda of Iraq in 1999; and during 2003-2006 it fought against the American occupation of Iraq. Named *The Islamic State in Iraq* (ISI) in 2006, it has continued combating the Shiite government headed by Nuri al Maliki with the help of Sunni tribes that were alienated by this government. Simultaneously in 2011 another offshoot of Al Qaeda, JN, was founded by Muhammad al-Jawlani, as part of ISI, and subsequently as part of ISIS. In 2013 JN split away but has remained an extension of Al Qaeda, whereas ISIS became independent of Al Qaeda. In 2014 ISIS changed its name to the Islamic State (IS) under the leadership of Abu Bakr al Baghdadi, who named himself the new "Muslim Caliph," namely the successor of the prophet Muhammad. Both these militant organizations are in conflict, but occasionally they cooperate with each other. JN's fighters are mostly Arabs and periodically cooperated with FSA and other moderate Syrian groups. But it also cultivated the militant Khorasan organization, fought against Hezbollah and committed suicide bombing in Damascus and Aleppo.[10]

In comparison, ISIS is more fanatic, cruel and larger than JN. They recruit many non-Arab Muslims and non-Muslim Europeans converting to Islam. Financed with contributions from wealthy Muslims in the Gulf, bank robberies, levying taxes and drawing income from oil sales, this organization has created a force of some 50,000 fighters, including former Iraqi Baathist officers.

Employing open trucks and using semi heavy weapons (they also captured several Iraqi tanks and Syrian fighter jets) they occupied large territories in Iraq, including the oil producing city of Mosul, Tikrit, which is Sadam Hussein birthplace and Falluja, some 70 km west of Baghdad, defeating a disintegrating new Iraqi army. Practically erasing the Iraqi-Syrian border, ISIS occupied also large parts of northern and northeastern Syria, including a part of Aleppo, Tabaqa airport, part of Dayr Azur, as well as several oil fields. IS established its headquarters in Raqqa in northeast Syria and is still fighting to take the Kurdish city of Kobani on the Syrian-Turkish border. This Sunni militant organization fought, persecuted and brutally executed Kurds (Sunnis), Sunni-Arab "hypocrites" (secular), Turkmens (mostly Sunnis), Yazidis, Christians and particularly Shiites and Alawis, creating deep fear among the population.[11]

Thus, it appeared in 2014 that ISIS was about to occupy Iraq and Syria, and establish a new militant Islamic Caliphate. This Islamic state may have spread into neighboring Arab countries and totally change the geostrategic and ideological environment of the entire region. This scenario was also based on a new phenomenon of a growing current of highly motivated youngsters from Arab, Muslim, American and European countries, fighting alongside ISIS, and committing atrocities against captive prisoners.[12]

In reality, however, this scenario proved to be farfetched, or exaggerated. To begin with large parts of the territories occupied by IS are desert, while the Bedouin tribes that helped them were motivated by political and financial interest, not by ideology; and subsequently some of them changed their alliances and joined the government forces. In addition, most Muslim in the region and beyond – Sunnis and Shiites alike – consider the concept of ISIS a distortion of Islam ("Shiite and Sunni institutions in Egypt, Iraq, Saudi Arabia and Iran agreed to denounce and condemn extremists [ISIS] deeming their acts to be in direct conflict with Islam").[13] But apart from this ideological backing, Syria and Iraq have been supported in the war against IS and JN by military airplanes from the US, European and Arab countries, as well as by Iranian forces, Hizballa fighters, Shiite militias from Iraq,Iran and Pakistan and Kurdish fighters from the region. Turkey has also changed its anti-Kurdish tactics though not regarding Iraqi Kurds. As a result of these military endeavors ISIS lost most of its territorial gains in Iraq and Syria, except for Mosul, in northern Iraq, which is under siege as of this writing in April 2017, and Raqqa, in northern Syria, the "capital" of ISIS.

To sum up this discussion, it seems that the geostrategic configuration in the region is changing not only by crucial domestic developments, but also by the political-military involvement of regional and global powers. Syria is a major case study in this critical process.

The changing domestic and geostrategic configuration of the region: the impact of the Syrian civil war

As indicated above, the uprising in Syria started as a peaceful process by low class inhabitants of villages and small towns, which were impoverished by the social economic policies of Bashar, as well as by years of draught. Neglecting the wellbeing of peasants and workers, Bashar promoted the new middle class of the privileged urban bourgeoisie. Initially he tried to appease the protesters by promising economic benefits, but he soon resorted to brutal measures, to suppress the spreading protest. In reaction and inspired by the uprising in Tunisia and Egypt, growing numbers of Syrians employed arm violence against the regime. But using heavy arms, tanks, airplanes and chemical weapon, the regime has endeavored to crash the rebellion.

Indeed, the Syrian civil war has claimed, since 2011, the lives of some 500,000 people, hundreds of thousands wounded and some 11 million refugees out of some 23 million inhabitants, mostly inside Syria, as well as the destruction of infrastructure and rural and urban neighborhoods.[14] The country is divided among several major forces: Bashar's government that controls about 50% of the country (with some 70% of the population), including the major cities of Damascus, Homs, Hamah, Aleppo and the Latakia province that is mostly inhabited by members of the Alawi sect, which is 12% of the population and Bashar's main support group. His government is also backed by most Christians (some 10%), Druze (4%), Circassians, Turkmens and some Kurds. Significantly, not a few Sunni Arabs, out of the 65% of the majority, also cooperate with the regime for social and economic interests. In contrast, most Kurds, some 10% of the total population, oppose Bashar and have established three autonomous enclaves in north and northeastern Syria, called west Kurdistan or Rojava. Several parts of the region are dominated by ISIS and JN, which lately joined forces with another rebel group and changed its name to Jabhat Fath Al-Sham, namely: the Front for Conquering Greater Syria. This includes strategic positions along, or near, Syrian borders with Iraq, Turkey, Lebanon, Jordan and Israel. In addition, many Syrian opposition groups – religious and secular – control various areas in different parts of the country. They are mainly The Free Syrian Army (FSA), two Islamic fronts including Muslim Brothers and the Free Men of Greater Syria, Ahrar al-Sham. Simultaneously, several civilian opposition groups emerged, representing various political and communal sections of the population, in different parts of the country. All of them have demanded the removal of Bashar and his regime, replacing them with a "democratic state that spreads freedom and social security...devoid of ethnic, gender, religious or political discrimination." Even the MB declared that their aim was not an Islamic state, but an egalitarian democratic one.[15] Initially, these groups were organized in the "Syrian National Council," headed by Burhan Ghalion, a Sorbonne University professor. However, owing to personal, political and sectarian differences and splits, a new umbrella organization was established in November 2012: "The Syrian National Council of the Revolutionary Forces and Opposition." These bodies are affiliated to various armed groups, notably the FSA, but have failed not only to topple Bashar, but also to efficiently employ the various military organizations. These organizations lack effective coordination and heavy weapons, and are backed by different regional and global powers. For example, the FSA is supported by some Western and Arab countries; the Muslim Brothers – by Turkey and Qatar, while other Salafi groups – by Saudi Arabia. Jordan has created, with US help, a special force mostly composed of Syrian refugees, in order to combat Bashar's regime.[16] Israel, which has benefited from disarmament of Syrian chemical weapons, has remained officially neutral. However, it has periodically attacked Syrian military sites and convoys that supply sophisticated arms to Hezbollah. Israel is also providing medical and logistic aid to Syrian opposition groups, possibly also to JN.[17] But while Israel has played so far only a marginal role, the two other regional powers – Iran and Turkey – are more significantly involved in the Syrian civil war.

The role of Turkey

Although calling for the fall of Bashar, Turkey has not taken advantage of its special strategic location (900 km of a common border) and its great military power to topple Bashar with the help of the US and Arab countries. This is mainly to avoid an open conflict with Iran and Russia, Syria's chief allies. However, Ankara permitted thousands of volunteers – Muslims and non-Muslims – to cross its territory and join ISIS and JN to fight Bashar. Yet, allegedly Ankara plotted with these militant organizations to combat another common enemy, namely the Kurds of Northern Syria. Turkey is indeed treating the Kurdish Democratic Union Party (PYD) in Syria as a threat to its national security; since PYD has been affiliated to the Kurdish Workers' Party (PKK), Ankara's internal arch enemy. Turkey is concerned lest the Syrian Kurds would help the PKK in its subversive activities, even though Ankara and the PKK signed in 2013 a ceasefire agreement. Erdogan himself warned the PKK and the Syrian Kurds: "we will not allow a terrorist group (PKK) to establish camps in Northern Syria, being a threat to Turkey. If there is a step which needs to be taken against the terrorist group, we will definitely take it."[18] Ankara also requested Tehran to prevent its Kurds from helping the PKK, although both parties have taken opposite sides regarding Bashar's regime. With regard to the Iraqi Kurds, Ankara has recognized the Kurdish regional government (KRG), headed by Masoud Barzani, despite strong opposition by the Shiite government in Baghdad. This bold Turkish step derives from close trade relations (mainly oil) with the KRG and its promise not to help the PKK and the PYD.[19] Nevertheless, the KRG troops – Peshmerga – were dispatched to help the besieged Kurds in the town of Kobani, on the Syrian-Turkish border. Ankara initially did not use its army to fight the IS warriors that occupy part of the city and killed many Kurds. Only in Nov. 2014, under US pressure, Ankara permitted Peshmerga fighters to cross thru its territory and fight IS in Kobani. Reportedly the Turkish army has also trained Peshmerga troops, as well as Iraqi soldiers, to fight the IS.[20]

On other regional policy issues too, Turkey did not score significant gains. For example, Erdogan lost a good ally, then president Morsi of Egypt, with whom Turkey aimed to "create a new democratic axis of power."[21] Following Morsi's removal, Erdogan harshly criticized the military coup in Egypt against the democratically elected government, and the two countries suspended diplomatic relations in late 2013. Instead, Egypt and Saudi Arabia have joined forces against Turkey, competing with it over regional supremacy and leadership of the Sunni Muslim community. On its part, Saudi Arabia succeeded in inducing Qatar, Turkey's ally, to join the Gulf Cooperation Council (GCC) lead by Riyad.[22] Turkey also rivaled with Saudi Arabia over influencing Muslim opposition groups in Syria as well as over the Israeli-Hamas conflict. Turkey openly supported Hamas and harshly criticized Israel during the recent Gaza war in July-August 2014, whereas Saudi Arabia (and Egypt) tacitly backed Israel.

Israel's potential role

Although Israel was not involved in the "Arab Spring" uprisings, including in Syria, it may potentially play a significant role in shaping the new geostrategic configuration of the region. To begin with, the disarmament of Syria's chemical weapons as well as the wearing down of its army, have granted Israel further strategic military advantage. By contrast, however, the deployment of Russian warplanes and other military systems in Syria have added a new concern to Israel security. Consequently, many Israeli decision makers would prefer to continue working with "the devil" they know, Bashar, who is pragmatic and secular, much preferable to the Islamic fanatics. Other Israelis consider Bashar as a highly potential threat in the long run, since he is allied to Iran and Hezbollah – the archenemies of Israel. Therefore these Israelis conclude that their country should side and cooperate with Sunni Muslim countries, which consider the Shiite alliance as deadly enemy.

It is true that Egypt (and tacitly also Saudi Arabia and Jordan) sided with Israel during its war against Hamas in Gaza (July-August 2014), but many other Arab and Muslim countries as well as millions of Arabs and Muslims severely condemned "Israeli aggression" and criticized it for failing to settle the Palestinian problem.[23] PM Netanyahu and other leaders believe that the Palestinian problem can be settled indirectly thru Egypt and other moderate Arab states, thus outflanking the Palestinian Authority. However, this seems to be wishful thinking. For example, President Sisi of Egypt has stated several times that Israel must settle this problem directly with the Palestinians, and should agree to the creation of a Palestinian state ("But first a Palestinian State must exist");[24] only then can Egypt help with security arrangements between Israel and the Palestinian state. It would appear then that unless Israel first settles the Palestinian issue Sunni Arab states would not openly accept Israel as a strategic partner in the conflict with the Shiite alliance.

Israel apart, the crucial questions that are looming: Can a Sunni Muslim coalition, supported by the US, contain the Shiite alliance backed by Russia? Similarly, can a Sunni Muslim coalition or the Shiite alliance eliminate IS and JN – the new non-state actors in the region? A major key to these crucial regional issues lies in the Syrian civil war.

The Shiite alliance and Syria

It is evident that since the eruption of the Arab Spring upheavals, the members of the Shiite alliance have encountered severe problems and losses. Hezbollah,

Iran's ideological and strategic ally, lost many of its fighters in combat with Syrian opposition groups, but not its influence in Lebanon. Bashar has lost about half of his country to various opposition groups, particularly IS and JN, that are still holding parts of Syria regime. He is also hated by most Syrians, who have suffered immensely from his brutal actions. Owing to these cruel measures, including the use of chemical weapons against civilians, notably in 2013 and 2017, he became a pariah in most Arab states and the global community. In 2012 Damascus was ousted from the Arab League, while many members of the international community have harshly criticized it.

Turkey, Jordan and Qatar, but not Sisi's Egypt, have also adopted hostile attitudes toward Bashar, while Israel humiliated him by occasionally bombing Syrian strategic sites. The US also intended in 2013 to bomb such sites, in reaction to Damascus use of chemical weapon but changed its mind (see below). Iran and Russia, Bashar's chief strategic allies have encountered serious challenges from the US and European countries, notably: economic sanctions on Iran because of its nuclear program, and on Russia, owing to its aggression against the Ukraine.

These challenges, difficulties and constraints notwithstanding, Bashar has managed to stay in power for more than 6 years since the eruption of the rebellion, while his chances to continue his rule are not too slim. His close allies – Iran, Hezbollah and Russia – have not faltered, and will continue to support him. And despite its losses, Hezbollah has acquired military experience during the Syrian war, and is still backed by Iran. Iran itself has improved its regional and international standing through its agreement with P5+1 regarding its nuclear program. The economic sanctions against it were partly lifted as Iran gained more "legitimacy" with the International community. Furthermore, the threat of IS and JN to Iraq and Syria, have contributed to reduce their antagonism, and create common strategic interests between Sunni Arab countries and the US on the one hand, Tehran and Damascus on the other.[25] Fighting against IS has indeed become first priority for the US and some Arab countries, over their initial aim to topple Bashar. Thus, on the one hand, Washington has declared time and again that the Bashar must go; it also supported the moderate Syrian opposition and threatened

Damascus with air strikes. On the other hand, the US, manipulated by Russia in 2013, avoided air strikes on Syria, in return to Bashar's commitment to disarm his military from chemical weapons.[26] This commitment, which was largely implemented, has contributed to Bashar's survival and legitimacy in the eye of many Americans, Europeans, Arabs and Israelis. Significantly, former US officials and diplomats openly advocated for cooperation with Bashar against IS and JN.[27] US new president Donald Trump initially adopted a similar position and was ready to cooperate with Moscow to reach a political settlement to the Syrian crisis while allowing Bashar to stay in power. But following the Syrian Army's chemical attack on Khan Shaykhun, near Idlib on April 4, 2017, the US launched some 60 Tomahawk missiles against a Syrian air base near Hama, destroying some 20 Syrian warplanes. This bold US operation may have been accompanied by a change of Trump's attitude to Bashar, while straining his relations with Putin. Still Washington has not done its best to equip the moderate rebels with heavy weapons, as well as to forge a strong military coalition among these rebel groups and among the Sunni Muslim neighboring countries. Indeed, the split and conflict among the Sunni Muslim states and within the many Syrian rebel groups, have also helped Bashar to stay in power. Furthermore, many Syrian rebels and ordinary citizens are fed up and tired from this bloody war, and tend to reconcile with Bashar's regime.[28]

Throughout the civil war Bashar has demonstrated great stamina, cruelty and devotion, while efficiently controlling his army and security services (despite many defections). He did not agree to suggestions by Arab and European leaders to give up his rule, to go on exile or to make major changes in his government. He also rejected other diplomatic efforts to find political solutions to the crisis, notably: two international conferences in Geneva, on June 2012 and January 2014 as well as in Astana, Kazakhstan in early 2017. Earlier, Lakhdar Brahimi, an Algerian diplomat, appointed by the UN and the Arab League, failed to settle the Syrian crisis and resigned in February 2014.[29] And in June 2014 Bashar was "reelected" as president, in a public referendum, with 88.7% of the votes. In Dec. 2014 he stated that he intends to "stay in his position as president despite the prospect of a long and hard war against the rebels."[30]

Conclusions and prospects

The chances for Bashar to stay on in power are not slim, as stated before, mainly because the balance of power vis-à-vis his enemies is, in his favor. The US and its European and Arab partners are tacitly cooperating with him against IS and JN in Syria (and Iraq). Even if the US would be unable to fully defeat these organizations, it could stop their expansion and reduce their scope of control. This would enable Bashar to regain from the rebels lost Syrian territories, and he is likely to receive further support from his close allies – Hezbollah, Iran and Russia. For example, Hezbollah's leader, Hassan Nasrallah, stated already in 2013: "Our fighters, our *mujahiddun*, are present on Syrian soil, to confront all the dangers of the international, regional and *takfiri* (Muslim heretics, namely IS) attacks on this country and on this region."[31] Some 10,000 Hezbollah troops are deployed in Syria, in addition to approximately 10,000 Iranian operatives, such as the "Revolutionary Guards," "Al-Quds Force" and "Al Basij Group." Iran also supplies to Syria weapons and great sums of money, since it "sees the survival of the Syrian government as being crucial to the longevity of its own regime."[32]

Similarly, Russia has a vested interest in the survival of Bashar's regime ("Russia will continue to support Syria").[33] This, owing to its geostrategic interest: maintaining its presence in the area, its naval base in North-Eastern Syria (Tartus), as well as blocking the US influence in the region. Apart from substantial military and financial help, Russia has extended also enormous political and diplomatic assistance to Bashar. In addition to backing Damascus' stand at the UN, Moscow has periodically suggested peace talks between Bashar and the Syrian rebels.[34] In early 2017, Russia, Iran and Turkey have negotiated in Astana a new political settlement between Damascus and some rebel groups. Earlier in 2014 Moscow also backed a new initiative by the UN envoy, Staffan de Mistura. He suggested freezing the Syrian conflict by achieving local cease-fire agreements between the rebels and the government, leading to a comprehensive political settlement. Initially Bashar supported this plan, calling it "national reconciliation."[35] Under this title Bashar may also initiate a great reconstruction plan for the ruined infrastructure of his country, as well as for the rehabilitation of millions of Syrian refugees. To this end, he is likely to receive international aid and cooperation. Even the US and its Western and Arab allies may ease their pressure on Damascus and consider Bashar as a tolerable partner, preferable to IS and JN. Simultaneously, he is likely to take advantage of these options to push aback the IS and JN, reconcile with moderate oppositions organizations, by including them in a new government; this in coordination with Iran, Hezbollah and Russia. A crucial question is whether the new Trump administration would support such plan, or work against Bashar's government and his allies Russia and Iran.

Presumably, Damascus will continue to be an important partner to Shiite crescent under Tehran's leadership, alongside Hezbollah and possibly also Baghdad. Indeed if Bashar stays in power Hezbollah will continue to play a more important role in Lebanon, and will contribute to its territorial integrity. In Iraq too, the American-European-Arab military coalition, alongside Iran may succeed in defeating IS and hence contribute to the strengthening of the new Shiite government in Baghdad.[36] This government will continue to woo Sunni Arab tribes in Western Iraq, by offering them political and financial benefits to break their alliance with IS. In a similar vein, Baghdad is likely to seek the revival of a federal arrangement with the Kurdish Regional Government (KRG) in northern Iraq, to reinstate its unity, as well as to prevent the creation of a pan-Kurdish state. Iran and Turkey are likely to support such arrangement, to prevent separatist tendencies within their Kurdish communities, as well as in northern Syria. Arab states and the West may also back such plan, aiming at preserving Iraq territorial integrity. To be sure, such "rosy" scenario, namely maintaining the territorial integrity of Iraq, Syria and Lebanon, if materialize, may empower Iran's led Shiite crescent.

The opposite grim scenario is: the continuation of the domestic and regional conflicts – military, political and social – and the further disintegration of Iraq, Syria and Lebanon into religious, ethnic enclaves or states, such as: an Islamic state and north-eastern Syria; Kurdish autonomous regions in northern Iraq and northern Syria; a Syrian-Alawi state in central

Syria and the Latakia region as well as Shiite, Suni, Christian and Druze enclaves in Lebanon. It would appear that some of these enclaves or states will not be economically and politically viable, and will continue to fight one another. They may also continue to be under the influence of the regional powers – Iran, Turkey and Israel, as well as Russian and the US.

Finally, parts or a mixture of these two scenarios may also develop in view of a new balance of power between local, regional and global players, as well as under changing circumstances.

Notes

[1] This is a revised and updated version of my article, Strategic Upheavals in the Mediterranean and Middle Eastern countries since the "Arab Spring", *Journal of Balkan and Near Eastern Studies*, vol. 18, No. 4 July 2016, pp. 352-350.

[2] Khalil al-Anani, Whither Political Islam, *Al-Jazeera*, December 24, 2013; Zvi Bar'el, *Ha'aretz*, January 16, 2014; *New York Times*, January 14, 2014

[3] Syrian Center for Political & Srrategic Studies, Washington DC, 2013 pp. 58ff *Syria Transition, Road Map*.

[4] I. Alvarez-Ossaro, "Syrian Struggling Civil Society", *Middle East Quarterly*, Spring 2012, pp. 23-32; Tam Hussein, *Al Majalla*, 29 November 2013.

[5] There are several studies on attitudes and values related to democracy and Islam, e.g. M Tessler, Islam and Democracy in the Middle East, *Comparative Policies*, April 2002, pp. 337-354.

[6] A. Moussali, *The Islamic Quest for Democracy, Pluralism and Human Rights*, University Press of Florida; N. Lahoud, *Political Thought in Islam*, , London & New York: Routledge, 2005, p.4.

[7] J. L. Esposito & J. O. Voll, *Islam and Democracy*, New York: Oxford University Press, 1996; M. Hatina & U M. Kupferschmidt (eds.), *The Muslim Brothers* (Hebrew.), Tel Aviv: HaKibutz HaMeuhad, 2012, p.67.

[8] M. Ma'oz, *Asad – The Sphinx of Damascus*, London & New York: Grove Press, 1989, pp. 149ff.

[9] Power of Vacuum in the Middle East, *New York Times*, 5 January, 2014; Y. Schweitzer, & S. Goldstein-Ferber, *Al-Qaeda and Internationalization of Suicide Terrorism*, Tel Aviv: JCSS, 2005; Y. Schweitzer and A. Oreg, *Al-Qaeda's Odyssey to the Global Jihad*, , Tel Aviv: INSS 2014.

[10] *BBC News*, 4 October 2014; *Al-Safir*, 19 August, 2014; *The Daily Beast*, 14 November, 2013.

[11] *New York Times*, 8 & 26 November, 2014.

[12] *The Guardian*, 22 June, 2014; *The New York Times*, 8 October, 2014.

13 *Al-Monitor*, 15 December, 2014.
14 See for example F. Ajami, *The Syrian Rebellion*, Stanford: Hoover Institute Press, 2012, *passim;* Eyal Zisser, *Syria – Protest, Revolution & Civil War (*Hebrew), Tel Aviv: Tel Aviv University, 2014, *passim.*
15 *Road Map*, p. 84; *Al-Majala*, 29 November, 2013; *The Wall Street Journal*, 15-16 February, 2014.
16 *RT,* 12 March, 2013; *Fox News*, 25 March, 2013; *The Times of Israel*, 2 January, 2015.
17 *BBC News,* 30 August, 2014, *Ha'aretz*, 7 December, 2014.
18 J. Dorsey, *Huffington Post*, 8 August, 2012.
19 *Al-Jazeera*, 16 November, 2013; *Al-Monitor*, 7 February, 2013.
20 *Reuters*, 22 November, 2014.
21 *The New York Times*, 9 September, 2011; Hasan, Kosebalaban, *Perceptions*, Autumn, 2011, p. 109.
22 *Ha'aretz*, 24 November, 2014.
23 *Al Jazeera TV,* 10 July, 2014.
24 *Al Arabiyya TV,* 23 November, 2014.
25 *The New York Times*, 7 January, 2014; *Ha'aretz*, 16 January & 24 June, 2014.
26 *LA Times*, 15 November, 2013.
27 *The New York Times*, 7 January, 2014; *Al-Monitor,* 1 September, 2014;CNN,4-6 April, 2017.
28 *Al-Monitor*, 16 September, 2013.
29 *The Wall Street Journal*, 15-16 February, 2014;Al-Jazeera,14 March, 2017.
30 *The Guardian*, 4 June 2014; *Paris Match*, cited in *Yediot Ahronot*, 5 December, 2014.
31 *The New York Times*, 14 November, 2013; S. Cagaptay, *The Washington Institute for Near East Studies*, 29 January, 2013.
32 *The Telegraph*, 21 February, 2014; *Middle East Monitor*, 1 January, 2015.
33 *Huffington Post*, 13 December, 2014; *BBC News,* 15 June 2012.
34 *Al-Arabiyya TV,* 30 January, 2012, 29 November, 2013; *BBC News*, 27 January, 2014; *Al-Monitor*, 10 December, 2014.
35 *UN News Centre*, 3 November, 2014; *Al-Monitor*, 3 December, 2014; *Ha'aretz*, 15 December, 2014.
36 *The Guardian & The New York Times*, 4 November, 2014.

[2]
SOME POLITICAL AND LEGAL ASPECTS OF HYDRO-CARBON EXPLORATION AND EXPLOITATION IN THE EASTERN MEDITERRANEAN

Rauf Versan

Political aspects

The Mediterranean, as the etymology of the word suggests, is a strategically important area: it stands at the middle of three continents – Europe, Asia and Africa.

The politics and economics of the Eastern Mediterranean are in a state of change and the region remains an extremely turbulent and unstable area. The ongoing civil war in Syria and the involvement of foreign powers therein, the political transition in Egypt after the Arab Spring, the emergence of Turkey as a leading regional power, tensions in Gaza, strains between Turkey and Israel and the long-standing dispute between Turkey and Cyprus – all have had an impact upon the geopolitical stability of the region. Because of the complexity of this long list of issues and the close interaction between many of them, there are no hard and fast solutions to the problems of the region. Parallel to these, there is uncertainty concerning the evolution of regional security, underscored by various, partly unknown, factors in the related security environment.

The implications of these developments concerning the geopolitics of the region are manifold, leading to a situation wherein the interplay of politics, economics and law becomes all too evident.

Exploration in the seabed and subsoil of the Eastern Mediterranean began in the late 1960s and early 1970s with well drilling in the shallow shelves of Israel and Northern Sinai.[1] The wells were found to be dry, but still this drilling gave important indication as to the geomorphological infrastructure of the Eastern Mediterranean region. Further drillings in the late 1970s and mid 1980 were successful and light oil was found offshore Sinai, although its production was not commercially viable.[2]

Exploration in the Eastern Mediterranean gained momentum in 1999 when natural gas deposits were discovered west of Ashkelon and the Gaza strip. The Gaza Marine gas field, discovered some 25nm off the Gaza coast has not been developed so far, mainly for political reasons.[3]

Palestine's maritime borders are not yet fixed, but are likely to be greater than the 20 mile nautical limit set under the Oslo Accord. The final borders will be settled in future negotiations between Israelis, Palestinians and Egyptians. It is to be noted that Israel currently respects Palestinian hydrocarbon exploration rights in the area under Oslo (including Gaza Marine), despite the fact that the area is under Israeli military control.[4]

With these discoveries, considerable amount of geophysical data were collected, not only in respect of these localities, but the greater area of the Levant Basin.

Further discoveries were made in 2009 in offshore Israel in the so-called Tamar field and in the Leviathan field, yielding respectively 9.7 tcf and 16 tcf of gas. Noble, an American company that is engaged in the production of Israel's gas, says that the gas from Tamar field, which began flowing in 2014, already supplies 45% of the country's electricity. But production from the much larger Leviathan fields, farther west, is slow.[5]

It is believed that there are other natural gas reserves offshore Turkey and Cyprus.[6]

Turkey occupies a crucial position in natural gas transit by virtue of its geographical location between continental Europe, the world's second-largest gas market, and the natural gas reserves of the Caspian basin and the Middle-East.[7] It plays an important part in oil and natural gas supply movement from Russia, the Caspian region, and the Middle-East to Europe. Since 2005, Turkey has also been engaged in exploration in the seabed and subsoil of its maritime territory in the Mediterranean Sea. Turkish Petroleum Company (TPAO) has carried out seismic surveys offshore Antalya, Mersin and Iskenderun. In November 2011, TPAO and Shell signed joint operation agreements to conduct oil and natural gas exploration off Antalya.

Turkey has recently increased its exploration activities in the Eastern Mediterranean. It has purchased a new and technologically advanced seismic research vessel and ordered another one to be commissioned in the State Mining and Exploration Institute (MTA).

Actually, the Turkish State Petroleum Company is licensed by the Turkish Government to conduct exploration in a much wider area in the Eastern Mediterranean Sea which Turkey claims to be its continental shelf and which partly overlaps with the Exclusive Economic Zone (EEZ) claimed by the Republic of Cyprus in the west and southwest of the island.

The Republic of Cyprus began preparing the ground for offshore hydrocarbon exploration in the early 2000s. It signed EEZ delimitation agreements with Egypt in 2003, Lebanon in 2007 and Israel in 2010. With these agreements, the outer limits of a 52 square kilometer exploration area south of the island were demarcated. The area comprises 13 blocs. The Republic of Cyprus launched in 2007 its first international tender, and in 2008 a US company was awarded a three year license in Block 12.[8] Following further seismic surveys, this company, having already made various discoveries nearby in Israeli waters, was authorized by the Republic of Cyprus to begin the first exploratory drilling in Block 12. Drilling commenced in 2011 and it was announced in December 2011 the discovery of an estimated 200 billion cubic meters of natural gas in what is called the Aphrodite field.[9]

In February 2012, the Republic of Cyprus announced a second international tender for exploration licenses in the remaining 12 blocks. This time, a great number of international companies participated in the tender. Agreements were signed with an Italian-South Korean consortium for blocks 2, 3 and 9 and with a French firm for blocks 10 and 11.[10]

Oil companies including the Italian consortium and France's TOTAL may find plentiful of gas in these given areas. If not, Cyprus's gas venture will depend upon getting it elsewhere, perhaps from Israel's Leviathan field.

But can Israel sell gas to its neighbours in the existing political climate? And how can the Palestinian dimension be accommodated into this regional gas supply framework? Israeli Prime Minister Netanyahu has expressed his desire to improve Israel's relations with its neighbours. The demand for gas in countries such as Egypt, Jordan and Cyprus could provide Israel a significant geopolitical opportunity to meet this demand, even if only partially, in the right situations. However, Israel's Arab neighbours face domestic resistance to such deals because of Israeli-Palestinian dispute. On the other hand, while Cyprus has reached an agreement on its EEZ with Israel, Turkey contests Cyprus's claims to offshore gas fields. As Cyprus proceeds to develop the Aphrodite field, tensions may arise, and indeed increase, between Turkey and Cyprus, as well as between Turkey and other states doing business with Cyprus, such as Israel and Egypt.

Legal aspects

i. General Considerations Concerning the Settlement of Continental Shelf and Exclusive Economic Zone Boundaries

The existence and establishment of continental shelf and Exclusive Economic Zones substantially increased the number and size of the maritime boundaries between coastal states. Various surveys have identified over 400 international maritime boundaries throughout the world.[11] The increase has been due partly to the emergence of new states and the breaking-up of the Soviet Union. It is also conceivable that a new generation of boundaries will result from climate change and accessibility to resources in the Arctic waters. Although many of the boundaries already settled relate only to the continental shelf, they are likely to be reviewed and renegotiated also within the context of the EEZ delimitation.

The operation of the rules and principles by which the continental shelf and EEZ are established is an important matter because the institution of these areas has produced new kinds of boundaries to be settled, and also new kinds of boundary disputes. The whole matter is now compounded by the convergence of the continental shelf and EEZ boundaries which, as a result, has given rise to questions of 'single maritime boundaries.'

The law concerning these questions has developed mainly from the rules adopted in the Continental Shelf Convention of the 1958 United Nations Conference on the Law of the Sea (UNCLOS I), the rules of the 1982 UN

Convention on the Law of the Sea (UNCLOS III), from state practice reflected in very many boundary agreements and also from a massive jurisprudence of international courts and tribunals, most notably the International Court of Justice. It is important to keep in mind, however, that the case law pertains to disputes essentially on which agreement proved impossible and that the majority of boundaries have been settled by agreement.

During UNCLOS III, the delimitation of the continental shelf and EEZ boundaries, which were discussed jointly, proved to be one of the most difficult questions to be negotiated. States participating at the Conference manifested themselves generally in two approaches, one (relying on the 1958 Convention) arguing that the premise for delimitation should be the equidistance line, the other (invoking the North Sea Continental Shelf Cases[12]) that delimitation should be effected on equitable principles. In the end, a compromise between these two positions was reached, but in such a way as to provide the relevant articles of UNCLOS with a high level of abstraction; they lay down the aim of delimitation, but without indicating the method, or methods, by which delimitation could be effected by the states. Under these articles, the primary legal principle concerning continental shelf boundaries is that, if possible, they are to be settled by agreement in accordance with equitable principles.[13] A principle to similar effect exists also in respect of EEZ boundaries.[14]

Since UNCLOS became law in 1994, many boundary agreements which are negotiated have been agreements that aimed at fixing a single maritime boundary for both the continental shelf and the EEZ. Only a small number of agreements have been made, which establish individual boundaries for the continental shelf and EEZ respectively. This development is explained on the basis that previously there was no need to delimit a single boundary when the only extended claim to coastal state jurisdiction validly recognized was the continental shelf. But although the 1982 Convention established the right of a coastal state to claim an EEZ up to 200 miles, together with an identical criterion for delimiting the continental shelf, it appears to overlook the possible impact of this development on the question of delimitation. Instead, as mentioned above, it contains separate Articles for the delimitation of the shelf and the EEZ boundaries.

Whether the continental shelf and EEZ boundaries should necessarily be coextensive and, if so, what legal rules and principles will apply to delimitation by a single boundary are questions which require important consideration. For these questions, UNCLOS remains silent. Would Articles 74 and 83 of the UNCLOS have any application for the single maritime boundary? International courts and tribunals on a number of occasions accepted explicitly that the single maritime boundary is an institution of state practice and international case law rather than UNCLOS,[15] but without effectively going into why these Articles apply to cases of delimitation of the single maritime boundary.[16] They have also stated that these Articles reflect customary international law.[17] It could thus be argued that Articles 74 and 83 are relevant and applicable in respect of any delimitation of an undelimited area between the territorial sea and 200 miles from the coastal baselines, whether the states concerned are parties to UNCLOS and whether they seek an agreement for a single maritime boundary or separate EEZ and continental shelf boundaries. In the case of states not parties to UNCLOS, the applicable law would be not Articles 74 and 83, but rules of customary international law having the same content, unless such states have persistently objected to such rules during the process of their making.

ii. Third states' interests in boundary settlements

The rules and processes by which the continental shelf and EEZ boundaries could be settled bilaterally take on added complexity when the boundaries in question involve the possibility, even necessity, of a multilateral settlement.[18] Such settlements can be achieved on the basis of direct negotiations between all the states concerned. This mode of settlement has the benefit of allowing the states to define the parameters and timetable of the negotiations and to enable the issues to be reviewed as a whole, with weaknesses in one area possibly compensated by gains in another area. In situations where direct negotiations are unsuccessful or deemed unpreferable, resort to international judicial adjudication is possible.

The submission of multilateral maritime boundary disputes to international courts and tribunals raises several issues both of substance and procedure. In the first place, it requires a special agreement which is binding on all the states concerned and which defines the disputed zone as between the parties. It would be extremely difficult for the parties to agree on a definition which would not encroach upon the adopted position of either one or the other. Even if such a difficulty is overcome, there still remain the difficulties not only of handling three or four sets of pleadings as opposed to two, but also of laying down the appropriate criteria and methods, as well as taking into consideration a wider scope of 'relevant circumstances.' It is conceivable, for example, that the decision of the court or tribunal on the 'equitableness' of a certain criteria, method and 'relevant circumstances' between two parties might be affected by adverse considerations relating to the interest of the remaining states. In the North Sea Continental Shelf Cases the International Court of Justice fortunately found that the interests of The Netherlands and Denmark vis-à-vis The Federal Republic of Germany were so similar that the cases were treated as if it was a bilateral dispute.

More important in practical terms is the potential need to apply appropriate principles of law and devise suitable techniques in a system which has hitherto developed within the framework of two contesting parties, not three or four. A tripartite or quadripartite boundary settlement by international adjudication is still a novelty. Experience of state practice in this regard is limited.

Concluding observations

It is in the interest of states that there should be clear and predictable legal rules and principles for international maritime boundary delimitation so that effective standards can be developed on the basis of which boundary problems can be negotiated, resolved and, if need be, adjudicated upon peacefully. Given the political and economic sensitivity related to boundary problems, the availability of such standards and the possibility of recourse to them take on added significance. Such rules and standards also serve as a protection for states against expansionist aspirations by their neighbours.

On the other hand, individual cases of delimitation between states have their own peculiarities emanating from the special features of the maritime areas concerned. These may include the coastal configurations, the presence of islands with their own configurations, seabed geomorphology, habitat of the natural resources, and finally the demographic, economic and legal backgrounds of the states and regions concerned.

The fact that the Mediterranean is a semi-enclosed sea means that states in the region have additional duties of cooperation in accordance with Article 123 of UNCLOS. According to this article, coastal states of an enclosed or semi-enclosed sea "should cooperate with each other in the exercise of their rights and in the performance of their duties under this Convention." It also requires states to "endeavor" to coordinate their activities in relation to certain specific areas, including conservation and exploitation of living resources, marine scientific research and protection and preservation of the marine environment. By virtue of the character of the Mediterranean as a semi-enclosed sea, it is likely, and even actually the case, that the establishment of marine zones and the delimitation of the maritime boundaries will have an impact on several other states.

Finally, the existence of discernable and country specific interests of individual coastal states, on the one hand, and the need to formulate general rules and principles with a view to applying them in order to control and prevent situations from escalating into international conflicts, on the other hand, leads to an environment where the efficacy of international law will depend on its carefully assessed and balanced application.

Notes

[1] See US Energy Information Administration, Eastern Mediterranean Region, Full Report, August 15, 2013, p.1.
[2] Ibid.,1-2.
[3] Ibid., 5.
[4] Palestine is also entitled to a fishing zone under the Israeli-Palestinian Interim Agreement, 1995, which had been restricted in extent by Israel for security reason. See Israeli-Palestinian Interim Agreement on the West Bank and the Gaza Strip, 28 September 1995. Under the Ceasefire Agreement of 26 August 2014, it was agreed

that Palestinian fishermen would be allowed to sail within 6 nm of the Gaza Strip. See: http://mfa.gov.il/MFA/ForeignPolicy/Issues/Pages/Israel-accepts-Egyptiancease fire-26-Aug-2014.aspx.

5   See M.Ratner, Natural Gas Discoveries in *The Eastern Mediterranean*, Congressional Research Service, 15 August 2016, 13.

6   Cf. A. Giannakopoulos, The Eastern Mediterranean in the Light of Recent Energy Developments and Their Impact, in *Energy Cooperation and Security in the Eastern Mediterranean; A Seismic Shift towards Peace or Conflict?*, Research Paper No.8, February 2016, Tel Aviv University, 11.

7   See generally, S. Zemach, Eastern Mediterranean Development- 1: Levant Basin presents narrowing resource opportunities, Oil and Gas Journal, 4.6.2015, http://www.ogj.com/articles/print/volume-113/issue-4/exploration-development/east-mediterranean-development-1-levant-basin-presents-narrowing-resource-opportunities.html.

8   Ibid.

9   See n. 5, 8.

10 Ibid.

11 See C. F. Schofield and M. Pratt, Cooperation in the absence of maritime boundary agreements: The purpose and value of joint development, The Aegean Sea 2000, Proceedings of the International Symposium on the Aegean Sea, 5-7 May 2000, 152.

12 North Sea Continental Shelf Cases (Federal Republic of Germany v. Denmark; Federal Republic of Germany v. The Netherlands), ICJ Rep. 1969, 3.

13 Art. 83/1. See P.Weil, The Law of Maritime Delimitation- Reflections, 1989, 79-81.

14 Art.74/1. See Weil, ibid.

15 See, for example, Maritime Delimitation and Territorial Questions Between Qatar and Bahrain (Qatar v. Bahrain), ICJ Rep. 2001, 40; Arbitration between Guyana and Suriname (Annex VII Tribunal), International Law Reports, Vol.139, 2007, 566.

16 See, for example, Case concerning the Land and Maritime Boundary between Cameroon and Nigeria (Cameroon v. Nigeria, Equatorial Guinea intervening), ICJ Rep. 2002, 303, paras. 285-286; Maritime Delimitation in the Black Sea (Romania v. Ukraine), ICJ Rep. 2009, 61, paras.17, 31; Delimitation of the Maritime Boundary in the Bay of Bengal (Bangladesh/ Myanmar), ITLOS Rep.2012, 4, paras. 182-184.

17 See, for example, Qatar v. Bahrain Case, 167; Territorial and Maritime Dispute (Nicaragua v. Colombia), ICJ Rep. 2012, 624, parag.139.

18 See Weil, op.cit., 252-256.

[3]
THE EASTERN & CENTRAL MEDITERRANEAN ERA OF OIL AND GAS/IMPORTANCE FOR THE EUROPEAN ENERGY SECURITY

Anthony E. Foscolos

Introduction

Beyond 2020, the European Union will face a natural gas deficit of 440 bcm/year, Figure 1, and over 2 billion barrels of oil, Figure 2, due to the rapid depletion of oil and gas fields in the North Sea.

The chapter indicates how these shortcomings can be resolved by relying on the hydrocarbon resources, which are located in the Eastern and Central Mediterranean Sea.

Confronting the European natural gas deficit

The current natural gas deficit of the European Union of 240 bcm/year is satisfied by importing 136 bcm/year from Russia, 30 bcm/year from Algeria, 24 bcm/year in the form of LNG from Qatar and the remaining in the form of LNG, from Nigeria and Trinidad-Tobago, Figure 3.

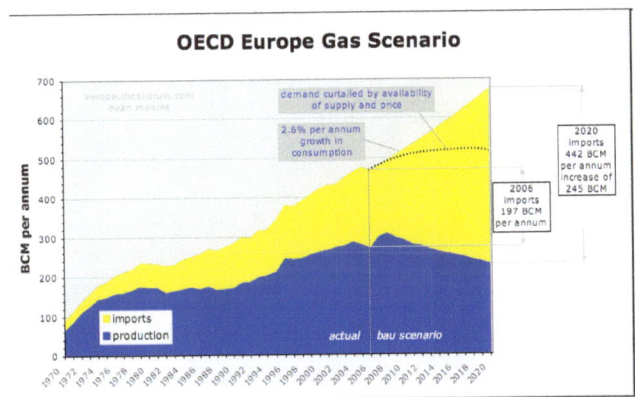

Figure 1: OECD Europe Gas Scenario (http://europe.theoildrum.com/node/4361).

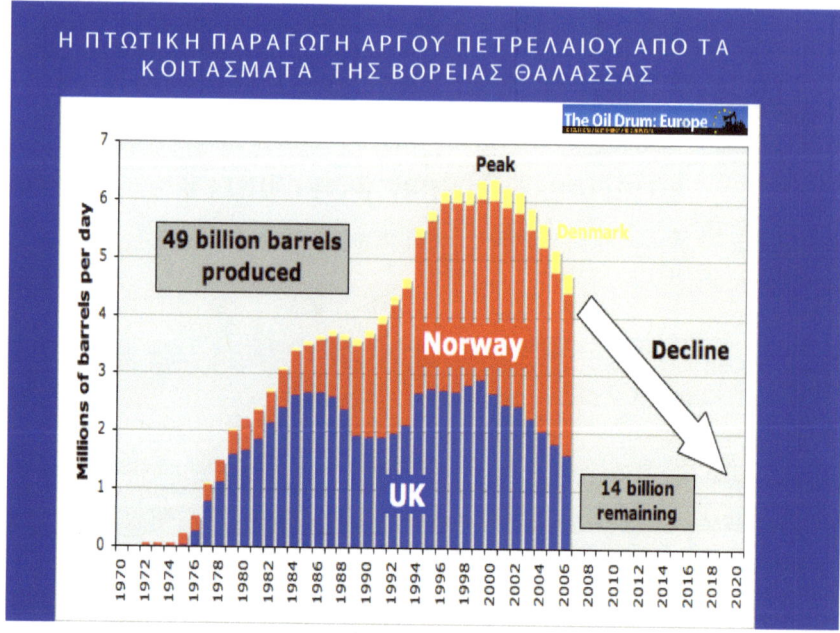

Figure 2: North Sea Petroleum declining production by Euan Mearns, 2009, The Oil Drum Europe.

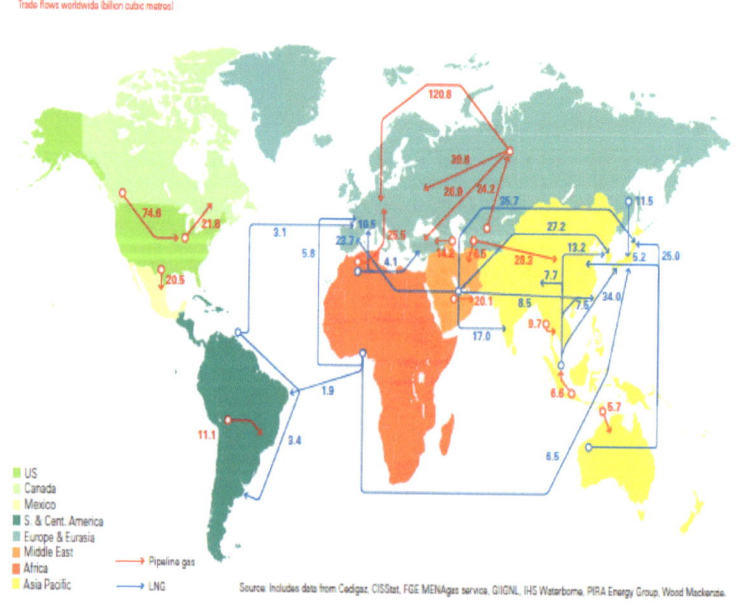

Figure 3: Gas shipments by pipelines and LNG (BP Statistical Review of World Energy 2014).

The additional deficit of 200bcm/year which is forthcoming beyond 2020 can not be satisfied neither from Russia, nor from the North Africa, nor from USA as some European parliamentarians believe.

The reasons are the following:

1. Based upon the data provided by BP Statistical Review of World Energy, 2014, Russia's natural gas reserves stand at 33 tcm. The annual production stands at 630 bcm/year and the exports at 231 bcm/year. The remaining, roughly 2/3 of the production is consumed internally. Hence, the available amount for export is 11 tcm out of which 6.9 tcm is already committed for the next 30 years, while an additional 2 tcm are allocated for China leaving only 2.1 tcm of natural gas for other customers. Since Europe beyond 2020 will need 200bcm/year or 6 tcm for the next 30 years, it is apparent that Russia cannot be considered as the nation to meet Europe's natural gas demands. In addition, the European Union does not want to obtain any more natural gas from Russia because they do not want to be totally dependent on Russia's natural gas supplies. Practically and politically, Russia cannot fill the European natural gas vacuum of 200 bcm/year for the next 30 years.

2. Based upon the data provided by BP Statistical Review of World Energy, 2014, Egypt and Libya have stopped supplying the European Union with natural gas while Algeria has reduced the export of natural to Europe from 70 bcm/year to 30 bcm/year. Obviously, the North African States cannot commit 200 bcm/year of natural gas to Europe.

Based upon the data provided by BP Statistical Review of World Energy, 2014 USA has 9.3 tcm natural gas deposits. The annual production stands at 680 bcm/year while the consumption at 730 bcm/year. Obviously, a nation that imports natural gas can not export its resources to Europe even if shale gas reserves of 14 tcm prove to be correct and economically exploitable.[1]

Based upon 2 USGS Technical Reports, Fact Sheets 2010-3027[2] and 2010-3014[3] the technically recoverable natural gas deposits from the Nile

Cone and the Levantine basin, excluding the natural gas deposits of offshore Cyprus, offshore Crete and the Ionian Sea, stands at 345 tcf (trillion cubic feet) or 9.8 tcm which is more than what USA has 330 tcf. In addition, these 2 basins should have 3.4 billion barrels of oil and 9 billion barrels of gas liquids, Figure 4. These data show the immense importance of the Eastern Mediterranean as an energy supplier for the European Union.

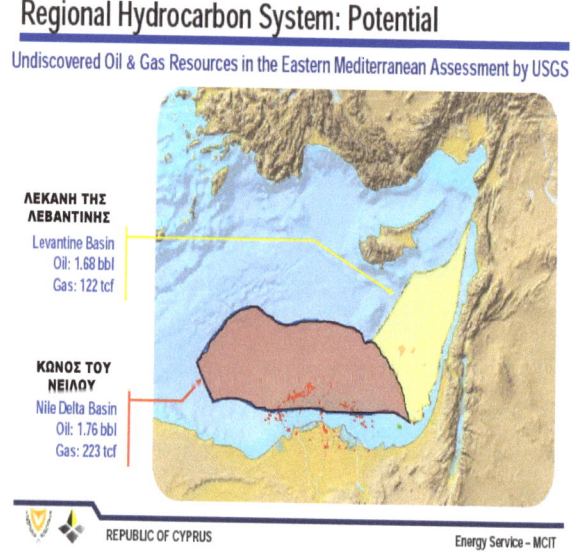

Figure 4: *Hydrocarbon potential of Nile Delta basin and Levantine Basin, USGS Technical Reports 2010-3014 and 2010-3027.*

Table 1 indicates the natural gas resources of all Eastern and Central Mediterranean Countries with different probabilities. This table indicates that with a probability of 50%, the natural gas reserves in the Eastern and Central Mediterranean are 16.3 tcm. These reserves classify the Eastern and Central Mediterranean basin as the second worldwide natural gas basin. The first one is the Western Siberian basin with 643 trillion cubic feet (18.2 trillion m³) of natural gas. The third worldwide natural gas basin is the Rub Al Khalil basin in Algeria with 425 trillion cubic feet (12.1 trillion m³), the fourth is the Greater Gawar Uplift in Saudi Arabia with 227 trillion cubic feet (6.4 trillion m³) and fifth the Zagros Foki Belt with 212 trillion cubic feet (6.0 trillion m³). Figure 5 indicates the natural gas wealth of the Eastern and Central Mediterranean in respect to what is encountered in North America and the Western Siberian basin.

Figure 5: Proven reserves of natural gas in Northern America and Western Siberia basin and 50% probable natural gas reserves in Eastern Mediterranean basin.

Table 2 indicates the amount of gas discovered by Noble Company which is also ascertained by EIA, 2013[4] and MIT, 2013[5]. These proven reserves allow the proposed by DEPA, the National Greek Gas Company, to carry 15 bcm/year of natural gas to the European Union for 25 years, Figure 6. This is an identical amount which TANAP/TAP natural gas pipeline will carry from Shah Deniz Gas Field of Azerbaijan, Figure 7.

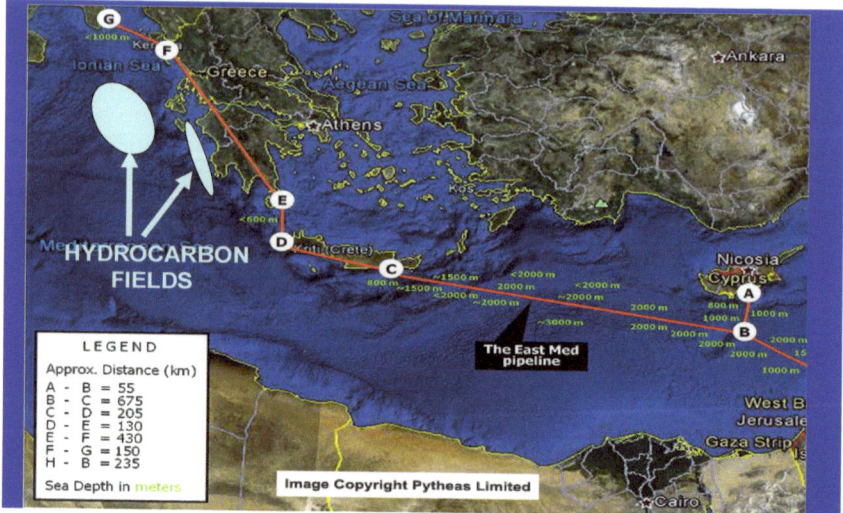

Figure 6: Proposed East Med natural gas pipeline to carry 10-15 bcm/year from Israel and Cyprus to Europe. Beyond 2020 the European Union will need 200 bcm/year.

The already discovered natural gas in Eastern Mediterranean, 1.2 tcm, is more than the natural gas reserves of Azerbaijan, 0.9 tcm, BP Statistical Review of World Energy 2014.[6]

Figure 7: TANAP/TAP natural gas pipeline to carry 15 bcm/year. from Shah Deniz, Azerbaijan to European Union.

Table 1 shows that Israel has proven reserves of natural gas 900 bcm out of which 40% can be exported, while Cyprus has proven reserves of 200 bcm and highly probable, at least 1,800 bcm while Greece has at least 3,500 bcm in offshore southern Crete and in the Ionian Sea we might have at least another 500 bcm. Therefore, assuming that Greece and Cyprus expedite their exploration and exploitation program the following amount of natural gas can be exported beyond 2025 for the next 30 years, Figure 8:

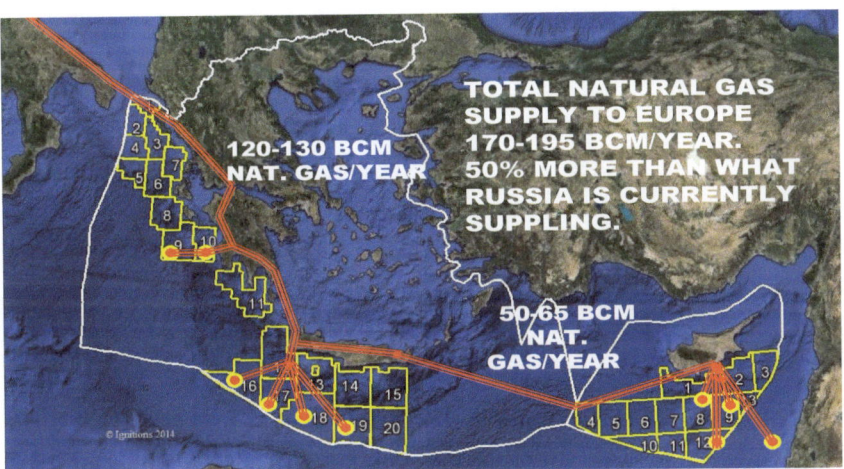

Figure 8: Potential of annual natural gas supply from Eastern Mediterranean (Israel and Cyprus) 50-65 bcm/year and Greece 120-130 bcm/year • Conversion Factors: 1 Barrel of Oil Equivalent (boe) = 155,373 Cubic Meters (m3) = 5,467 Cubic Feet (cf).

Table 1: Expected (Possible) Conventional Natural Gas Reserves In Eastern and Central Mediterranean in Trillion Cubic Meters (tcm).

EEZ OF COUNTRIES	RESERVES 95% PROBABABILITY	RESERVES 50% PROBABABILITY	RESERVES 5% PROBABABILITY	ACCURACY
EGYPT	3.4[1]	5.8[1]	12.1[1]	20%
ISRAEL	0.9	1.5[2]	3.5[2]	30%
CYPRUS	1.2	2.0[2]	4.5[2]	30%
LEBAN.+ SYRIA	0.9	2.0[1]	5.0[1]	40%
GREECE	1.9	4.5[3]	8.8[3]	50%*
TOTAL EASTERN & CENTRAL MEDITERANEAN	8.3	16.3	33.5	50%*

[1] USGS Technical Reports 2010-3014 and 2010-3027.
[2] USGS Technical Reports + Data from the Cypriot Hydrocarbon Public Company (KPETYK).
[3] Bruneton et al., 2011, Foscolos, et. al., 2013, PGS 2011.
* Inaccurate estimates due to sparse data. Reserves, however, have been extrapolated based on geological similarities (converging plates, mud flow volcanoes and accretionary prism complexes) of southern offshore Crete, Greece with the highly prolific hydrocarbon areas of the Barbados Ridge, West Timor, Indonesia and the Andaman-Nicobar islands, Myanmar.

Table 2: Reserves and Exportable amounts of natural gas reserves from Israel and Cyprus, Noble Energy, Inc.[1].

GAS FIELDS	RESOURCES (TCF)	% EXPORT	EXPORT= VOLUMES (TCF)
TAMAR	10.0	50	2.0*
DALIT	0.5	75**	0.4
LEVIATHAN	18.9	50	9.5
DOLPHIN	0.1	75**	0.1
TANIN	1.2	75	0.9
KARISH	1.8	75	1.4
TAMAR SW	0.7	75**	0.5
APHRODITE	9.0[2]	100	9.0
TOTAL	42.2		23.8

[1] www.sigmalive.com/files/download.pdf
[2] Aphrodite gas field has 5 tcf of natural gas while the satellite field in block 12 has at least an additional 4.05 tcf of natural gas bringing the total to 9 tcf.. Data from Noble Energy Inc.
* 50% of uncontracted volumes.
** Up to 100% at discretion of MEWR (Ministry of Environment and Water Resources).

- Israel exportable amount 360 bcm or 12 bcm/year
- Cyprus exportable amount 1,800 bcm or 60 bcm/year
- Greece exportable amount 3,500 bcm or 116 bcm/year
- Total exportable amount from Eastern Mediterranean and offshore Crete and the Ionian Sea 5,660 bcm or 188 bcm/year

The remaining 12 bcm/year will be supplied from Azerbaijan in order to reach the needed 200 bcm/year of natural gas. As a result the total European natural gas deficit of 440 bcm/year beyond 2020 will be met, provided that Russia can keep her commitment, as follows:

188 bcm/year (42.7%) from Eastern Mediterranean
    (Israel, Cyprus and Greece.

120 bcm/year (27.3%) from Russia

36 bcm/year (8.2%) from Algeria,

84 bcm/year (19.1%) as LNG
    from Qatar, Nigeria, Trinidad-Tobago and other nations

12 bcm/year (2.7%) from Azerbaijan

Total 440 bcm/year

Hence, a complete coverage of the European natural gas deficit. Natural gas can be exported to Europe either by pipelines, Figure 9, or by CNG and/or LNG, Figure 10 and 11. This development will undermine Russia's natural gas dominance of the European market with all its ramifications for Russia's economy.

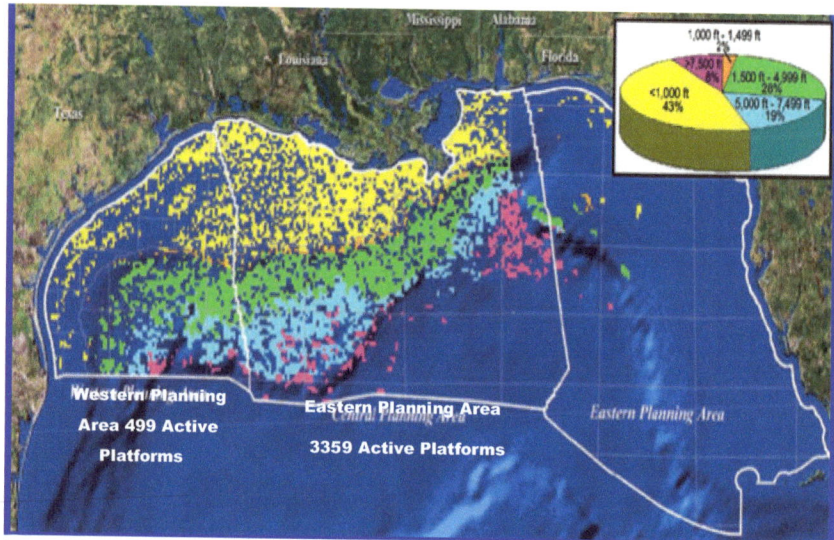

Figure 9: 3,858 offshore active platforms in the Gulf of Mexico producing 1.5 million barrels of oil/day and 46 bcf (billion cubic feet)/day natural gas.

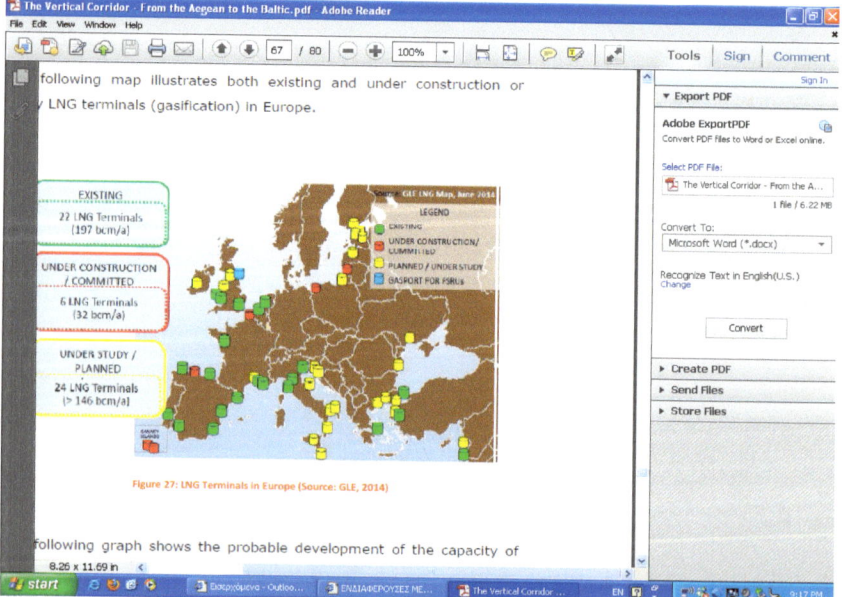

Figure 10: LNG stations in Europe.

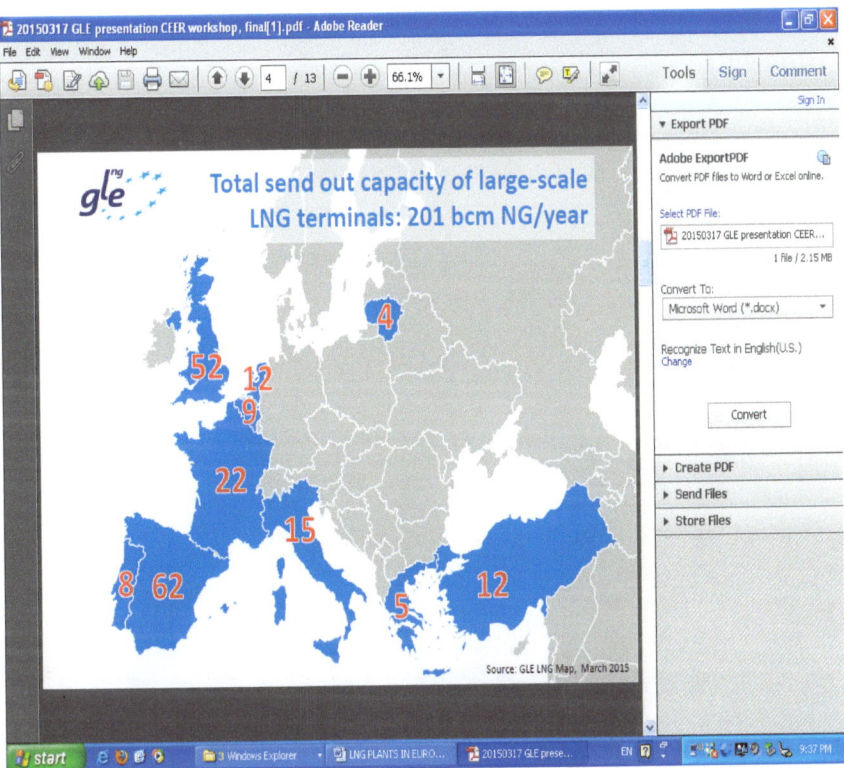

Figure 11: Total LNG in bcm/year to be delivered www.sigmaline.com/files/download/pdf.

Confronting the European oil deficit

Table 3 indicates that the proven and highly probable oil reserves of Israel, Cyprus and Greece amount to 14.5 billion barrels. Based on a rule of thumb the daily production is 1/10,000 of the reserves which means that Eastern and Central Mediterranean can supply the European Union with, at least 1,450,000 barrels/day. This amount can increase to 2,500,000 barrels/day if EEZ between Egypt, Greece and Cyprus is materialized. The latter will allow the exploitation of the Herodotus basin which is estimated to have 12.5 billion barrels of oil. Two fifths of Herodotus basin belongs to Egypt, two fifths belongs to Greece and one fifth to Cyprus.

Table 3: Proven, highly probable and probable conventional Southern Crete and the Ionian Sea Oil Reserves (Bbo) in Eastern Mediterranean and Offshore.

EEZ OF COUNTRIES	PROVEN RESERVES	HIGHLY PROBABLE	50% PROBABLE
EGYPT	4.0[1]	1.8[3]	5.5[5]
ISRAEL	2.0[2]		
CYPRUS	1.5[2]		1.5[5]
LEBANON		1.0[3]	
GREECE		11.0[4]	5.5[5]
TOTAL	7.5	13.8	12.5[5]

[1] BP Statistical Review of World Energy 2014

[2] Data from Noble Energy Inc.

[3] USGS Technical Reports of 2010

[4] Statements by the ex Prime Minister Samaras and Minister of Energy and Climatic Change Yiannis Maniatis

[5] Total estimate of Herodotus basin by BEICIP/FRANLAB based upon TGS-NOPEC geophysical data and Krois et. al., 2009

General Discussion

To exploit all this hydrocarbon wealth, a large number of active offshore platforms are needed. By comparing the size of the area in the Gulf of Mexico, USA, some 600,000 km², the amount of hydrocarbons reserves, 17 billion barrels of oil and less than 2 tcm of natural gas and the number of active offshore platforms needed, 3,858. Figure 9, with the EEZ of Cyprus and Greece, roughly 600,000 km² which has 15 billion barrels of oil and 3.1 tcm, Table 2, 95% probability, then it is reasonable to anticipate the same number of active platforms to be deployed in Eastern and Central Mediterranean Sea.

Conclusions

1. Europe is currently facing a deficit of 240 bcm of natural gas/year. It is anticipated that by 2020, it will carry an additional deficit of 200 bcm of natural gas/year. At the same time, a deficit of over 1.8 billion barrels of oil/year is predicted. Both deficits are attributed to the high depletion rate of the oil and gas fields in the North Sea.

2. Neither Russia, nor North Africa or even USA can help the European Union to meet this additional natural gas energy deficit of 200 bcm/year. The same applies to the oil deficit.

3. Geological, geophysical and geochemical data indicate the existence of very large hydrocarbon concentrations in the Eastern Mediterranean Basin (Lebanon, Israel, Palestine, Egypt and Cyprus) along with offshore southern Crete and the Ionian Sea. If exploration and exploitation of the hydrocarbon fields is expedited, Israel, Cyprus and Greece can supply the European Union with at least 188 bcm/year, thus covering the additional European Union gas deficit which is forthcoming after 2020. Moreover, some of the European Union oil deficit can be also covered by producing 1,400,000 barrels/day. This amount can be augmented to 2,500,000 barrels/day if Herodotus Basin is exploited by Egypt, Greece and Cyprus.

4. The production of oil and gas from Eastern and Central Mediterranean needs a safe marine environment.

Notes

[1] BP. 2014. World Energy Resources, 45, http://www.bp.com/content/dam/bp-country/de_de/PDFs/brochures/BP-statistical-review-of-world-energy-2014-full-report.pdf, accessed 2 April 2017.

[2] United States Geological Survey S(USGS), 2010. Undiscovered oil and gas of the Nile Delta Basin, Eastern Mediterranean. Fact Sheet 2010-3027. Feb. 2010.

[3] United States Geological Survey (USGS), 2010. Assessment of undiscovered oil and gas resources of the Levant Basin Province, Eastern Mediterranean. Fact Sheet 2010-3014, March 2010.

[4] EIA (U.S. Energy Information Administration), 2013. Overview of oil and gas in the Eastern Mediterranean region, 1-29, https://www.eia.gov/beta/international/analysis_includes/regions_of_interest/Eastern_Mediterranean/eastern-mediterranean.pdf, accessed 3 April 2017.
[5] MIT Energy Institute, 2013. Interim report for the study: Monetization pathways for Cyprus. Economics for Project Development Options,1-92.
[6] BP, World Energy Resources, 2014, 45.

[4]
A FRAMEWORK FOR THE SUSTAINABLE DEVELOPMENT OF EAST MED'S HYDROCARBONS, THE EASTERN MED'S "TRIANGLE OF FIRE" AND THE CASE OF SOUTH/EAST CHINA SEA

Sotiris N. Kamenopoulos

Eastern Mediterranean's "Triangle of Fire" and a framework for the sustainable development of East Med's Hydrocarbons

One hundred years after the Middle East's Sykes-Picot Agreement, geopolitics and world resources are still inextricably linked in each nation's economic, social, and physical development. No longer do nations exist in isolation; they are interdependent upon each other.[1] The stake of mineral and/or natural resources could be a factor for regional tensions in many places of the world. Natural resources are probably associated with conflicts[2] and peace is more likely to fail due to conflicts related to natural resources because access to such resources is an especially valuable prize worth fighting for. Resource wars constitute a new feature in the international arena and a threat to global security.[3] Resource wars are armed conflicts revolving to a significant degree over the pursuit or possession of critical materials.[4] The total number of conflicts between 1946 and 2008 was 285 while the total number of natural resources conflicts between 1946 and 2008 was 117.[5]

The following factors may be considered when dealing with the geopolitical aspects of mineral resources:

a) The world population is expected to increase.[6]

b) Demand for mineral resources, and especially for petroleum and other liquid fuels, is expected to rise in the future.[7]

c) The global Gross Domestic Product (GDP) is expected to increase.[8]

d) Some of the mineral resources deposits are located in areas that are contested or politically unstable.[9]

e) Significant indicators to capture and measure/rank potential geopolitical risks related to strategic mineral resource projects are the following: political stability, corruption, security apparatus, conflict history, and political rights/civil liberties.

The Eastern Mediterranean has been particularly vulnerable to political conflicts, even prior to the offshore gas discovery. The latter development has only complicated the issues further.[10] The world after the turmoil of "Arab Spring" became almost unpredictable. No social scientist or political analyst in either the West or the Arab world itself claims to have predicted the Arab Spring.[11] Since 2010, after the political upheavals of the "Arab Spring," a number of political events followed in some of the states of Eastern Mediterranean region. In order to have a better view on the events that occurred in the Eastern Mediterranean region since 2010, a time and event table was constructed (Table 1). Events are indicative, but they can be relative qualitative indicators of the activities that have been developed in the region since 2010.

If someone wants to create a model picturing the current geopolitical situation in the Eastern Mediterranean he/she could borrow useful concepts from other scientific fields. For example, in the field of fire safety, three elements are required in order to create a fire: an ignition source (heat), oxygen, and fuel.[12] These three elements are often called the "Triangle of Fire." In order to prevent the fire mishap, someone has to remove one of the three abovementioned elements. The geopolitical condition in the Eastern Mediterranean region could be simulated in a similar way by applying the "Triangle of Fire" metaphorically, in a manner of a "fire mishap" waiting to happen; this mishap should be prevented. At a first glance, it seems that the discovery of potential hydrocarbon offshore deposits in the region functioned as the "igniter" and/or the causal factor of a geopolitical/geo-economic combustion that was spread rapidly. The "oxygen" of subject geopolitical combustion could be simulated by the economic stakes/

values related to the probable hydrocarbon discoveries. The amount of probable natural gas reserves in the Eastern Mediterranean may be enormous, as the economic benefits indeed.[13] Based upon the geological similarities and their vast experience in both the Eastern Mediterranean and the West Timor trough, the Southern basin of Crete is equivalent to the Levantine basin.

Table 1. Time and event table for Eastern Mediterranean region.

TIME	EVENT
June 2010	Conflict aboard "Mavi Marmara". The Israeli Navy took over a flotilla of international aid ships headed to the Gaza.[14] The Israeli-Turkish relations deteriorated until June 2016.[15]
July 2010	Greek Prime Minister George Papandreou visited Israel[16]
October 2010	First publications on Greek websites regarding the existence of probable offshore hydrocarbon fields in the south of Crete[17]
December 2010	Noble Energy announces significant discovery at Leviathan offshore Israel.[18] Cyprus and Israel signed deal demarcating sea borders.[19]
February 2012	Benjamin Netanyahu became the first Israeli Prime Minister to visit Cyprus.[20]
October 2013	Greek Prime Minister Anthony Samaras visited Israel.[21]
April 2014	Israel places for the first time a Military Attaché in the Israeli Embassy in Athens, Greece.[22]
August 2015	Large gas field in Mediterranean discovered off Egypt was announced by the Italian energy company ENI.[23]
November 2015	First visit of Greek Prime Minister Alexis Tsipras to Israel.[24]
December 2015	Greece, Cyprus and Egypt end trilateral talks with broad declaration.[25]
January 2016	Second visit of Greek Prime Minister Alexis Tsipras to Israel[26]
March 2016	Israel-Greece-Cyprus hold trilateral parliamentary meeting[27]

This result implies that the potential to discover natural gas and oil offshore Crete is very strong.[28] The "fuel" of the geopolitical combustion could be simulated by the geopolitical competition/antagonisms between the regional powers. Figure 1 depicts the Eastern Mediterranean "Triangle of Fire." The challenge in the case of the Eastern Mediterranean region is to prevent a probable geopolitical "mishap," thus formulating a balance control between the regional powers. As in the case of real fires, someone has to remove one of the three elements, or all of them, in order to prevent the "fire." The three "mishap" prevention alternatives in the case of Eastern Mediterranean region could be the following:

1. Reduce the probability of "ignition:" use of a process/mechanism to allocate the hydrocarbon deposits amongst regional stakeholders, or
2. Control the level of "oxygen:" use of a process/mechanism to allocate the economic stakes amongst regional stakeholders, or
3. Remove "fuel:" use of a process/mechanism to diminish the competition/antagonism between regional stakeholders, reduce geopolitical risks, and increase regional security.

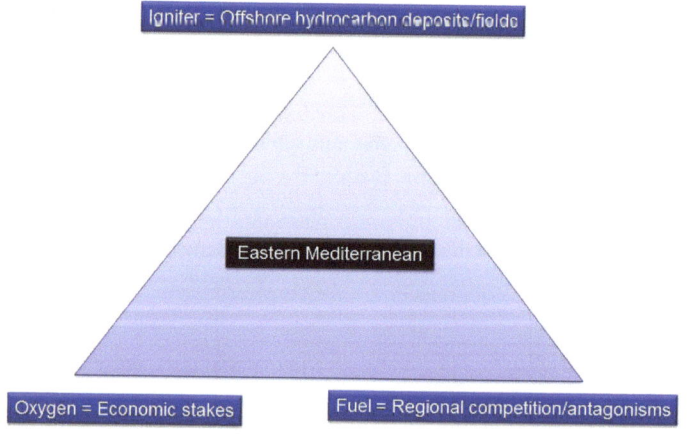

Figure 1: The Eastern Mediterranean "Triangle of Fire" model.

The fishbone diagram of Figure 2 was developed to represent the "effect" of each stakeholder to the balance of Eastern Mediterranean's "Fire Triangle." It was based on inputs from Table 2. These "effects" are considered dynamic, meaning that they may be subject to changes at any time. The "effects" of different stakeholders may make the development of offshore hydrocarbon projects a very complicated task in the Eastern Mediterranean region. Figure 2 shows that currently it seems most of the stakeholders have taken the necessary steps to improve relations with each other through trilateral agreements; perhaps the only conflict that remains unresolved is that between Cyprus and Turkey making peace in the region wishful thinking.

The efforts of all stakeholders involved in the Eastern Mediterranean region should be the construction of a roadmap for the sustainable development of hydrocarbons/energy resources. A pre-specified context that will frame the surroundings in which the involved stakeholders perform their tasks is considered essential for the sustainability of offshore hydrocarbon projects in the Eastern Mediterranean region. Recognizing the need to move forward and develop offshore hydrocarbon projects in a sustainable manner, a plausible framework for the sustainable development of Eastern Mediterranean Offshore Hydrocarbon Projects is proposed in Figure 3. Any recommended action for the establishment of a sustainable framework should be within the context set off by the "Brundtland Commission,"[29] the Rio Summit (AGENDA 21),[30] and the Rio+20[31] recommendations. The proposed framework for the sustainable development of Eastern Mediterranean offshore hydrocarbon projects may include fundamental elements that contribute to a holistic sustainable platform.

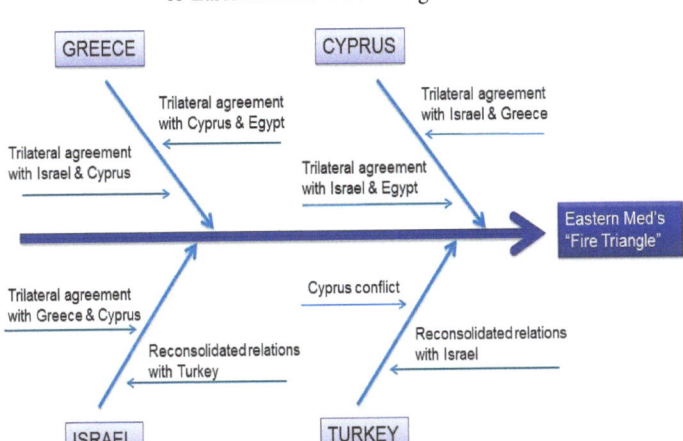

Figure 2: Fishbone diagram representing the "effect" of each stakeholder to Eastern Med's "Fire Triangle".

The proposed framework may include the following parts (Figure 3):

- ✔ Five components represented as circles: (geo)economy, society, environment, technology, and (geo)politics.
- ✔ Three controlling/limiting factors: (geo)policy, (geo)governance, and (geo)stakeholders.
- ✔ A number of output quantities to be used in decision making: (geo)indicators.

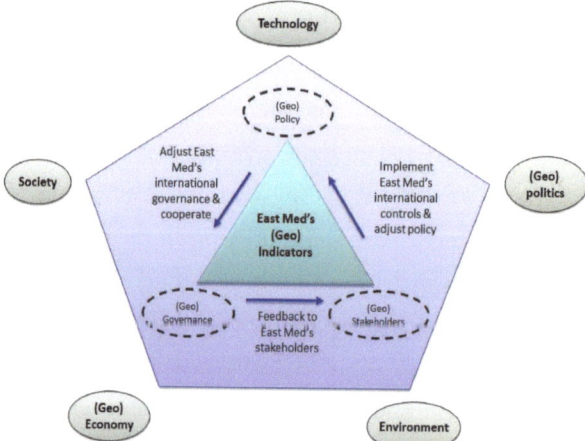

Figure 3: Plausible framework for the sustainable development of Eastern Med's Offshore Hydrocarbon Projects (based on work by Kamenopoulos et al).

The proposed plausible sustainable development framework is based on previous work by Kamenopoulos et al[32] and it is adjusted in order to fit the (geo)conditions of Eastern Med's "Fire Triangle" model.

The first three basic components (economy, society, and environment) were developed by the "Brundtland Commission" in 1987 and they are considered the main pillars of global sustainable development. The component of technology is a key concept of sustainable development: it may resolve the economic, social and environmental problems that make current sustainable development paths unsustainable.[33] The component of geopolitics may be considered as a must in any suggested sustainable development framework since the hydrocarbons are considered vulnerable to geostrategic and geopolitical risk. The geopolitical pillar of the proposed framework may be concentrated at the Eastern Med's "Fire Triangle."

The three controlling/limiting factors of the plausible framework are related in a counterclockwise manner (Figure 3) and this internal process would be considered as a closed loop. (Geo)governance would be considered the sum of the many ways individuals and (international) institutions, public and private, manage their common affairs[34] in the Eastern Mediterranean region. (Geo)governance is based on the achievement of preset objectives that best fits the needs of societies, influenced by complex (geo)political scenarios, which affect the environment and the economies. In order to meet the objectives, (geo)governance designers utilize specific tools (regulations/laws/rules) that ultimately lead to the formation of (geo)policy. (Geo)policy would not be considered a static notion: it is adjusted under the specific fluctuating conditions and needs of stakeholders. Stakeholders receive the feedback from the implemented governance; the adjusted policies lead toward the adjustments of governance/supervision and so forth. The next step would be the development of a decision support mechanism which will incorporate selected (geo)indicators and assist decision makers/stakeholders to better assess the impact of any Eastern Med's Offshore Hydrocarbon project from the sustainability point of view and in a holistic manner. The selection of indicators should be based on the five proposed components/pillars of Figure 3. The overall process which details how the plausible framework would be applied in the case of Eastern Med's offshore hydrocarbon projects is presented in Figure 4.

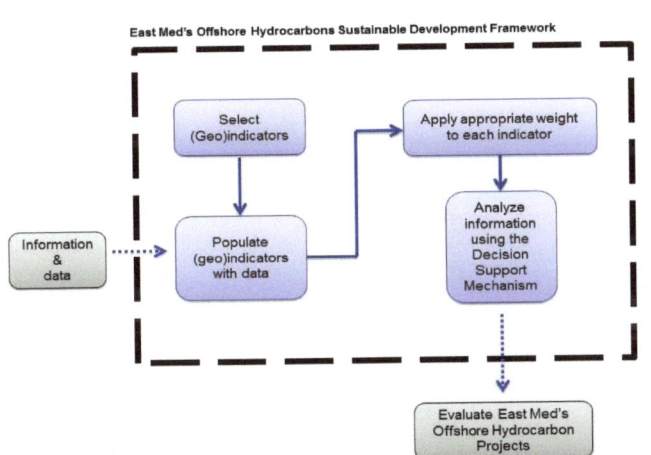

Figure 4: Application of the plausible framework in the case of Eastern Med's Offshore Hydrocarbon Projects (based on Kamenopoulos et al).

Eastern Mediterranean vs. South/East China Seas

In 2001 a geographical world map was published showing candidate/probable global contested areas for conflicts related to natural resources: oil/natural gas/ pipelines, water systems, and gems/mineral and timber.[35] The map (Figure 5) was used as an indicator for potential violence in the contested areas whose ownership of natural resources would be a subject of severe dispute. Klare's map did not include the Mediterranean region; yet it included, amongst others, the East and South China Seas. After ten years, in 2011, three regions seemed to be the most challenged areas for global navies: the Arctic, the Eastern Mediterranean, and the South/East China Seas[36] (Figure 6). These regions may have a common ingredient: all three of them can probably have high potential to uncover reach deep-sea oil/natural-gas fields/deposits. In 2011, due to *America's Pacific Century*[37] dogma (known as the "American Pivot" or rebalance toward Asia) it seemed that the Mediterranean region would no longer be in the spot of the geopolitics. However, the burst of the Arab Spring and the later Syria crisis proved that the Mediterranean region probably is and perhaps will be for a long period of time in the spot of the geopolitics together with the South/East China Seas region.

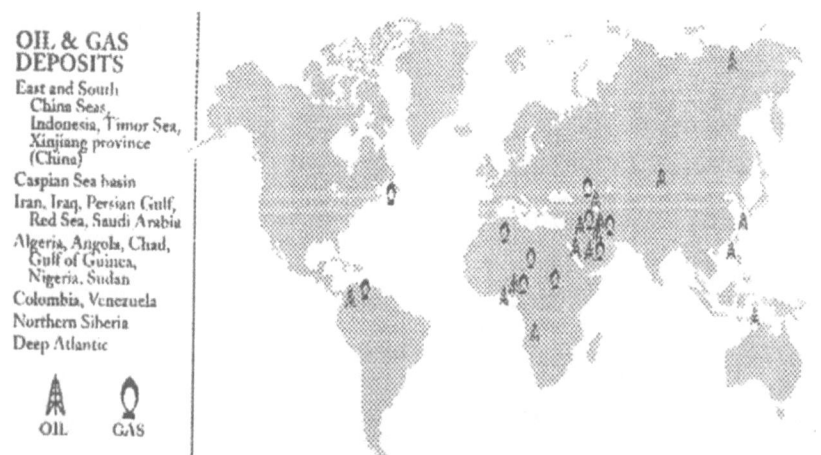

Figure 5: Michael Klare, The New Geography of Conflict, Foreign Affairs, May/June 2001, pp. 49-61.

The comparison between the cases of Eastern Mediterranean and south/east China Seas may be used as a useful and yet challenging support tool for several direct as well as indirect stakeholders involved in the geopolitical decisions, especially in the Eastern Mediterranean region. This comparison may be used as a magnifier in order to help reveal, clarify and examine the root causes of tensions. Thus, it may be utilized as a tracer for the designing of a sustainable peace roadmap in the Mediterranean region. The attempt, effort and aim of the following paragraphs are to unfold any probable qualitative variables of the South/East China Seas region that might be comparable to the case of Eastern Mediterranean region. The aim is not to create an in-depth analysis on subject variables. Such an in-depth analysis would be the scope of a larger scientific study and should include several stakeholders.

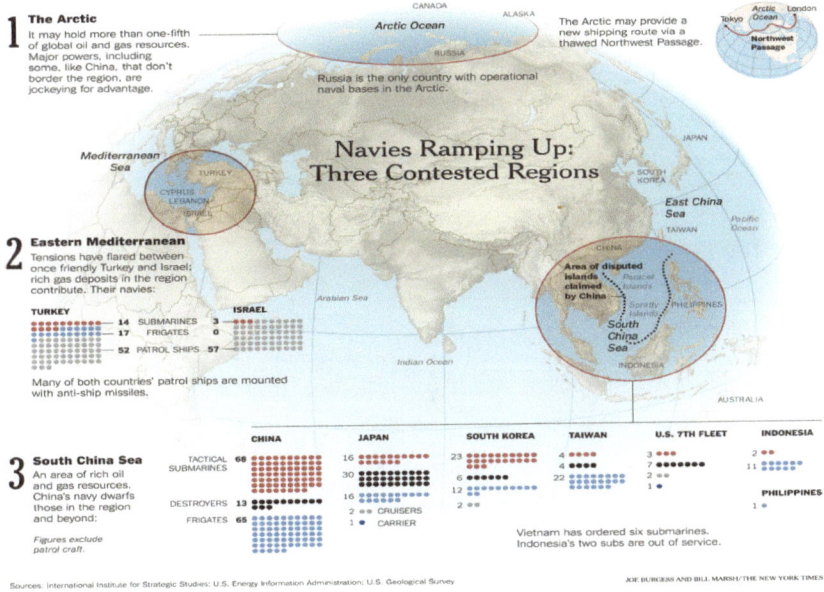

Figure 6. Mark Landler, A new era of gunboat diplomacy, The New York Times, 12 November 2011, http://www.nytimes.com/imagepages/2011/11/13/opinion/13gunboat img.html, accessed 27 June 2016.

The hypothesis formulated is that in limited variables the current conditions and/or framework and the practices and/or procedures followed by stakeholders in the case of South/East China Seas region may be relatively comparable to the case of Eastern Mediterranean region.

The methodology that will be used in order to prove the abovementioned hypothesis is the *comparative method*. (CM).[38] The reasoning behind the selection of this method is the following:

- ✦ The CM allows us to discover an empirical relationship among variables.

- ✦ The number of cases (alternatives-N) that the CM deals with is too small to permit systematic control by means of partial correlations.

- ✦ The CM focuses the comparative analysis on "comparative" cases and allows examining the small number of N alternatives under the features of a large number of important characteristics (variables).

For the purposes of this paper the number of alternatives (cases) to be compared is two (N=2):

❏ The Eastern Mediterranean region
❏ The South/East China Seas

In both cases probably there are many stakeholders involved. In the case of Eastern Mediterranean region the feasible direct and indirect stakeholders are: Israel, Turkey, Greece, Cyprus, Egypt, Russia (indirect) and U.S (indirect). In the case of South/East China Seas the stakeholders are: China, Vietnam, Malaysia, Philippines, Japan, Brunei and U.S (indirect). In a recent development that might act as a guide and might be relevant to the case of the Eastern Mediterranean Sea, the Permanent Court of Arbitration in Hague reached a decision over a case brought by the Philippines in 2013 against China's South China Sea claims. The Court said that it finds no legal basis for China's claim to historic rights to resources within the claimed zone.[39] Although Chinese navigators and fishermen, as well as those of other states, had historically made use of the islands in the South China Sea, there was no evidence that China had historically exercised exclusive control over the waters or their resources, the Court said. China had violated the Philippines' sovereign rights in its exclusive economic zone by (a) interfering with Philippine fishing and petroleum exploration, (b) constructing artificial islands and (c) failing to prevent Chinese fishermen from fishing in the zone.

Table 2 summarizes the framework of the problem.

Table 2: Framework of the problem.

Alternatives	Stake	Stakeholders	Tools
Eastern Mediterranean	Mineral resources	Israel, Turkey, Greece, Cyprus, Egypt, Russia and US	UNCLOS - EEZ
South/East China	Mineral resources	China, Vietnam, Malaysia, Philippines, Japan, Brunei and US	UNCLOS - EEZ

The next step would be to identify the set of variables under which the two alternatives could be compared with each other. In order to do so, a report,[40] which provides background information and issues for US Congress on maritime territorial and exclusive economic zone (EEZ) disputes in the East China (ECS) and South China Sea (SCS) involving China could be utilized as a main guide to identify aforementioned variables. Although this report focuses on how several disputes may affect US strategic and policy interests, it may provide specific variables from the point of view of one potentially important stakeholder. Finally, in both cases the issues of Economic Exclusive Zones (EEZ) and United Nations Convention of Law of the Sea (UNCLOS) seems to play a role within the framework of the problem. Table 3 summarizes the potential sub-variables in the case of South/East China Seas and comparative comments regarding the case of Eastern Mediterranean region.

Table 3: Potential qualitative variables and comparative comments for the two studied cases.

Sub-Variable #	Case of South/East China Seas/ Potential Qualitative Variables	Case of Eastern Mediterranean region Comparative Comments
1	...Coastal states under UNCLOS have the right to regulate economic activities in their EEZs but do not have the right to regulate foreign military activities in their EEZs...	Israel and Turkey have neither signed nor acceded either the Convention or the Agreement. Greece, Cyprus, Egypt, and Russia have signed and ratified the Agreement. The US has signed the Convention but has not ratified it. Yet, in 2012 Secretary of State Hillary Clinton gave her remarks on the Law of the Sea Convention before the Senate Committee on Foreign Relations. In accordance to Ms. Clinton's remarks: ...one could argue, that 20 years ago, 10 years ago, maybe even five years ago, joining the convention was important but not urgent. That is no longer the case today. Four new developments make our participation a matter of utmost security and economic urgency...[41]
2	...Although the maritime disputes at first glance may appear to be disputes over a few seemingly unimportant rocks and reefs in the ocean, these disputes are considered important by China, other countries in the region, and the United States for a variety of strategic, political, and economic reasons...	In 1996 during the Greek-Turkish crisis over the Imia islands in the Aegean sea some U.S officials were referring to Imia islands as "some rocks".[42] In addition, ...while it seems that such minor pieces of land would not be of major concern, the issue has explosive potential (...) The tiny (...) islands support practically no life or economic possibility, are inhabited only by several happy seagulls and grazing goats and were considered no more than navigation hazards until the incident ... of 1996.[43]
3	...The South/East China Seas contain significant fishing grounds and potentially significant oil and gas exploration areas...	The Eastern Mediterranean region also contains potentially significant oil and gas exploration areas.
4	...The presence of valuable fish stocks and potential existence of large hydrocarbon resources under the East and South China Seas exacerbate the complicated claims...	The presence of potential existence of large hydrocarbon resources under the Eastern Mediterranean region[13] may also intensify the complicated claims amongst stakeholders.

5	. . . China wants to achieve a greater degree of control over its near-seas region in order to achieve a broader goal of becoming a regional hegemon in its part of Eurasia . . .	Turkey is perceived by regional countries as a would-be regional hegemon.[44] The first indication scenarios regarding the rerise of Ottoman Empire seem to appear at least since 2011 via geopolitical think tanks such as Wikistrat.[45] It should be noted that during the Ottoman Empire both Israeli and Greek states did not exist.
6	. . . Significant portions of the world's oceans are claimable as EEZs, including high-priority US Navy operating areas in the Western Pacific, the Persian Gulf, and the Mediterranean Sea . . .	The U.S Navy 6th Fleet operates at Mediterranean sea.[46]
7	. . . China is pursuing a goal of becoming a regional hegemon in its part of Eurasia, and that achieving a greater degree of control over its near-seas region is a part of this effort. From a US standpoint, such an effort would be highly significant, because it has been a long-standing goal of US grand strategy to prevent the emergence of a regional hegemon in one part of Eurasia or another . . .	Turkey is perceived by regional countries as a prospective regional hegemon. The first indication scenarios regarding the rerise of Ottoman Empire seem to appear at least since 2011 via geopolitical think tanks such as Wikistrat. It should be noted that during the Ottoman Empire both Israeli and Greek states did not exist.
8	. . . China is a party to multiple maritime territorial disputes in the South/East China Seas, including in particular the following: - a dispute over the Paracel Islands in the SCS, which are claimed by China and Vietnam, and occupied by China; - a dispute over the Spratly Islands in the SCS, which are claimed entirely by China, Taiwan, and Vietnam, and in part by the Philippines, Malaysia, and Brunei, and which are occupied in part by all these countries except Brunei; - a dispute over Scarborough Shoal in the SCS, which is claimed by China, Taiwan, and the Philippines, and controlled since 2012 by China; and — a dispute over the Senkaku Islands in the ECS, which are claimed by China, Taiwan, and Japan, and administered by Japan...	Turkish disputes in the Aegean Sea.

9	... The position of the United States and most countries is that while the United Nations Convention on the Law of the Sea (UNCLOS), which established EEZs as a feature of international law, gives coastal states the right to regulate economic activities (such as fishing and oil exploration) within their EEZs, it does not give coastal states the right to regulate foreign military activities in the parts of their EEZs beyond their 12-nautical-mile territorial waters ...	Israel and Turkey have neither signed nor acceded either the Convention or the Agreement. Greece, Cyprus, Egypt, and Russia have signed and ratified the Agreement. The US has signed the Convention but has not ratified it. Yet, in 2012 Secretary of State Hillary Clinton gave her remarks on the Law of the Sea Convention before the Senate Committee on Foreign Relations. In accordance to Ms. Clinton's remarks ... one could argue, that 20 years ago, 10 years ago, maybe even five years ago, joining the convention was important but not urgent. That is no longer the case today. Four new developments make our participation a matter of utmost security and economic urgency ...
10	... China makes regular use of China Coast Guard (CCG) ships to assert and defend its maritime territorial claims, with Chinese Navy ships sometimes available over the horizon as backup forces. ... particularly in terms of confronting or harassing foreign vessels that are similarly lightly armed or unarmed . .) China also uses civilian fishing ships as a form of maritime militia, as well as mobile oil exploration platforms, to assert and defend its maritime claims..."	In October 2014 a seismic Turkish frigate and two additional Turkish vessels entered the EEZ of Cyprus.[47] For that reason the EU Parliament voted on a resolution "on Turkish actions creating tensions in the exclusive economic zone of Cyprus." [48] In April 2016 a Turkish coast guard patrol boat threatened to arrest fisherman sailing in Greek waters.[49] In accordance to a Greek defence website in 2015 there were more than 1,200 territorial water violations by Turkish vessels. The vast majority of violations were made by fishing vessels.[50]
11	... Frequent patrols by Chinese Coast Guard ships—some observers refer to them as harassment operations—at the Senkaku Islands ...	Same as previous comments.

12	. . . As part of his prepared statement for the same hearing, Robert Scher, then-Deputy Assistant Secretary of Defence, Asian and Pacific Security Affairs, Office of the Secretary of Defence, stated that "..our military activity in this region is routine and in accordance with customary international law as reflected in the 1982 Law of the Sea Convention . . .	Israel and Turkey have neither signed nor acceded either the Convention or the Agreement. Greece, Cyprus, Egypt, and Russia have signed and ratified the Agreement. The US has signed the Convention but has not ratified it. Yet, in 2012 Secretary of State Hillary Clinton gave her remarks on the Law of the Sea Convention before the Senate Committee on Foreign Relations. In accordance to Ms. Clinton's remarks: . . . one could argue, that 20 years ago, 10 years ago, maybe even five years ago, joining the convention was important but not urgent. That is no longer the case today. Four new developments make our participation a matter of utmost security and economic urgency . . .
13	. . . The strategy of the US is to prevent China becoming a regional hegemon in East Asia, and potentially as part of that, preventing China from controlling or dominating the south/east China seas . . .	Turkey is perceived by regional countries as a prospective regional hegemon. The first indication scenarios regarding the rerise of Ottoman Empire seem to appear at least since 2011 via geopolitical think tanks such as Wikistrat.[81] It should be noted that during the Ottoman Empire both Israeli and Greek states did not exist.
14	"…In conjunction with the Department of State and the U.S Coast Guard, the U.S has dramatically expanded their maritime security assistance in south/east China seas regional countries in recent years …"	It seems that the US Coast Guard intents to be involved in the security issues of Eastern Mediterranean region. In May 2016, the deputy chief of U.S Coast Guard visited Athens, Greece showing the US interest in refugee flows and security conditions in the Eastern Mediterranean. The U.S showed their interested on the situation in the Aegean wanting help with the US Coast Guard.[51]
15	. . .The Defence Threat Reduction Agency (DTRA) is helping to construct a Philippine National Coast Watch Center in Manila that will assist the Philippine Coast Guard (PCG) in assuming increased responsibility for enhancing information sharing and interagency coordination in maritime security operations . . .	Same as previous comment.

16	. . . A key element of U.S DoD's approach to maritime security in Southeast Asia is to work alongside capable regional partners. . . . The US joined trilaterally to achieve these goals. . . . In November 2014, President Obama, Prime Minister Abe, and Prime Minister Abbott hosted their first trilateral meeting and agreed to expand maritime cooperation, trilateral exercises, and defence development.	The US has made several trilateral naval exercises in the Mediterranean sea.[52] In addition trilateral agreements have been made between Israel-Greece-Cyprus and between Greece-Egypt-Cyprus.

As it can be seen from Table 3, sixteen potential sub-variables of the South/East China Seas were identified that may form common sets of variables with the case of the Eastern Mediterranean. The next step will be to identify if some of the sub-variables are repeated; thus the number of probable comparable/common sub-variables would be grouped to develop a set with a limited number of variables. Further analysis of the information in Table 3 shows that the following sub-variables are the same or repeated thus they may be grouped to a smaller number of variables.

- Sub-variables 1, 9, 6, and 12: this set of sub-variables is grouped forming the variable of "UNCLOS/EEZ."
- Sub-variables 3 and 4: this set of sub-variables is grouped forming the variable of "Existence of Resources."
- Sub-variables 5, 7, and 13: this set of sub-variables is grouped forming the variable "Local Hegemonism."
- Sub-variables 2 and 8: this set of sub-variables is grouped forming the variable of "Disputes over Unimportant Rocks."
- Sub-variables 10 and 11: this set of sub-variables is grouped forming the variable of "Harassment Operations."
- Sub-variables 14 and 15: this set of sub-variables is grouped forming the variable of "US Coast Guard's Role."
- Sub-variable 16: forms a variable on its own; the variable of "Trilateral Agreements."

Consequently, the total number of sub-variables may be reduced to a set of seven variables under which the two alternatives could be considering as relatively comparable and/or similar with each other. These final variables are:

- ❏ UNCLOS/EEZ
- ❏ Existence of Resources
- ❏ Local Hegemonism
- ❏ Disputes over "Unimportant" Rocks
- ❏ Harassment Operations
- ❏ US Coast Guard's Presence/ Role
- ❏ Trilateral Agreements

As it was mentioned in a previous paragraph the aim of this effort is not to perform an indepth analysis on the abovementioned seven variables. An indepth analysis would be the scope of different scientific studies. The challenge would be to identify at which level the two alternatives (South/East China Seas vs. Eastern Mediterranean) are similar with respect to the behavior of some of the stakeholders involved and with regard to the seven variables.

Conclusions and recommendations

This paper was based on two pillars. The first pillar concerned the critical geopolitical challenges in the Eastern Mediterranean. The establishment of prevention mechanisms might be considered important in order to avoid probable geopolitical "mishaps" in the Eastern Mediterranean region. The current geopolitical situation in the Eastern Mediterranean has been modeled as a "Triangle of Fire." Under this model three "mishap" prevention alternatives were recommended. Furthermore, the "effect" of involved stakeholders to the balance of Eastern Mediterranean's "Fire Triangle" was acknowledged. These "effects" should be considered dynamic, meaning that they may be subject to changes constantly. A plausible framework for the sustainable development of Eastern Mediterranean Offshore Hydrocarbon Projects was also proposed. The proposed framework may include five components (geo-economy, society, environment, technology, geopolitics), three controlling/limiting factors (geo-policy, geo-governance, geo-stakeholders), and a probable number of output quantities to be used in decision making: geo-indicators. The aim would be to develop a decision support mechanism, which will incorporate selected geo-indicators and assist decision makers/stakeholders to better assess the impact of any Eastern Med's Offshore Hydrocarbon project from the sustainability point of view and in a holistic manner.

The second pillar was related to the cases of Eastern Mediterranean and South/East China Seas. In order to better understand the geopolitics of Eastern Mediterranean region a hypothesis was formulated stating that under current conditions and the practices/procedures followed by geopolitical stakeholders the case of Eastern Mediterranean region may be relatively similar to the case of South/East China Seas region. In order to prove the abovementioned hypothesis a preliminary comparison between the two cases was conducted in order to identify potential qualitative variables that may support subject hypothesis. During the analysis seven variables were identified. Yet, the existence of these variables does not necessary prove the hypothesis before an in-depth multi-stakeholders analysis occurs. For that reason in-depth analysis is considered essential in order to support several stakeholders involved in the geopolitical decisions and design a sustainable peace roadmap that will make the eastern Mediterranean region into a region of tranquility.

Notes

[1] B. Davis, Geopolitics, world resources, and survival: A role playing game, *Geopolitics*, 1982, v. 81, n. 2, 56-6.
[2] M. Conant, Resources and conflict: Oil-the likely contingencies, *The Adelphi Papers*, 1981, v. 21, n. 167, 45-50.

3   S. Peters, Coercive western energy security strategies: 'resource wars' as a new threat to global security, *Geopolitics*, 2004, v.9, n.1, 187-212.
4   P. Le Billon, The geopolitics economy of resource wars, *Geopolitics*, 2004, v.9, n.1, 1-28.
5   S. A. Rustad and H. Malmin Binningsbø, A Price Worth Fighting for? Natural Resources and Conflict Recurrence, *Journal of Peace Research*, 2012, v.49, n.4, 531–546.
6   United Nations, ed., World population projected to reach 9.6 billion by 2050, 2013, at: http://www.un.org/apps/news/story.asp?NewsID=45165, accessed 20 June 2016.
7   U.S. Energy Information Administration (EIA), ed., International Energy Outlook, Chapter 2: Petroleum and other liquid fuels, 2016, http://www.eia.gov/forecasts/ieo/liquid_fuels.cfm, accessed 28 June 2016.
8   Organization for Economic Cooperation and Development (OECD), ed., Environmental Outlook to 2050: Climate Change Chapter, 2011, http://www.oecd.org/env/cc/49082173.pdf ,accessed 21 June 2016.
9   S. Kamenopoulos, Z. Agioutantis, K. Komnitsas, and P. Partsinevelos, A New Tool for the Geopolitical Assessment of Rare Earth Elements projects, 7th International Conference on sustainable development in the Minerals Industry, 12-15 July 2015, Vancouver, Canada.
10 W. Khadduri, East Mediterranean gas: Opportunities and challenges, *Mediterranean Politics*, 2012, 17, 1, 111-117.
11 J. Goodwin, Why we were surprised (again) by the Arab Spring, *Swiss Political Science Review*, 2011, v.17, n.4, 452-456.
12 U.S National Fire Protection Association-NFPA, ed., All about fire, http://www.nfpa.org/news-and-research/news-and-media/press-room/reporters-guide-to-fire-and-nfpa/all-about-fire, accessed 5 July 2016.
13 A. Foscolos, Implementation of the Greek Exclusive Zone and its financial and geopolitical benefits, 2014, http://probeinternational.org/library/wp-content/uploads/2011/10/19052011_Foscolos_NEW1.pdf, accessed 4 July 2016.
14 Y. Katz, Nine dead in vicious conflict aboard 'Mavi Marmara', *The Jerusalem Post*, 1 June 2010, http://www.jpost.com/Israel/Nine-dead-in-Vicious-conflict-aboard-Mavi-Marmara, accessed 4 July 2016.
15 Reuters, ed., Turkey, Israel sign deal to normalize diplomatic relations, 28 June 2016, http://www.nbcnews.com/news/world/turkey-israel-sign-deal-normalize-diplomatic-relations-n600186, accessed 4 July 2016.
16 A. Tziampiris, Athens meets Israel, *The National Interest*, 4 August 2010, http://nationalinterest.org/commentary/athens-meets-israel-3779, accessed 04 July 2016.
17 Greek website *Newsbomb*, ed., An Alaska of hydrocarbons south of Crete, 25 October 2010, http://www.newsbomb.gr/ellada/apokalypseis/story/3058/uparxei-mia...-alaska-se-petrelaio-sto-kritiko-pelagos, accessed 4 July 2016.
18 Noble Energy official website, ed., Noble Energy announces significant discovery at Leviathan offshore Israel, 29 December 2010, http://investors.nobleenergyinc.com/releasedetail.cfm?ReleaseID=539152, accessed 4 July 2016.

[19] Israeli website *Haaretz*, ed., Cyprus and Israel signed deal demarcating sea borders, 17 December 2010, http://www.haaretz.com/israel-news/cyprus-and-israel-sign-deal-demarcating-sea-borders-1.331160, accessed 5 July 2016.

[20] A. Stergiou, Turkey-Cyprus-Israel relations and the Cyprus conflict, *Journal of Balkan and Near Eastern Studies*, Turkey-Cyprus-Israel relations and the Cyprus conflict, 2016, v.18, n.4, 375-392.

[21] S. Koutzanis, Samaras in Israel, Greek newspaper *Protothema*, 7 October 2013, http://www.protothema.gr/politics/article/316927/sto-israil-tha-vrisketai-simera-to-apogeuma-o-prothupourgos/, accessed 4 July 2016.

[22] Greek website On Alert, ed., Israel places for the first time a Military Attaché in the Israeli Embassy in Athens, 7 April 2014, http://www.onalert.gr/stories/to-israel-topothetei-gia-ptori-fora-akoloutho-amynas-stin-athina/33637, accessed 5 July 2016.

[23] Israeli website *Haaretz*, ed., Largest-ever' Gas Field in Mediterranean Discovered Off Egypt, Italian Energy Giant Eni Says, 30 August 2015, at: http://www.haaretz.com/middle-east-news/1.673619, accessed 4 July 2016.

[24] Greek website *Protothema*, ed., Visiting Tsipras in Israel shows that it is man of surprises, 26 November 2015, http://www.protothema.gr/world/article/530784/jerusalem-post-i-episkepsi-tsipra-sto-israil-deihnei-pos-einai-anthropos-ton-ekplixeon/, accessed 4 July 2016.

[25] Greek website *e-kathimerini*, ed., Greece, Cyprus and Egypt end trilateral talks with broad declaration, 9 December 2015, http://www.ekathimerini.com/204199/article/ekathimerini/news/greece-cyprus-and-egypt-end-trilateral-talks-with-broad-declaration, accessed 4 July 2016.

[26] Greek website *Protothema*, ed., Prime Minister Tsipras visits Israel accompanied by nine ministers, 27 January 2016, http://en.protothema.gr/pm-tsipras-visits-israel-accompanied-by-nine-ministers/, accessed 4 July 2016.

[27] Israeli website Israel National News, ed., Israel-Greece-Cyprus hold trilateral parliamentary meeting, 6 March 2016, http://israelnationalnews.org/2016/03/israel-greece-cyprus-hold-trilateral-parliamentary-meeting/, accessed 4 July 2016.

[28] A. Bruneton, E. Konofagos and A. Foscolos, Cretan gas fields: A new perspective for Greece's hydrocarbon resources, Pytheas Market Focus, 30 March 2012, http://images.derstandard.at/2013/08/21/greece_crete.pdf, accessed 31 March 2017.

[29] United Nations, ed., Report of the World Commission on Environment and Development: Our Common Future, 1987, http://www.un-documents.net/wced-ocf.htm, accessed 6 July 2016.

[30] United Nations, ed., Agenda 21, https://sustainabledevelopment.un.org/outcomedocuments/agenda21, accessed 6 July 2016.

[31] United Nations, ed., Rio+20 Conference, https://sustainabledevelopment.un.org/rio20.html, accessed 6 July 2016.

[32] S. Kamenopoulos, Z. Agioutantis, K. Komnitsas, A framework for sustainable mining of Rare Earth Elements, in Borges De Lima and W. Leal Filho, eds., *Rare Earths Industry: Technological, Economic, and Environmental Implications*, Amsterdam, Elsevier Publication, 2015, Chapter 7, 111-120.

33 United Nations, Earth Summit 2002, Science and Technology as a Foundation for Sustainable Development Summary by the Scientific and Technological Community for the Multi-Stakeholder Dialogue Segment of the WSSD PrepCom IV Meeting, Prepared by the International Council for Science (ICSU) and the World Federation of Engineering Organizations (WFEO), who were invited by the WSSD Secretariat as the organizing partners for the Dialogue Segment for the Scientific and Technological Communities. This document has been prepared in consultation with the InterAcademy Panel (IAP), the Third World Academy of Sciences (TWAS) and the International Social Sciences Council (ISSC).

34 United Nations Development Program-UNDP, ed., Reconfiguring Global Governance-Effectiveness, Inclusiveness, and China's Global Role, 2012, http://www.undp.org/content/dam/china/docs/Publications/UNDP-CH_Global_Governance_Report_2013_EN.pdf, accessed 6 July 2016.

35 M. Klare, The new geography of conflict, *Foreign Affairs*, May/June 2001, 49-61.

36 M. Landler, A new era of gunboat diplomacy, *The New York Times*, 12 November 2011, http://www.nytimes.com/2011/11/13/sunday-review/a-new-era-of-gunboat-diplomacy.html?_r=0, accessed 27 June 2016.

37 US Department of State, ed., Hillary Clinton: America's Pacific Century, 2011, http://www.state.gov/secretary/20092013clinton/rm/2011/11/176999.htm, accessed 27 June 2016.

38 A. Lijphart, Comparative politics and the comparative method, *The American Political Science Review*, v.65, n.3, September 1971, 682-693.

39 T. Daiss, Philippines Wins South China Sea Case against China, Court Issues Harsh Verdict, *Forbes*, 12 July 2016, http://www.forbes.com/sites/timdaiss/2016/07/12/philippines-wins-south-china-sea-case-against-china-court-issues-harsh-verdict/#df5bbd63a0ac.

40 R. O'Rurke, Maritime Territorial and Exclusive Economic Zone (EEZ) Disputes Involving China: Issues for Congress, Report Prepared for Members and Committees of U.S Congress, Congressional Research Service, 27 April 2016.

41 US Council of Foreign Relations, ed., Clinton's Testimony on the Law of the Sea Convention, May 2012, http://www.cfr.org/global-governance/clintons-testimony-law-sea-convention-may-2012/p28340, accessed 30 June 2016.

42 Greek newspaper *To Vima*, ed., The night of Imia, http://www.tovima.gr/relatedarticles/article/?aid=99051, accessed 30 June 2016.

43 S. Mann, The Greek-Turkish Dispute in the Aegean Sea: Its ramifications for NATO and the Prospects for Resolution, M.A. Thesis, National Security Affairs, U.S Naval Postgraduate School, Monterey, California, March 2001, https://www.hsdl.org/?view&did=450238, accessed 30 June 2016.

44 E. Oğurlu, Rising tensions in the Eastern Mediterranean: Implications for Turkish Foreign Policy, Instituto Affari Internazionali, Working Papers 12/04, March 2012, http://www.iai.it/sites/default/files/iaiwp1204.pdf , accessed 31 March 2017.

45 T. Barnett, ed., Turkey re-rise of the Ottoman Empire?,http://thomaspmbarnett.com/globlogization/2011/3/28/turkey-re-rise-of-the-ottoman-empire.html, accessed 5 July 2016.
46 L. Simon, Sea power and US forward presence in the Middle East: Retrenchment in perspective, *Geopolitics*, 2016, v.21, n.1, 115-147.
47 Greek website *Greek Reporter*, ed., Turkish "Barbaros" vessel enters Cyprus EEZ Zone without permission, 20 October 2014, http://greece.greekreporter.com/2014/10/20/turkish-barbaros-vessel-enters-cyprus-eez-zone-without-permission/, accessed 5 July 2016.
48 Natural Gas, ed., EU leaders condemn Turkey's escalation of Cyprus conflict, 3 November 2014, http://www.naturalgaseurope.com/eu-leaders-condemn-turkey-escalation-cyprus-conflict, accessed 5 July 2016.
49 Greek newspaper *Proto Thema*, ed., Episode in Oinousses: Turks threatened to arrest Greek fisherman, 29 April 2016, http://www.protothema.gr/greece/article/574267/epeisodio-stis-oinousses-tourkoi-apeilisan-na-sullavoun-ellina-psara/, accessed 30 June 2016.
50 Greek website Militaire.gr, ed., 1200 Turkish territorial waters violations in the Aegean in 2015, http://www.militaire.gr/1200-%CF%84%CE%BF%CF%85%CF%81%CE%BA%CE%B9%CE%BA%CE%AD%CF%82-%CF%80%CE%B1%CF%81%CE%B1%CE%B2%CE%B9%CE%AC%CF%83%CE%B5%CE%B9%CF%82-%CE%B1%CE%B9%CE%B3%CE%B1%CE%B9%CE%BF/, accessed 30 June 2016.
51 Greek newspaper *Kathimerini*, ed., US support to refugee, http://www.kathimerini.gr/861037/article/epikairothta/politikh/sthri3h-hpa-sto-prosfygiko, accessed 30 June 2016.
52 America's Navy, ed., Trilateral Naval Allies Successfully Conclude Exercise Noble Dina 2016, http://www.navy.mil/submit/display.asp?story_id=94245, accessed 30 June 2016.

[5]
RUSSIAN FEDERATION'S FOREIGN POLICY IN THE EASTERN MEDITERRANEAN SINCE THE END OF COLD WAR: GEOECONOMIC AND GEOPOLITICAL PARAMETERS

Andreas Stergiou

Introduction

Interpreting Moscow's foreign policy in Eastern Mediterranean renders a very difficult task. In geopolitical terms, the region's highly explosive political-national and religious sectarian complex well manifested on the numerous conflicts that have occurred historically there, have repeatedly provoked fluid and changing patterns of alliances both among the regional players and the great powers.

According some observers, the Mediterranean does not make up for Russia a more or less coherent region but pursues different policies towards the countries of the region on the ground of developing relations with at least four types of actors: North Africa and the Middle East, the southern EU members, countries involved in the challenges the Kremlin faces in the Black Sea region and the United States, as Moscow's worldwide policies are captured by an idea of redrawing the negative consequences of a US centered world order.[1]

Other scholars, however, have argued in favor of the distinct character of the Russian Federation's foreign policy in the Eastern Mediterranean discerning three different periods in the Kremlin's presence in the region since 1991: the stage of retreat during the 1990's, the phase of recovery in the first decade of 2000's and the years of global destabilization after the Arab Spring. This division is based on the various Russian presidents' attitude to toward the region. Under president Boris Yeltsin, Russia was satisfied with the role of an observer, while the take-over of the presidential power by Vladimir Putin in 2000 marked a decisive turn in Kremlin's course. The Eastern Mediterranean became one of the most important aspects of the Russian foreign policy swiftly transforming it into a zone of geopolitical and geoeconomic competition between Russia and Western States.[2]

Though, there is not a specific department in the Russian Foreign Ministry dealing exclusively with the Eastern Mediterranean, this chapter argues that the respective region does constitute both an international subsystem and a field of particular interest for Moscow. The chapter's main argument is that current developments regarding Russia's foreign policy in the region might seem to be novel, but in fact, they date back to the Cold War and beyond, indeed to at least the eighteenth century. Accordingly, it is argued that Moscow's policy, both during the Cold and the Post Cold War, has been characterized essentially by continuity, notwithstanding some exceptions.

Against this background, the Eastern Mediterranean is defined as a level of analysis in terms of international relations theory. More explicitly, in order to conceptualise the regional conflicts and security threats within a certain recognisable theoretical framework, the study is going to employ theoretical and analytical tools emanating from the well-known Copenhagen School. In fact, the so-called regional security theoretical complex construction is deemed very suitable in this regard, as it represents a valuable analytical tool for the understanding of the contextual dimensions of most security problems that are interrelated with geography and history. Given that international security is a relational phenomenon, suggesting that it is about the way collectivities relate to each other in terms of threats and vulnerabilities, the dynamics of security problems are located within the units themselves, concerning the respective case, the countries of the region, as well as between them. In that sense, the subsystemic level of analysis examines the same processes of securitization from different angles and their insights are complementary for the understanding of specific security problems.

According to the Copenhagen School[3] a regional security complex is a durable empirical phenomenon with historical and geopolitical roots. Moreover, it has security dynamics of its own that are distinguishable and analytically separable from the global or the unit level dynamics. Given the fact that states and societies are non-mobile units whose actions rarely threaten the survival of distant collectivities, it can be suggested that security – especially, when it is related with threats located on the military, political or societal sectors – is frequently associated with proximity.

Moreover, the Regional Security Complex is composed of at least two proximate units whose major processes of securitization and desecuritization are so interlinked that their security problems cannot reasonably be analyzed or resolved apart from one another. The inclusion of units in a Regional Security Complex arises from the interplay of their security problems rather than from their recognition or awareness of their belonging in this region. The presence of a distinct set of intense and inward looking security relationships determines both the existence of a Regional Security Complex and its exact boundaries as it represents the sole available criterion for the inclusion or exclusion of units in that complex. In this sense, a Regional Security Complex, in that case the Eastern Mediterranean subsystem, is a geographical entity comprising units whose security is deeply interdependent in terms of a mutually felt threat or a shared common interest.

Russia's foreign policy in the region confirms, as it will be showcased, in many ways regional security complex's theses. First of all and overall, Moscow's course has been driven and decisively shaped by the traditional, originated in the Cold War threat feeling towards the USA. Of key-importance for understanding, Russia's Post-Cold War Strategy is the energy factor that has been used to secure Russia's hegemonic position as traditional energy supplier of the West, which provoked a response from Washington, played out along the lines with the mutual felt threat theoretically conceptualized by the Copenhagen school.

Every time a geopolitical and geoeconomic shift of power happened or loomed in the Eastern Mediterranean, Moscow sought to address the challenge by establishing energy and defence cooperation with almost every country in the region. It avoided to take a clear stance and tried to offer a counterbalance to the real or perceived threat. To that purpose it paid respect equally to societal and state factors acting in the various countries. While forging an energy deal for example with a government, it promoted a pro-Russian atmosphere in that country by using one or more political parties. The Syria War added an imponderable variable to the power architecture of the greater Middle East, causing the Kremlin to rapidly change its former strategy and to undertake, for the first time since WWII, military action in the region. Moreover, for the first time since Afghanistan in the 1980's, the Russian military has been in direct combat with rebel forces trained and supplied by the C.I.A. This, however, marked a groundbreaking moment in the history of Russia's presence in the Eastern Mediterranean since the nineteenth century, which is marked by a remarkable continuity,[4] amounting to what has been called "a new Cold War".

This chapter seeks to shed light on Kremlin's policy in the region from the end of the Cold War until now using both secondary sources and primary sources, i.e. interviews conducted with people from several countries who are acquainted with the thematic complex and a few recently declassified documents.

The Cold War background

Like Imperial Russia, the Soviet Union followed, for geopolitical but also for pure economic reasons, a policy of "fishing in muddy waters," i.e. of a slow but steady penetration into the Eastern Mediterranean countries. However, this penetration was achieved mainly through indirect tactics. Rather than make territorial demands and send in their armed forces to annex, the Soviets, as also their allies, supported various political groups and governments with a view to weakening Western influence and extending Soviet influence southward. They also capitalized on the mishandling of the Cyprus issue by Western countries so as to encourage the Greek and Greek-Cypriot governments, directly or indirectly, to pursue a nonaligned policy.

In the first instance outright Soviet control of the Arab-Mediterranean region or at least denial of Western control offered many geostrategic and geopolitical advantages to Moscow. Gaining the upper hand became crucial to the assertion of the USSR status of a great power, a guardian and a vanguard of the Socialist camp. On this front, the first Soviet purpose was to maintain paramountcy in the Communist and left oriented parties. The second was to project the image of an omnipresent and reliable great power. Against this background should be understood the imposing Soviet naval presence since the 1960's and the following Soviet naval build-up there.[5]

Indeed, the use of naval force, a tactic documented in the repeated presence of the Russian fleet and a great number of medium range delivery vehicles as well as various nuclear weapons in the Eastern Mediterranean, turned out to be a powerful gambit of demonstrating Moscow's interest in the region. Its tiny military base at Tartus on Syria's Mediterranean coast, a stronghold outside the former Soviet Union, provided the necessary logistical support. Thanks to it, Soviet warships were not forced to return to their Black Sea bases through the Bosporus Strait, controlled by Turkey. For this reason Moscow remained a close ally of Syria since the 1973 Arab-Israeli war and regularly supplied Syrian military in conflicts, while its civilian technical advisers worked irregularly on Russian built air defence systems and repair planes and helicopters in the country. Furthermore, the introduction of Soviet tactical nuclear weapons into the Mediterranean put an additional nuclear threshold that should be calculated in any great power confrontation.[6]

The forum of the United Nations, on which all the socialist countries aligned their voting behavior with Moscow's aspiration in the region, provided another appropriate setting for the Soviets in order to promote their goals. Indeed, in the 1950s the Soviet Union and Eastern European bloc countries supported with great determination Greece's efforts to internationalize the Cyprus Question in the UN General Assembly.[7] The motives behind this tactic are obvious: Moscow was trying to hinder a NATO inspired settlement of the problem, which might have enhanced the influence of the Western camp in the region as well as to exploit and escalate possible tensions in it. In that way, it turned in favor to the Arab world in the early 1960s and even threatened to attack Israel in both the 1967 Six Day War and 1973 Yom Kippur War, though the Soviet Union was one of the first states to support the creation of Israel in 1948.

However, due to the delicate balance of power and the overall fluid geopolitical situation, the Soviets could never afford any other policy for securing in the long-term its economic and political interests than sticking absolutely and cynically to a risky and complex policy of balance. More precisely, it had to carefully avoid to military commit itself at the side of a country or at least to offer substantial economic and political support to any country of the region, thereby putting at risk its relations with another. Therefore, in its attempt to keep all sides satisfied, the Kremlin followed a contradictory policy in the Mediterranean. In times of peace and stability this relative inconsistency was not apparent, but when tensions came to a head and Moscow was forced to choose sides, it became clear that Moscow would prefer to adopt an ambiguous and equivocal stance, appeasing one side so as not to jeopardise the progress it had made in its relations with another. This stance can be clearly seen in the differing Russian positions in the Syria-Turkey conflict and in the Greco-Turkish confrontation over the Aegean Sea.[8]

Only mid-1980s in the context of Gorbatchev's "new thinking," when many traditional strategic dogmas were challenged, Soviet policy in the greater region experienced some change. In particular, the "new thinking" suggested that Soviet interests would be best served not by attempts to exploit regional tension for unilateral gain, but by efforts to work with the United States to stabilize conflict situations, as it was reflected on the support Soviets offered to the improvement in relations with Israel and the moderate Arabs and Arafat's new pragmatism.[9]

On the other side, the Western powers' strategy there during the Cold War was closely intertwined with three main factors: the region's energy resources, the establishment and continued existence of Israel, and the maintenance of NATO's southeastern flank. The permanent control by the West was kept solid by:

- The admission of Greece and Turkey to NATO in the 1950s;
- The deployment, since 1946, of the US Sixth Fleet in the Mediterranean;
- The strategic alliances of Israel with the US and Turkey since the end of 1940s;
- Israel's 1979 Camp David peace accords with Egypt.

However, these events meant that Greece and Cyprus, Turkey's traditional enemies, were prevented from establishing close ties with Israel, and as Ankara secured for Israel the strategic advantages it needed, those relations lessened in importance.[10]

Furthermore, local geopolitical crises and unpredictable political developments repeatedly proved how fragile the Western-led balances were. Typical examples that should be analysed on the ground of new unpublished material in the book were the US President L.B. Johnson' notorious letter to Turkish President Inönü, aimed at avoiding a direct confrontation between Greece and Turkey within the context of the bicommunal riots in Cyprus in 1963-1964. Of course he had also exerted similar pressure on Greece, while the USSR threatened Turkey with military action. At any event, Johnson's letter would have far reaching consequences, because it caused grief and frustration. Inönü felt personally hurt and initiated a shift in foreign policy towards greater independence from Washington. From then onwards Turkey's loyalty to NATO declined. Ankara began to flirt with Moscow, with various ramifications during the Cold War. A significant reverberation was Turkey's decision to permit the Soviets to move a complete fleet into the Mediterranean through the Bosporus Straits in 1967. In the same vein, the Western attitude during the 1974 Turkish invasion in Cyprus led to the withdrawal of Greek forces from NATO and the increase of anti-American and anti-Western sentiments.

Another example is the Greek Socialist Party's (PASOK) foreign policy agenda and rhetoric in the eighties. Indeed, in contrast to other European countries, which in the eighties were characterized by the cultural dominance of the 'New Right,' Greek politics were overwhelmed by the PASOK's rise, which came to power in October 1981 to the detriment of the more left wing parties. In particular, PASOK's foreign policy preelectoral rhetoric as well as its bizarre European policy and pro-Arab World and pro-Eastern Europe orientation during its administration (1981-1989) accounted for a significant part of its political supremacy. Its stance also raised serious Western concerns about Soviet infiltration in the eastern Mediterranean, which could be eased only in the nineties, after PASOK had been ousted from power.

The Post-Cold War era

Following the disintegration of the Soviet Union, relations between Russia and the countries of the region have been marked by cooperation, but also by rivalries and competition. Russian-Turkish relations constitute a typical example in this respect. Despite numerous agreements in the fields of economy, technology, science, culture, health and tourism, Russia never stopped regarding Turkey as a threat and competitor to its interests in Central Asia and Caucasus, where Russian and Turkish ambitions clashed actively and repeatedly for dominance. The traditional ties of Turkey's Kemalist establishment with the USA and Turkey's aspirations of using its key geostrategic, geo-economic position to fill the geopolitical vacuum occurred in the region after the collapse of the USSR, put obstacles in the improvement of Turkish-Russian bilateral relations. The territorial conflict between Azerbaijan and Armenia provided an additional bone of contention. As widely known, Armenia occupied Nagorno-Karabakh and seven surrounding Azeri districts in 1993. While Russia upheld Armenia's claim to the occupied territory, Turkey was the most ardent supporter of the Azeri positions in the international arena.[11]

However, the Iraq war in 2003 and the establishing of a de facto Kurdish state in Iraq as a result of the US-invasion substantially affected US-Turkish relations, precipitating as side-effect an improvement in Russian-Turkish relationship. That bilateral progress was also favored by the gradual diminishing of the tensions in Central Asia as well as Russia's emergence as a profitable market for Turkish entrepreneurs. Particularly the energy parameter of those ties played a guard role.[12]

The clinching of various energy deals was designed to enforce Turkey's drive to become a regional hub for gas and oil transits[13] as well as to help Moscow to diversify supply routes and potentially maintain its monopoly on natural gas shipments from Asia to Europe. Turkey, which has been highly dependent on Russian energy (especially gas) supplies, allowed Russia's Gazprom to use its sector of the Black Sea for the South Stream pipeline to pump Russian and Central Asian gas to Europe bypassing Ukraine and Russia and join a consortium with the aim to build the Samsun-Ceyhan oil pipeline from the Black Sea to the Mediterranean. As it has been asserted by some experts,[14] this has been coinciding with Gazprom's aims to control the entire value chain on the European Market. Therefore it sought to dominate the construction and operation of prestige projects like Nord Stream and South Stream gas pipelines, just as Transneft, the other Russian energy giant, sought to exert influence over oil projects, like the Trans-Black Sea Burgas-Alexandroupolis pipelines.

On the other side of the Aegean, Athens' relationship to Moscow in the 1990's was decisively influenced by the Balkan turbulences. FYROM's recognition by Kremlin by its contentious (at least in Greek eyes) constitutional name "Macedonia" was a blow for Greece's foreign policy at that time, since it had been fully waded into an international campaign to preempt usage of the name "Macedonia" by the international community for the new founded state.

However, the Balkan drama prepared the soil for a close Greek-Russian cooperation. Athens partially interpreted the Balkan instability in the context of the Greek-Turkish conflict, as Greek officials feared that Turkey might detect a "window of opportunity" in the Balkan turmoil for the improvement of its position vis-à-vis Greece. The fragmentation of Yugoslavia – coupled with the deterioration of Greek relations with Albania and Bulgaria at the same time– also generated in the Greek security perceptions a threat of a possible "Islamic encirclement" due to the Muslim population resided in those countries. Those fears were strengthened by Ankara's strategy to sign with the most south eastern european countries bilateral trade and military cooperation agreements and to offer them promises of economic, military and political aid.[15]

These Turkish strategic gambits provoked a joint Greek-Russian response, after the demise of the Soviet Union and the disappearance of the so-called Communist Threat in Balkan, Greece suddenly found it had mutual interests with Russia in opposition to their common rival, Turkey. That is why Greece had permitted Russia to establish a significant presence in Cyprus and also explored with Russia the possibility of bringing oil from the Caucasus and Central Asia to the Mediterranean through a Bulgarian-Greek pipeline bypassing Turkey and other Muslim countries.[16]

Apart of it Russian and Greeks shared, in general, similar views on conflict resolution in former Yugoslavia and supported the preservation of the existing geopolitical status quo in Balkan, thereby defending the permanence and safeguarding of state sovereignty and inviolability of borders by virtue of former international treaties. Within the NATO, Athens showed the greatest understanding for Russian concerns against the NATO expansion and repeatedly urged to be given the most serious consideration to them. Moscow reciprocated by supporting some Greek positions on bilateral issues with Turkey. Unlike during the Cold-War period, the Russian Foreign Ministry and DUMA recognized Greece's right to expand its territorial waters from 6 to 12 miles in Aegean[17] and took favorably to Greece's position in the Imia crisis in January 1996.[18]

Despite NATO-restrictions in the 1990's, Greeks and Russians proceeded to a defence cooperation. Russian state companies retained the big procurement from the Greek state to modernize 501 military tanks BMP-1 Greece had received in the framework of the restructuring of the conventional forces in Europe Treaty from the GDR-Republic reserves.[19]

In the period 2004-2009 the conservative Karamanlis government viewed a closer relationship with the Federation of Russia as a chance to upgrade Greece's geopolitical and geo-economic profile and attempted to forge a comprehensive strategic partnership with Russia. Accordingly Athens pursued an upgraded energy and defence cooperation, which, however, negatively affected Greece's traditional relationship with the United States. Would the construction of these two pipelines enhance the strategic importance of Greece on the one side, would it on the other side increase Greece's energy and defence dependence on Russia. Indeed, in December 2007, Athens announced its intention to buy some armored personnel Russian tanks (420 BMP-3M) of approximately 1.2 billion euros worth, thus becoming the only NATO member state to directly purchase military material from Moscow. The main project, however, of this strategic partnership should be the construction of gas and oil pipelines from Russia via the Black Sea to Bulgaria and Greece bypassing the Straits, the so-called Burgas-Alexandroupoli pipeline. That opposing to the Nabucco pipeline project, long favored by the US, was endorsed by the Greek Parliament with overwhelming multipartisan support in August 2009. However, both the energy and the defence project did not survive EU and US reactions, which coupled with budgetary concerns led to a repealing a few years later.[20]

A key component of Kremlin's policy in the region and an apple of discord within the Western powers has been over the decades Cyprus, not only because of its strategic importance. Both Soviet and Post-Communist Russia maintained a consistent policy of engagement in relation to Cyprus with a view to weakening the island's ties with the West and extending Soviet influence southward. More precisely, they supported various Cypriot political and social groups and movements, which were in favor of a nonaligned policy for the Island Republic. For this reason, Moscow has traditionally declared its commitment to safeguarding Cyprus's state sovereignty and neutrality in order to avoid the pro-NATO militarization of the island. Nevertheless the support never went beyond equivocal and diplomatic statements calling for a peaceful resolution of the conflict and active involvement of the United Nations through the in general unrealistic option of the convocation of a broad international conference on the issue.[21]

Official Cypriot-Russian relations date back to the 1960's, when the USSR established diplomatic relations with the newly independent Republic of Cyprus. In 1982, the two states signed an agreement on double taxation avoidance. As a result, at the beginning of the 1990s, Cyprus was one of the few capitalist countries with an institutional framework for Russian capital outflows and inflows from Cyprus already in place. The island rapidly became one of the favored destinations for Russian capital. Some scholars believe that money laundering and tax evasion were the main driving forces behind capital movements.[22] From the early 1990's onwards Russians were among the most active non-resident portfolio investors to the Cyprus Stock Exchange with the overwhelming majority of the invested money deriving from Russian capital flight. Cyprus' accession into the European Union in 2004, albeit it induced a large volume of legislative changes to bring Cyprus into line with the EU, did not halt this tendency. Cypriot capital was also a major investor in Russian securities market. These investments are often considered to mean the return of Russian capital. To a large extent these outbound investments act as safety nets for Russian companies to protect themselves from uncertainties in the domestic environment.²³ However, the top position of Cyprus may also indicate that many foreign companies trading with Russia use Cypriot subsidiaries in order to take advantage of the favorable taxation in Cyprus.²⁴

In October 2010, the two countries signed a new agreement (Convention for the Avoidance of Double Taxation of Income and Property) to avoid double taxation, which further increased the flow of investment. The common characteristic of all the double tax treaties Cyprus signed, is that all reduce or eliminate the normal withholding taxes imposed by the contracting states on dividends, interest and royalty payment. Cyprus does not impose withholding tax on payments of dividend, interest and royalties paid by international business companies. Therefore, the Cyprus international company is mostly used to receive dividend interest, royalties and capital gains from the other treaty country so that the withholding tax is reduced. The interest and royalty payment is in most cases a deductible expense in a high tax jurisdiction, whereas the capital gain is exempted from tax.²⁵

The defence cooperation flourished too. Since the Republic Cyprus until today has not been constrained by any alliance restrictions, could easily resort to the acquisition of Russian arms, as it decided systematically to do from the mid 1990's onwards. On 4 January 1997 proceeded to the acquisition of T-80, TOMA and BMP-3E military tanks as well as some six batteries of advanced TOR-M1 and S-300 anti-aircraft as well as antiballistic ground-to-air missiles. Both Washington and Ankara strongly reacted against the installation of the S300 missiles in Cyprus. Washington was concerned that the deployment of S300 missiles in Cyprus would bring the Eastern Mediterranean under Russian control. Thus, it exerted pressure over Athens and Nicosia to cancel the acquisition of the missiles, repeatedly stating: "this action would not contribute to stability and thus would constitute a seriously troubling factor."²⁶

According to the declassified presidential records which former US President Bill Clinton recently made public, he was very bothered by the deal as he regarded it as a "terrible" development because of the "Russian connection" and hence asked Tony Blair to exercise pressure on Cypriot President Glafkos Klerides to stop the delivery of the missiles.²⁷

Ankara, at its side labeled the agreement as "a culmination of provocations against Turkey and an attempt to over militarization of the island"²⁸ and initially lobbied Moscow against it. However, when it became obvious that Russia was determined to implement the deal, Turkey threatened to strike the Russian vessels carrying the missiles to Cyprus. In response, Moscow described Turkish threats as an outright provocation and *casus belli*. After more than two years of a diplomatic tug-of-war, the Greek and Cypriot Government finally bowed to US pressures and made a retreat. The missiles were bought but installed not on Cyprus but on Crete in September 1999, where they first were tested 14 years later![29]

In April 2004, during a very important session of the UN Security Council on the future of Cyprus in a climate of great expectation coupled with uncertainty, Russia was the only country torpedoing a UN resolution. That resolution was meant to provide sufficient security guarantees for the implementation of the so-called Annan Plan that had been proposed by the UN Secretary General. The respective plan was strongly supported by the United States and the United Kingdom with the aim to precipitate a "pro western" solution in the Cyprus problem. In this case Putin's Moscow succesfully dealt a diplomatic blow exploiting rivalries between the Western states[30] involved in the Cyprus Improglio. The vehicle for the materialization of the gambit was an old Moscow ally, the powerful Cypriot Communist Party-AKEL, of whose many professional party cadres studied in Moscow or in other former socialist countries. By seeking an alibi to reject the plan the party had persistently demanded for more security guarantees before the plebiscite which the UN Security Council resolution was supposed to offer.

In favor of Russia's interests in the region has also been AKEL's Cold-War resentments motivated anti-NATO stance.[31] While membership of NATO is not a requirement for EU membership, most EU members are part of the alliance. Cyprus and Malta are the only two entrants in 2004 that are not members of the organization. Notably, even those EU members, officially maintaining a policy of neutrality in their external relations, have opted to join the Partnership for Peace. Cyprus is the only country choosing to act in a different way despite increasing reaction by all parties across the political spectrum because of AKEL's resolute objections.

Furthermore, some newspaper reports[32] have even suggested that Cyprus may be being used by Russia as a shipment route to provide, in violation of the EU arms embargo, assistance to the government of Bashar al-Assad; a claim repeatedly denied by Nicosia.[33]

The energy factor as a catalyst in the ongoing reconfiguration in the balance of power in the Eastern Mediterranean

Following the Russian-Ukrainian crisis in 2006, the increasing significance of the energy security issue and the Western perceived necessity of diversifying the routes and sources of gas supplies to the European Union moved to the top of the list of EU priorities in its external relations, as was announced in the Second Strategic Energy Review in 2008. In 2010 about 80% of EU gas imports still derived from only three suppliers: the Russian Federation, Algeria and Norway. This heavy dependence on so few suppliers occasioned the European Commission to make the concept of diversification a cornerstone of its energy policy in the wider context of a common energy policy, enabling the EU to "speak with the same voice" on the need for sufficient diversity of exporters.[34] In spite of that, Russia is still the main supplier of oil, gas and coal to the European Union, as well as one of its main providers of uranium. In 2013, Russia supplied 39% of the gas, 33% of the crude oil and 29% of the solid fuels imported by the EU.[35]

Therefore, there has been a serious interest by Western European and US companies in gas supplies from the Caspian region (from Azerbaijan, Iran, Iraq and Turkmenistan – especially since the president of the last country changed in late 2006/early 2007[36]) – and hence EU-US political support for the so-called Southern Gas Corridor and Trans-Adriatic pipeline (TAP), the supply routes running from Azerbaijan via Turkey to Europe.

The discovery of natural gas resources in the Eastern Mediterranean since the late 2010s has also predictably attracted EU/US interest, given the enormous European demand for the relatively cleaner power of natural gas as well as attempts to create a competitive, interconnected and well-functioning internal market and develop a coherent and collective external strategy. The latter would also allow EU countries to both diversify and secure their gas supply from abroad.[37]

Furthermore, this would coincide with Washington's long pursued aim of putting an end to Moscow's tactic of using its natural gas exports to exercise economic and political influence in Europe.[38] The Kremlin believes that the domestic energy industry should be organized into two legal regimes. Unlike the oil-companies that should be private, gas companies (Gazprom) should be state-run companies for two reasons: first in order to control gas prices on which so many people depend (Gazprom controls about 90% of the Russian market) and second because Gazprom's activities are fully intertwined with Russia's foreign policy.[39]

However, as it is widely known, due to a series of diplomatic confrontations between 2008 and 2012, the relationship between Israel and Turkey has entered a period of great tension, following fifty years of close and successful cooperation. After Turkish-Israeli ties became strained, in a classic example of "the enemy of my enemy is my friend," Israel and Cyprus and, by extension, Greece, came together to form a defence economic alliance which could, under certain conditions, be turned against vital Turkish interests in the region. The economic benefit expected from the substantial natural gas and oil resources discovered in the Exclusive Economic Zones of Israel and Cyprus has also contributed to the materialization of an unprecedented political, military and energy relationship.

Nevertheless, the EU-Cyprus-Greece-Israel cooperation conflicts with Turkey's geopolitical aspirations in the region by underlining the special nature of this closed international subsystem marked, as suggested in the framework of Security complex analysis, by economic and political threats associated with proximity. Turkish economic and political elites would view a possible export route to European markets through the Mediterranean, connecting Israel, Cyprus and Greece, as a threat to their own ambition to transform Turkey into the major non-Russian transit route for gas sales and a regional energy hub.[40] Ankara has been contesting the fact that the areas with gas reserves in the eastern basin of the Mediterranean, stretching from the Levant coast to southern Crete and maybe beyond, are situated in clearly divided national waters, thereby ignoring Republic Cyprus' rights and jurisdiction over the maritime areas of the island.[41]

Furthermore, Turkey repeatedly threatened Cyprus with military action, even while US-company Noble Energy was still carrying out exploratory drilling off the island's southern coast, thereby creating tensions in the region by dispatching Turkish military vessels. As a result, the recently forged Israel-Cyprus-Greece alliance has a well-shaped military character. Indeed, in spring 2012, Israel and the United States invited Greece to join them in joint military exercises through which Israel sought to replace the strategic depth it had lost after the cancelling of defence exercises with Turkey.[42] At the same time, Washington has been trying to mediate between Israel and Turkey to resolve the crisis in their bilateral relations, but also between Turkey, Cyprus and Greece in a bid to resume negotiations to settle the Cyprus conflict.

Within the framework of the geopolitical and geoeconomic shift of power looming in the region, Turkey initially turned to Moscow, seeking to foster its energy cooperation with Russia – also in the field of nuclear power – in order to counterbalance these US-EU plans in the Eastern Mediterranean, fueling a new form of US-Russian rivalry in the region. For its part, Russia tried to address these daunting geopolitical challenges by establishing energy and defencedefence cooperation with almost every country in the region. The motives behind these actions are obvious: Moscow is prepared to undertake preemptive action against anything that can undermine its hegemonic position as energy provider to the European Markets and to the countries of the Eastern Mediterranean.

In December 2011, Russia and Turkey signed an agreement on the South Stream natural gas pipeline, allowing Russia to build the South Stream gas pipeline through Turkey's exclusive economic zone. On the same day, Gazprom signed an annex to its gas contracts with the Turkish corporation BOTAS, which allows it to increase the supply of Russian gas, possibly leading to a significant reduction in its price.[43]

In July 2012, President Vladimir Putin visited Israel to promote a Gazprom deal with the Israeli government (formally as the guest of honor to inaugurate a monument to the Red Army soldiers who defeated Hitler in World War Two) that would give it control of Tamar's gas and access to the Asian market for its liquefied natural gas.[44] A few months later, however,

Russia started negotiations with the Palestinian Authority on a possible development of the Gaza Marine Field.[45]

The Israeli-Russian relationship is quite complicated. With the emergence of Putin, Israel seems to have found the closest thing to a friend it has ever had in Moscow. In 2014 Putin was one of the few world leaders to support Israel's Operation Protective Edge against Hamas. After Russia annexed the Crimea, Israel abstained from voting on a United Nations resolution condemning Russian actions – which in UN diplomatic vocabulary is actually equivalent to voting against it.[46] Notably, Russia is Israel's largest supplier of crude oil and a big recipient of agricultural imports from Israel. Russia's deployment of advanced surface-to-air S-400 missiles, though, has been of grave concern to Israel, as Tel Aviv fears the transfer of advanced weapons from Iran or Syria to archenemy Hezbollah, apart from Israel's fear of a militarily strong Iran. The more critical of Israel's treatment of Palestinians, particularly of its settlement policy in the West Bank the European Union became, the more common ground Tel Aviv found for cooperation with Moscow. For several years, Gazprom's main concern has been that Israel's entry into European gas markets would severely undermine the company's market power.

From 2013 onwards and especially under President Abdel Fattah el-Sisi Moscow also revived its strong relationship with Egypt as it became obvious in the array of cooperation agreements on trade and nuclear energy have been signed. Moscow and Cairo have also deepened military cooperation, while Egyptian diplomacy has appeared to have paved the way for the Saudi-Russian rapprochement. Egypt has also very quietly endorsed the Russian approach to resolving the Syrian conflict, as it supports preserving the Syrian state and its institutions, including President Bashar al-Assad regime.[47]

In 2013-2014 Russia made moves towards more challenging alternatives. In May 2013, Russian companies were allowed to build and own a 20 billion US Dollar nuclear power plant on Turkey's southern Mediterranean coast. At the same time, Russian companies (Gazprom and Russian Railways) attempted to purchase Greece's main state-run gas and oil company (DEPA), one of the participants in the South Stream project and the main gas supplier to the Greek market, and the Greek Hellenic Railways Organization (OSE) in order to control energy and transport infrastructure. However, it is a common secret in Greece that, before the Russian companies' intention materialized, EU institutions intervened and repealed the project. Relying on the legal background of the EU Third Energy Package, which does not allow gas producers to possess their own gas transportation systems at the same time (although Azerbaijan's SOCAR bought out Greek gas transporter, DESFA), the EU Commission raised objections to the deal. The EU Commission raised objections to the deal and Gazprom was compelled to withdraw interest in the Greek gas firm.

In October 2013, Russia and the Lebanon signed an energy cooperation Memorandum of Understanding for developing natural gas fields off the Lebanon's shore. Several Russian companies also bid for the Lebanese exploration tender, while the Russian state-owned Soyuzneftegaz Company clinched an agreement with the Syrian Ministry of Energy in December 2013, in order to explore in its Offshore Block 2.[48] That very promising 25 year deal signed with the Damascus' regime appears to have been an additional driving force behind Moscow's gambit to further bolster Assad, as it is estimated that the existing energy finds in the Levant Basin extend into Syria's offshore territory.[49]

Moreover, since the beginning of the Syrian crisis, Moscow has gradually augmented its naval presence in the region. Since 2011, Moscow has repeatedly dispatched *fleets* of five or six combat ships to the Mediterranean with frigates, cruisers and aircraft carriers to conduct military drills. The Russian fleet's activities in an area that is very sensitive for NATO, obviously connected with the civil war in Syria, have no precedent since the Cold War in terms of size of forces involved, the measures employed, the territorial span, the number of exercises or the scheduling and methodology of the drills. The intensity of the activities of the Russian Navy in the Mediterranean and the military means engaged are comparable, in due proportion, to the Soviet fleets' moves during the Vietnam War.[50] It has of course to be noted that the US has again become equally rumbustious in the area, as well as in the Black Sea, further fueling tensions.

Within the same context, in August 2013 the Kremlin submitted an official request to rent the Andreas Papadopoulos airfield near Paphos, even though since 2012 Russian naval vessels had been using the Limassol port for refuelling. Eventually in February 2015 and despite US opposition, Cyprus agreed to allow some Russian naval ships to make stops at its ports with the aim of countering terrorism and piracy; in return, Russia agreed to provide debt relief[51] to the Republic of Cyprus, restructuring the 2.5 billion euro bailout loan it had given Cyprus in 2011.

There are numerous Russian companies based in Cyprus today. Although there is still a lot of pressure on Russian companies to repatriate assets, while Russian related businesses are believed to make up around 10% of the Cypriot economy. Most of them are located in Limassol, where a Chamber for Russian Companies, Russian schools and Orthodox Churches have been established as well as a Russian language television and radio service has been set up. Cypriot law allows those who buy a house worth 300,000 euros or more to claim permanent residency rights, while those who spend five million euros of more on property can apply for passports. According to an estimate by Morgan Stanley Cypriot entities, often owned by rich Russians, lent 40 billion US Dollars a year to Russia from 2007 and 2011. About 25 percent of Russian foreign direct investment moves through Cyprus, frequently in a "round trip" process that serves to lubricate the Russian economy. About 40,000 Russians live on the island with real estate and businesses in both, the Republic Cyprus and the Turkish break away area. In the second quarter of 2016 Cyprus was officially the biggest source of foreign direct investment in Russia (2.8 billion US Dollars). 525,000 Russians visited the island in 2015.[52]

Thus, it is not surprising that Russians were unhappy with a positive result of the two years long ongoing negotiations between Greek-Cypriot and Turkish-Cypriot community (2014-2016), aimed at the reunification of the island. Western countries' intension to achieve an agreement to reunify the island in order to prepare the soil for a following energy deal aimed at lessening Europe's energy dependence on Russia has prompted Moscow's reaction.[53] Cypriot local press has repeatedly reported by the end of 2016 that Russian officials have attended an antiunification political gatherings, while there is evidence that Moscow might be using social and mass media, as well as ties to fringe nationalist political parties and the Greek Orthodox Church, to undermine the settlement talks.

Russia's policy in Syria and implications for the EU and regional players

Given the sanctions imposed on Russia because of its intervention in the Ukraine, Russia appears to look upon its involvement in Syria as a chance to lose the status of international pariah and to projecting power outside its region. Nevertheless, Russia's military involvement in the interstate affairs of the Eastern Mediterranean not only aims at undermining NATO's role in the security architecture in the region but also to demonstrate Russia's military capabilities and potential as alternative security provider in a region suffocating traditionally by instability.

Furthermore, the war in Syria constitutes the field of competition between EU countries and Russia, due to the latter's support for the Assad regime, which escalated into Moscow's active military engagement. The Russian military intervention in the Syrian Civil War began on 30 September 2015, following, according to media reports, a formal request by the Syrian government for military help against rebel and jihadist groups. The activities consisted of air strikes primarily in northwestern Syria against militant groups opposed to the Syrian government. A quarter of a century, after its withdrawal from Afghanistan, Moscow found itself again at war in a Muslim country beyond the perimeter of its historical empire.

The war in Syria had many side effects, as it affected the fragile geopolitical architecture of power in the region in many ways, revealing the validity of the regional complex securitization analysis. The most radical change was precipitated by the Russian-Turkish clash. Already, in October 2014, Ankara had illegally issued a NAVTEX order, thereby reserving areas in the Economic Exclusive Zone of the Republic Cyprus for seismic surveys, and dispatched a seismic vessel accompanied by Turkish warships in order to collect data. In reprisal, Greece, the Republic of Cyprus and Israel, this time with Russian participation, conducted a joint naval exercise in waters of the Eastern Mediterranean on the same days. Once again, it became obvious that no matter how important the US role in the region might be, the countries in the region still need Russian diplomatic and military support. It was the first episode in a gradual deterioration of Ankara-Moscow relations that was to culminate within the context of the Syrian crisis as Moscow threatened Turkey with counteraction should it continue its naval activity there.

Clouds over Turkish-Russian relations had already appeared during the 2014 Russian invasion of the Crimean Peninsula where roughly 300,000 Turkic-speaking Tatars still remain as a remnant of Ottoman history. The ensuing annexation of Crimea shifted the balance of power in the Black Sea at Turkey's expense. After the annexation of Sevastopol, Russia's Black Sea Fleet, largely designed to counter Turkey's naval strength in wartime, can be deployed at whim in the Black Sea. To supply its forces in Syria, the Russian navy has been relying on the so-called Syrian Express, a naval supply route from Sevastopol on the Black Sea to its Eastern Mediterranean naval facility at the Syrian port of Tartus. However, according to Article 20 of the Montreux Convention, which stipulates that in wartime Turkey, if a belligerent, has full discretion when allowing or preventing the passage of warships through the strait, potentially cutting Russia off from the Mediterranean. Therefore, Russia has been pushing for decades for a revision of the respective treaty.[54]

Russia's annexation of Crimea and action to support anti-government forces in the eastern part of the Ukraine, including alleged direct Russian military support for separatist militias in the Donbass region,[55] did radically change not only the Ankara-Moscow relationship but the whole Post Cold War paradigm of European security. Throughout the first half of 2014, Western governments were compelled to recognize that the two decades old policy of courting Russia as a partner in building Euro-Atlantic security had failed, and that a shift back to a more adversarial relationship was under way.[56]

Accordingly, NATO initially condemned Russian air strikes and urged Russia to stop supporting Syrian President Bashar al-Assad. However, after the terrorist attacks in Paris and the invoking of Article 42.7 of the NATO Charter by France, a rapprochement between Western countries and Putin vis-à-vis ISIS began to emerge. And yet, apparently out of the blue, on 24 November 2015, a Russian Sukhoi Su-24 aircraft was shot down by a Turkish Air Force F-16 fighter jet in an incident thought to be the first time a NATO country had shot down a Russian airplane in half a century. Notably, the incident triggered an open confrontation between Russia and

Turkey (Moscow imposed rigid sanctions against Turkey including imports of Turkish farm and other products, the non-extension of contracts for the 200,000 Turks working in Russia, a ban on Turkish companies in Russia and an end to charter flights between the countries) negatively affecting a possible NATO-Russia cooperation.

Turkey had already demanded backing from its NATO allies towards Syria in the summer of 2012, after Syrian troops had shot down a Turkish warplane. Consequently, immediately after the downing of the Sukhoi, it called for a meeting of NATO members under Article 4 of the organization's charter, which provides for consultations, when a member state feels its territorial integrity, political independence or security is under threat.[57] By shooting down the Russian airplane, Turkey signaled that it wanted action to be taken in Syria only under its supervision, enabling Ankara to put its terms in the post-war architecture of power in the region.

Over the past few decades, Turkey's focus has been on northern Syria and northern Iraq, a belt of former Ottoman provinces that naturally extend eastward from Turkey's Hatay province and are mostly populated by Kurds. Russia's involvement in Syria in defence of the Alawite government runs directly against Turkey's objective of expanding its own military footprint in Aleppo, keeping under control the Kurdish separatist activity, by trying to create a 'free stateless zone' and eventually replacing Syrian President Bashar al-Assad with a Sunni government friendly to Turkish interests. Yet this does not comply at all (to that extent for the first time since Turkey was incorporated into the North Atlantic alliance) with Western interests. Western countries have been heavily relying on Kurds and seeking Russian assistance in resolving the Syrian question.[58]

Apart of it, Turkey and the EU have a very serious mutual problem linked to the Syrian war, the huge wave of refugees. The military successes of Assad's forces backed by the Russian Federation in northern Syria in the first months of 2016 increased the number of refugees on the Turkish border and the threat of another wave of migration from the Middle East to the EU. The Assad regime's military successes mean that it is more and more likely that it will recapture the territories currently controlled by the opposition forces supported by Turkey. At the same time, Syrian Kurd troops and the Islamic State, both of which are hostile towards Ankara, have maintained their positions in northern Syria. If Assad's troops manage to reach the Turkish border, this will mean the elimination of Ankara's and the West's proxies in this part of the country, and Turkey's real influence will be dramatically reduced.[59]

On the other side, Russia seems to have multiple incentives, which are still in stark contrast to those of its Western "allies," to get involved in the war. Perhaps the most important one is to strategically divert the West from Russia's primary interests in Europe, that is, Russian predominance in East-Central Europe. It obviously wants Assad to remain in power and to use the conflict instrumentally in order to improve the Kremlin's bargaining position in its relations with the West.

More specifically, the Syrian campaign was Russia's attempt to retain the domestic prestige it won with the annexation of Crimea, to break out of the external siege laid by the West immediately afterwards, and to try to establish itself in the new global order as a great power. The deployment of the highly advanced S-400 missiles, while not forming part of the immediate operations against terrorist forces in Syria, establishes Russian control of the skies over much of Syria. This also serves as a warning to Turkey. However, they demonstrate, together with the increased Russian military personnel and heavy equipment (T-90 tanks, armored personnel carriers, artillery systems and surface-to-air missiles), Russia's military strength. As has been observed[60] Russia's new military boldness has left Western observers puzzled. Yet, it does not come out of nowhere: current Russian strategy is the culmination of a systematic military reform that has been insufficiently appreciated by the European Union and the US. Russia has implemented far reaching military reforms to create a more professional and combat ready corps of armed forces that can swiftly deploy abroad, backed by expertise in non-conventional warfare tactics such as subversion and propaganda.

Another very significant incentive for Moscow's military tactics is apparently the Muslim population of 20 million currently living in Russia, which is 40-50 percent larger than in 1989 and increasingly radicalized. It is widely predicted that at these rates, the majority cohort in the Russian Armed Forces will be Muslim by 2020. Despite its diplomatic offensives (notably after September 2001 and today), Moscow does not share

Washington's commitment to a "global war on terrorism." However, it does wish to keep jihadist out of Russia and the former USSR.[61]

For the Russians, ISIS constitutes a mortal enemy for two main reasons. First, it is a global jihadist organization that looks to all Muslim populated areas, including Central Asia and Russia's own North Caucasus, Tatarstan, and others. Second, a large proportion of its foreign fighters originated from former Soviet lands and from Russia itself. Once victorious in Syria and Iraq, these jihadists can return to their places of origin and make trouble there.[62] Within this context, an important part of Moscow's strategy is to eliminate as many as possible of these Russian based jihadists fighting in Syria. Many have indeed been killed, thus reducing the possibility of future terrorism in Russia.

Last but not least, as has already been mentioned, the prospecting energy 25 year deal Russia signed at the end of 2013 with the Damascus regime might be another incentive too for Russia's involvement in the Syrian war.

Against this background both the 22 February 2016 Russian-American declaration on Syria for a ceasefire and the 9 September 2016 US-Russia agreement to reduce violence in the Syrian conflict should be regarded as a diplomatic success for the Kremlin. Even though the declaration did not bring about any resolution to the conflict and even though it is highly uncertain that joint military targeting by the two powers against Islamic jihadists in Syria agreed in September 2016 will work out, both earned Russia the formal recognition of its role as a codecision maker in resolving the Syrian question. Moreover, the failure of the agreements in and of themselves will make it difficult for the West to criticize Russia's and Assad's tactics in the conflict. Russian Federation's foreign minister Lavrov's comment on the agreement that "it denounces arrogant sanctions" levied against Russia for its annexation of Crimea two years ago, speaks volume for the role Syria's Conflict plays in Kremlin's strategy.[63]

The temporary deterioration of the Turkey-Russia relations, however, turned the regional balances once again upside down, thereby confirming Copenhagen school's theoretical assumptions on the mutual felt threat. Given Turkey's dependence on Russian energy resources, Ankara turned back to Israel, seeking alternative energy suppliers and defence support against a possible

Russian aggression. As a gesture of goodwill towards Turkey's reconciliation with Israel, Ankara enabled Israeli activity within NATO, and permitted Israel to open an office at NATO headquarters in May 2016. Eventually in June 2016 Israel and Turkey reached a deal to normalise their fraught relations. Except the important economic and energy considerations the turn Syria war has got must be regarded as an additional incentive behind this development. It is widely known that Israel is deeply concerned with limiting the regional influence of its archfoe Iran, while Turkey and Iran, though cooperating in various sectors, have been remaining on opposing sides of the five year civil war in Syria.

Similar factors such as the revival of projects such as the natural gas pipeline, Russia's contract to build Turkey's first nuclear power plant and Syria Civil War, appeared to be among the incentives, which entailed the rapid improvement of Turkey-Russian relations in Summer 2016. It is no accident that Erdogan's first foreign trip since the abortive July 15 putsch in Turkey was to Russia just as Turkey's relations with traditional allies the United States and Europe showed once again increasing strain. An additional factor facilitating the rapprochement was that the Syrian Conflict turned out to be a war of attrition for both countries. Therefore, Ankara, Moscow and the Syrian government as well as Iran and Syrian rebel groups supported by Turkey felt compelled to negotiate a ceasefire by the end of December 2016, which was adopted unanimously by the UN Security Council on 31 December 2016. Though the deal that explicitly excludes factions deemed by the United Nations Security Council as "terrorists," is very fragile, it has been the most serious effort undertaken so far to terminate the nearly six year long war. Moscow's motive behind this cooperation appears to be the same as it has shaped its strategy all the years before in the region, to confirm Putin's long envisaged goal to transform Russia into an equal partner of West in the new world order and to encourage a strategic separation between Ankara and Western countries.

The role of Moscow friendly parties

In order to achieve their objectives in the years following World War II, not only in the Eastern Mediterranean, the Soviets developed a wide variety of tactics, including such gambits as deception, concealed penetration and subversion and so on. They especially sought corroboration at international meetings. It meant positive propaganda to endorse a regime, plus support against domestic opponents (except pro-Soviet Marxist–Leninists), encouragement to bolster local Communist parties and other Communist-friendly organizations as well as other pro-Moscow political and social organizations in order to put governments under pressure to follow a policy in line with Moscow's interests.

In this regard, the Soviets confronted in the Eastern Mediterranean some insurmountable obstacles. The Moscow led Greek Communist Party was outlawed in 1947, the Communist movement in Turkey had to fight against the Kemalist state and Islamic religion as well, whereas Iraqi Communists were suppressed by the Baathists and Kurd Communists were divided as a result of the anti-Communist course followed by the countries where Kurds lived. Hence, the most suitable for this mission could be no other than the most successful party among all Communist parties in the region -- the Communist Party of Cyprus, AKEL and the Greek Communist Party.[64]

Kremlin's tactic continued into the Post-Cold War era as well. As it has recently been revealed in the media, American intelligence agencies have been conducting a major investigation into Russian clandestine funding of European parties over the last decade as well as how the Kremlin is infiltrating political parties in Europe. The review reflects mounting concerns in Washington over Moscow's determination to exploit European disunity in order to undermine NATO, block US missile defence programs and revoke the punitive economic sanctions regime imposed after the annexation of Crimea. Although it has not been made know which parties could come into the probe but it is thought likely to include far-right groups including Jobbik in Hungary, Golden Dawn in Greece, the Northern League in Italy and France's Front National.[65]

This paradoxical "alliance" to the extend it exists, has to be put into a broader political context and it came into emergence in recent years across Europe. In many countries traditional political elites are being challenged by newer, smaller, and leaner parties from both left and right, which quite often capture the political agenda. Among other political and social features they are broadly sceptical about the EU, the United States, and are sympathetic to Vladimir Putin's Russia.[66] Beyond Europe, pro-Russian oriented parties or social groups are to be found in Israel, Egypt and elsewhere, but their impact on those countries' post Cold War course towards Russia has yet to be well documented.

Regarding Greece and Cyprus, however, it is worthwhile mentioning that both countries have been undergoing a profound identity crisis, as their previous, dominant political system, economy and reigning political culture have all been discredited, leaving a vast void. Especially, among the Greeks there is a strong belief that their country is not being accorded the recognition it deserves as a sovereign country. There is the wide spread view that it was Berlin's authoritative behavior which provoked EU-led austerity policy in Greece since 2010.[67] Furthermore, the kind of confidence that normally exists among EU partners has been shaken. It will take years of close interaction between Greece and the other EU members to reestablish it. After decades the debate on Greece's orientation towards West, in whose structures Greece had been firmly rooted since the end of Second World War and the East, remerged. However, this time it was not only the Communist party or some marginal political groups that argued for a reorientation toward the East and a confluence with Russian policy but various political forces in the right and left political spectrum and broad parts of the Greek Society.

A recent poll conducted in Cyprus, showed that a majority of Greek Cypriots favor granting Russia some military facilities on the island, with around a third supporting granting Moscow similar bases to those the British warplanes have been using to bomb Syria.[68]

Greece's heterogeneous pro-Russian camp includes parties with different political and ideological orientation and structure: Golden Dawn, Independent Greeks and SYRIZA. However after an internal crisis in the summer of 2015 and the then splitting off of some of its leading members, loosened its initial pro-Russian stance. The two governing parties, Independent Greeks and Syriza, are not in favor of an extension of EU sanctions against Russia and they oppose NATO military build up against Russia because they believe that such a development will harm relations between Brussels and Moscow and increase the possibility of large-scale war.[69]

On the other hand, the increasingly popular Neo-Nazi party Golden Dawn is a fierce opponent of Euro-Atlantic institutions and presents strong pro-Russian leanings. It has always had close connections with Russian extreme right parties and groups, and in recent years it is believed to have received under-the-table funding from Moscow. Being anti-European and anti-American, Golden Dawn sees Russia as Greece's "natural ally." As a consequence, Greece should disassociate itself from the West (i.e. the EU, NATO and the US) and offer Russia the long desired exit to the Mediterranean Sea in return for a Russian guarantee of Greek national security.[70]

Conclusion

The objective of this study has been to analyse Russia's foreign policy in the Eastern Mediterranean from the end of the Cold War until 2016. Based on the theoretical suggestions by the Copenhagen School of International Relations, it is argued that Moscow's foreign policy has been deployed in the framework of the EU-NATO-Russian antagonism, surrounding mainly energy and security issues that have been raging in the wider region since the 1990s. Exploiting the rifts and the conflicts repeatedly has emerged among the regional players in the last decade. Moscow tried to fill the economic and security vacuum which opened every time up. The Kremlin managed to maintain a delicate, low-key, and balancing strategy with its policies and to a longer, and more nuanced game in the region than perhaps any other player in the Post-Cold War. Overall there are two elements which compose Russian strategy in this region -- energy and military involvement. The energy factor is used to secure Russia's hegemonic position as traditional energy supplier of the West. Russia's military involvement has two dimensions -- the enhanced defence cooperation Kremlin has pursued with most of the countries of the region and the Syrian campaign. The latter was Moscow's attempt to retain the domestic prestige it won with the annexation of Crimea and to break out of the external siege that was laid down by the West immediately afterwards by trying to fit into the new global order as a great power. The deployment of weapons that do not comply with the scale of the military anti-rebels operations undertaken so far in Syria, have been meant to demonstrate Russia's military strength and to present the country as an alternative security provider in this unstable region.

Notes

1. A. S. Makarychev, Russia in the Mediterranean region: (Re)sources of influence, *The Yearbook of the European Institute of the Mediterranean* (IEMed) 2009,169-172.
2. P. Shlykov, Russian Foreign Policy in the Eastern Mediterranean since 1991, in S. Litsas and A. Tziampiris, eds, *The Eastern Mediterranean in Transition: Multipolarity, Politics and Power*, Farnham-Surrey: Ashgate, 2015, 31-32.
3. Cf. O. Wæver, Securitizing Sectors? Reply to Eriksson, *Cooperation and Conflict*, v.34, n.3, 1999, 334-340; O. Waever, Securitization-Desecuritization, in Lipschutz, R. ed., *On Security*, New York: Columbia University Press, 1995, 46-86; B. Buzan, People, *States & Fear: An Agenda for International Security Studies in the Post-Cold War Era*, 2nd edition, Hemel Hempstead: Harvester Wheatsheaf, 1991; J. Huysmans, The question of the limit: Desecuritisation and the aesthetics of horror in political realism, *Millennium*, v.27, n.3,1998,569-589; N. Tzifakis, Securitization and Desecuritization Dynamics in South-Eastern Europe (1992-1997), Lancaster University: Doctoral Dissertation, 2002, 4-29.
4. An additional reason might be the fact that the Russian Diplomatic Service consists, in part, of people who were still in service during the Communist period. There is no coherent foreign policy towards specific countries. Interview with Alexander Sotnichenko, Former Russian Diplomat in Israel and currently Associate Professor at the Saint Petersburg State University, School of International Relations.
5. I. Lederer, Historical Introduction, in Ivo Lederer and Wayne Vucinich, eds., *The Soviet Union and the Middle East: The Post-World War II Era*, Stanford University, Hoover Institute Publications, 1974, 2-3.
6. L. Whetten, The Soviet Presence in *The Eastern Mediterranean*. Washington: National Strategy Information Center, 1971, 32-35.
7. H. Faustmann, The United Nations and the Internationalization of the Cyprus Conflict 1949-1958, in: J. Ker-Lindsay/Oliver Richmond, eds., *Promoting Peace and Development in Cyprus over Four Decades*, Houndmills,NY, Palgrave, 2001, 3-49.
8. R. Eaton, Soviet Relations with Greece and Turkey, *Hellenic Foundation for Defence and Foreign Policy Occasional Papers No. 2*, 1987.

9 J. Hannah, At arms length: Soviet-Syrian relations in *The Gorbachev Era*, *The Washington Institute for Near East Policy-Policy Papers No.18*,1989, 5-8.
10 V. Fouskas, US Foreign Policy in the Greater Middle East during the Cold War and the Position of Cyprus, in H. Richter and V. Fouskas, eds., *Cyprus and Europe: The Long Way Back*, Mannheim and Möhnesee: Bibliopolis, 2003, 73-88.
11 A. Tekin and P.A. Williams, *Geo-Politics of the Euro-Asia energy nexus: the European Union, Russia and Turkey*, Basingstoke, Hampshire, Palgrave Macmillan, 2011, 160-161.
12 Cf. L. K. Yanik, Allies or partners? An appraisal of Turkey's ties to Russia, 1991-2007, *East European Quarterly*, v.41, n.3, 2007,,349-367; A. Sener, Turkish-Russian Relations after the Cold War 1992-2002, *Turkish Studies*, v.7, n.3, September 2006, 337-364.
13 Turkey is poor in energy resources neighbors the world's richest energy producing regions and hence it is strategically positioned to act as a type of bridge between Caspian and Middle Eastern oil and gas producers and western consumers.
14 A. Tekin and P.A. Williams, op. cit, 107 and 146-149.
15 See the excellent analysis by N. Tzifakis, op. cit., 290-304.
16 T. Michas, *Unholy Alliance: Greece and Milosovic' Serbia*, College Station, TX: Texas A&M University Press, 2002, 7-12.
17 Turkey recognizes the general validation of a state's right to expand its territorial waters to 12 miles and therefore it has made use of it in the Black Sea but it does not recognize Greece's right of extending its territorial waters specifically in the Aegean Sea, because it regards it as a claim against Turkey's national interests. However, this hinders the delimitation of the Exclusive Economic Zone and the exploitation of the possible energy reserves. Interview with the Professor of Law at the Istanbul University Rauf Versan, September 2014.
18 A. Pisiotis, Greece and Turkey in the concentric circles of Russian Post-Cold War Foreign Policy: Geopolitics, Oil and Religion, in C. Yiallourides and P. Tsakonas, eds., *Greece and Turkey after the End of the Cold War*, Athens: Caratzas Publisher, 2001, 409-422.
19 T. Tsakiris, Greek-Russian Relations, in G. Valinakis, ed., *Greece's Foreign and European Policy 1990-2010*, Athens: Sideris, 2010, (In Greek), 155.
20 A. Tziampiris, Greek Foreign Policy in the Shadow of the Debt Crisis: Continuity and New Directions, in P. Sklias, N. Tzifakis eds., *Greece's Horizons. Reflecting on the Country's Assets and Capabilities*, Athens: Konstantinos Karamanlis Institute for Democracy, 2013, 32-33.
21 A., Stergiou, Soviet policy toward Cyprus, *Cyprus Review*, v.19, n.2, fall 2007, 83-106. K. Liuhto, Russian gas and oil giants conquer markets in the West: Evidence on the internationalization of Gazprom and LUKoil, *Journal of East-West Business*, v.7, n.3, 2001, 35.
22 Central Bank of Cyprus, *Monetary Policy Report*, 2002, http://www.centralbank.gov.cy/nqcontent.cfm?a_id=10364&lang=en, accessed 3 April 2017; A. Hamatsou, *The Russian Presence in Cyprus*, (In Greek), Sygchrona Themata, vols.68-69-70, July 1998 – Mars 1999, 262-275.

23 K. T. Liuhto and S. S. Majuri, Outward foreign direct investment from Russia: A literature review, *Journal of East-West Business*, v.20, n.4, 2014, 199-200.
24 Central Bank of Cyprus, Monetary Policy Reports 2002, http://www.centralbank.gov.cy/nqcontent.cfm?a_id=10364&lang=en, accessed 3 April 2017 and 2010, http://www.centralbank.gov.cy/nqcontent.cfm?a_id=9837&lang=en, accessed 3 April 2017; E. Pelto, P. Vahtra, K. Liuhto, *Cyprus Investment Flows to Central and Eastern Europe - Russia's Direct and Indirect Investments via Cyprus to CEE*, Turun Kauppakorkeakoulu: Turku School of Economics and Business Administration, 2003,11-16; N. Fabry and S. Zeghni, Foreign direct investment in Russia: How the investment climate matters, *Communist and Post-Communist Studies*, v.35, 3, September 2002, 293-294.
25 Phidias, P., *The Role of Cyprus in Inward Investment in Russia*, Central and Eastern Europe. Cyprus: PricewaterhouseCoopers, 2002, 6.
26 Turkish Press Review and Cyprus Mail 1 October 1997; US Department of State Daily Press Briefing, 28 August 1998.
27 Clinton Presidential Records, declassified documents, Memorandum of Telephone Conversation between Bill Clinton and Tony Blair, 11 December 1998, 238. https://www.clintonlibrary.gov/
28 Anadolu Press, 21-25 September 1998 and 26 October 1998 and 3 November 1998.
29 C. Tsardanidis and Y. Nicolaou, Cyprus Foreign and Security Policy: Options and Challenges, in S. Stavridis, T. Veremis, T. Couloumbis and N. Waites, eds., *The Foreign Policies of the European Union's Mediterranean States and Applicant Countries in the 1990s Basingstoke*, Hampshire, University of Reading European and International Studies, 1998,181-182; *Turkish Press Review* and *Cyprus Mail*, 1 October 1997; US Department of State Daily Press Briefing 28 August 1998; Anadolu Press, 21-25 September 1998 and 26 September 1998 and 3 November 1998; Cyprus Mail 3 October 1997.
30 M. Katz, Exploiting rivalries: Putin's foreign policy, *Current History*, v. 103, n. 675, October 2004, 337-341.
31 Interview with the Sabanci University Professors of International Relations A. Evin and M. Müftüler-Bac, Istanbul September 2014.
32 Cyprus Releases Suspected Syrian Arms Ship, *Voice of America*, 10 January 2012; Russian-operated ship with bullets reaches Syria, *Reuters*, 13 January 2012; N. Bistis, Christofias, Munition and the hypocrites, (in Greek) *Protagon*, 18 July 2011.
33 In July 2011, confiscated munitions destined for Syria from Iran seized by the US Navy in January 2009 and stored in a naval base exploded, destroying Cyprus's largest power station killing 14 people in its worst peace time disaster and pushing it to the brink of seeking an EU bailout. According to the final investigation report on the accident submitted in October 2011, Communist President Dimitris Christofias seems to have promised Assad that the confiscated ship cargo would be returned to Syria. Source skai.gr ,2 October 2011.

34 S. Tagliapetra, Towards a new Eastern Mediterranean corridor? Natural gas developments. Between market opportunities and geopolitical risks, *Fondazione Eni Enrico Mattei Papers*, v.23, 2013.
35 M. Siddi, The EU-Russia gas relationship. New projects, new disputes?, *The Finnish Institute of International Affairs Briefing Paper*, v.183, n.3, 2015.
36 A. Jarosiewicz, The southern gas corridor. The Azerbaijani-Turkish project becomes part of the game between Russia and the EU, *Centre for Eastern Studies*, n.53, 2015, 9-10; Y. Kim and S. Blank, The new great game of Caspian energy in 2013-14: Turk stream, Russia and Turkey, *Journal of Balkan and Near Eastern Studies*, v.18,n.1, 2016.
37 S. Andoura and C. d'Oultremont, The role of gas in the external dimension of the EU energy transition, Notre Europe, *Jacques Delors Institute Policy Paper 79*, 2013.
38 A. Cohen and K. DeCorla-Souza, Eurasian Energy and Israeli Choices, *Jerusalem: The Begin-Sadat Center for Strategic Studies, Mideast Security and Policy Studies*, n. 88, 2011, 32-34.
39 Interview with A. Sotnichenko, former Russian diplomat in Israel and currently Associate Professor, Saint Petersburg State University, School of International Relations, Jerusalem, July 2013.
40 M. Eksi, The role of energy in Turkish Foreign Policy, *The Turkish Yearbook of International Relations*, v. 41, 2010, 62-65.
41 Y. Inan and M. Pınar Gözen, Turkey's maritime boundary relations, in: M. Kibaroglu, ed., *Eastern Mediterranean Countries and Issues*, Ankara: Foreign Policy Institute, 2009, 153-211.
42 An important annual naval event in the Mediterranean is the code named Reliant Mermaid that was first held in 1998 and originally involved Turkey. However, from 2011 onwards, after Turkey withdrew, Greece was invited to take its place. With Athens on board, the exercise was renamed Noble Dina and the overall mission of the training was changed from search and rescue exercizes to attack and defend scenarios that included repelling enemy assaults, anti-submarine warfare and aircraft operations as well as attacks on offshore natural gas and oil rigs.
43 A. Stergiou, Russian policy in the eastern Mediterranean and the implications for EU external action, European Union's Institute for Security Studies (ISS)-online-publications-opinions, 2012.
44 Israel needs both Russian diplomatic support and Russian know-how for the exploitation of the resources, while Gasprom has been keen to be involved in the exploitation of the new energy reserves but the right parties are against it. However, there are many resentiments from the Soviet and Russian support for the Arabs, interview with Alexander Sotnichenk.
45 S. Vogler and E. V. Thompson, Gas discoveries in the Eastern Mediterranean: Implications for regional maritime security, *The German Marshall Fund of the United States Policy Brief*, March 2015, 6.

⁴⁶ J. Cohen, Vladimir Putin is the closest thing to a friend Israel has ever had in Moscow, Reuters, 14 January 2016, http://blogs.reuters.com/great-debate/2016/01/14/vladimir-putin-is-the-closest-thing-to-a-friend-israel-has-ever-had-in-moscow/, accessed 1 April 2017.

⁴⁷ B. Siman, Russia seizing initiative in Eastern Med, Geopolitical Intelligence Service Report, June 2016.

⁴⁸ E. B. Günaydın, Can South-Eastern Mediterranean Gas be a supply for the EU?, *Istituto Affari International Paper*, v. 17, 2014, 5-6.

⁴⁹ S. Cropsey and E. Brown, Energy: The West's Strategic Opportunity in the Eastern Mediterranean, *Hudson Institute Paper No. 20*, 2014.

⁵⁰ The last combat readiness tests on this scale had been carried out by the Soviet army in the 1980s, as the Soviet Union maintained its 5th Mediterranean Squadron from 1967 until 1992. It was formed to counter the US Navy 6th Fleet during the Cold War, and consisted of 30-50 warships and auxiliary vessels between different periods. In the post-Cold War period, Russia sent ships to the region in 1995-1996 and in December 2008 and until January 2009. A. Wilk, Russian army justifies its reforms, Centre for Eastern Studies-Commentary, 26 June, 2013.

⁵¹ O. Razumovskaya, Cyprus signs deal to let Russian navy ships stop at its ports, *The Wall Street Journal*, 25 February 2015.

⁵² A. Kramer, Wealthy Russians ensnared as Cyprus crisis deepens, *The New York Times*, 22 March 2013 and L. Bershidsky, Why Putin would want the Cyprus talks to fail, Bloomberg, 16 January 2017, https://www.bloomberg.com/view/articles/2017-01-16/why-putin-would-want-the-cyprus-talks-to-fail, accessed 1 April 2017.

⁵³ S. Stefanini, Cyprus fears Russia could wreck reunification, *Politiko*, 12 January 2017, http://www.politico.eu/article/cyprus-fears-russia-could-wreck-reunification/, accessed 1 April 2017.

⁵⁴ Interview with the Sabanci University Professors of International Relations A. Evin and M. Müftüler-Bac, Istanbul, September 2014.

⁵⁵ The Kremlin denies that it has sent its forces to fight, but admits that individuals have a right to go and fight.

⁵⁶ The Military Balance, IISS - International Institute for Strategic Studies, 2015, Chapter Four: Europe, 57-58.

⁵⁷ A. Stergiou, Geopolitics: Greece, Cyprus and Israel change the military balance in the Mediterranean, *Geopolitical Information Service-GIS*, December 2013.

⁵⁸ K. Strachota and M. Chudziak, Turkey and the EU: The play for a security zone in Syria, *Centre for Eastern Studies Analyses*, 10 February 2016.

⁵⁹ Ibid.

⁶⁰ G. Gressel, Russia's quiet military revolution and what it means for Europe, *The European Council on Foreign Relations Policy Brief*, October 2015.

[61] J. Sherr, The new East-West discord, Russian objectives, Western interests, *Clingendael Institute Report*, December 2015, 69-71.
[62] D. Trenin, Putin's Syria gambit aims at something bigger than Syria, *Carnegie Analysis*, 13 October 2015.
[63] M. Menkiszak, The Russian-American declaration on Syria: A success for Moscow, *Centre for Eastern Studies, Analyses*, 24 February 2016; D. E. Sanger and A. Barnard, Russia and the United States Reach New Agreement on Syria Conflict, New York Times, 9 Sept. 2016.
[64] A. Stergiou, The Communist party of Cyprus and the Soviet policy in the Eastern Mediterranean, *Modern Greek Studies Yearbook*, University of Minnesota, v.30-31, 2014-2015, 206-207.
[65] n.a., Russia accused of clandestine funding of European parties as US conducts major review of Vladimir Putin's strategy, *The Daily Telegraph*, 16 January 2016.
[66] S. Dennison and D. Pardijs, The world according to Europe's insurgent parties: Putin, migration and people power, European Council on Foreign Relations, 27 June 2016,, paper, 1-3, http://www.ecfr.eu/publications/summary/the_world_according_to_europes_insurgent_parties7055, accessed 1 April 2017.
[67] Survey carried out by the Public Opinion Research Institute, University of Macedonia, April 2014, scientific supervisor G. Konstantinides.
[68] J. Gorvett, Nicosia holds the keys to Syria, the migrant crisis, and gas in the Eastern Mediterranean, *Foreign Affairs*, 12 January 2016.
[69] Cf. also Dennison and Pardijs, op.cit, 19-20.
[70] A. Klapsis, An unholy alliance, the European far-right and Putin's Russia, *Wilfried Martens Centre for European Studies*, 2015, 27-28.

Section B:
Regional Players

[6]
THE 'COMFORTABLE' QUASI-ALLIANCE OF ISRAEL, CYPRUS AND GREECE

Zenonas Tziarras

It is clear today that an axis of cooperation has gradually emerged between Israel, Cyprus and Greece, mainly since 2011, when the Republic of Cyprus (RoC) initiated exploration for the discovery of hydrocarbons in its Exclusive Economic Zone (EEZ).[1] Each of the three countries had its own reasons for entering this coalition. Yet Turkey and the energy factor were the two primary motivations that all three had in common. In light of this, the development of Greek–Turkish relations, the Cyprus Problem and Turkish–Israeli relations over the past decade have played an important role in the formation of this partnership. To be sure, the so-called 'shift' in Turkish foreign policy since the rise of the Justice and Development Party (AKP) came to power (2002), has also been decisive in leading the geopolitics of the eastern Mediterranean to the current state, and that is mostly because of the way Turkish–Israeli relations have been affected. Energy, on the other hand, was significant because of the profits it could entail.

Against this background, this chapter has three main goals: (i) to identify the collective and individual reasons behind the formation of the partnership among Israel, Greece and Cyprus; (ii) to examine the challenges and prospects of the partnership, especially in light of developments in Turkish–Israeli relations; and (iii) to suggest that the trilateral co-operation can be characterized as a 'comfortable' quasi-alliance. In so doing, the geostrategic needs of each of the three countries as well as the role of Turkish foreign policy are looked at within the regional security environment and an analytical framework of quasi-alliance formation. Thereby the 'comfortable' quasi character of the alliance can be better defined and its future prospects can be identified more easily.

The analysis reaches the conclusion that although the trilateral partnership of Israel, Cyprus and Greece has not developed into a traditional type of alliance, it has maintained the form of an informal 'comfortable' quasi-alliance driven by threat- and profit-related individual and collective motivations – including energy. The primary and most salient of these motivations – which worked as the 'glue' – has been their common perception of Turkey as a security threat and, perhaps to a lesser degree, energy-related interests. Moreover, although the cohesion of the quasi-alliance seemed to be threatened because of the gradual normalization of relations between Turkey and Israel since 2013, the quasi-alliance has reserved its cohesion.

Lastly, it is argued that despite the fact that the Turkey–Israel reconciliation could pose challenges to the quasi-alliance, the flexible nature of the relationship allows the development of bilateral relations with Turkey. On the other hand, it is suggested that the political comfort the quasi-alliance provides to its parties does not favor the deepening of relations and particularly the military aspect of the partnership. In other words, it is likely that it will not go farther than a loose and informal quasi-alliance without this precluding, however, a deeper cooperation.

Conceptual and analytical framework

Given that the object of analysis is the trilateral partnership or quasi-alliance between Israel, Cyprus and Greece, a working definition of alliances – the drivers behind their formation and their purposes – needs to be provided first. In this regard, it is clarified that this paper falls within the framework of neorealist understandings of alliances, though it remains focused on interstate and usually more ephemeral pacts rather than on long term or more institutionalized alliances such as the North Atlantic Treaty Organization (NATO). Additionally, it makes a distinction between energy and economic factors and attributes a special role to natural resources vis-à-vis the quasi-alliance in question. The role of energy resources is seen as partly dissociated from traditional economic considerations and as a separate factor in the overall relative power capabilities of a state, as is often the case in realism. As such, because of the importance of energy one could talk of energy security threat perceptions as well.

In neorealism, alliances and their interaction within the international system have always held a central position. Theorists like Hans Morgenthau[2] and Kenneth Waltz[3] made the case that alliance formation is a result of the anarchic international system and the balance of power within it that needs to be maintained as well as a result of states' quest for security. They also argued that not all states comprising an alliance share common or identical interests; they may serve identical, complementary or ideological interests (Morgenthau, 1993: 198–199; Waltz, 2010: 166). That is why this paper argues that the three states of the quasi-alliance are driven by both individual and collective motivations.

Advancing the understanding about power-acquisition strategies, Randall Schweller[4] argues that a state's security and survival are not the only motivations: the generation of profit should also be considered. Therefore, one could suggest that an alliance could pursue the simultaneous increase of profit and power as well. That is, material profits would contribute to a nation's relative power while the increase of its power through its alignment with other states would provide the circumstances under which it could secure or further its material capabilities and profits.

Apart from the power dimension, there is a general consensus in realism literature that the 'fear of other states'[5] plays an important role in the formation of alliances and thus an 'alliance is directed against a specific nation or group of nations' – it has balancing, deterrence or offensive purposes.[6] In a similar spirit, Stephen Walt sees security threat perceptions as central to alliance formation. Yet contrary to Morgenthau and Waltz, he sees alliances as answers to international security threats rather than to changing balances of power. He writes that 'states ally to balance against threats rather than against power alone', and he goes on to suggest that the level of threat is subject to geographical proximity, offensive capabilities and perceived intentions.[7] Following Walt's logic, this chapter accepts that the perception of an external threat is one of the motivations behind alliance formations as complementary to the above mentioned power and profit dimension.

Linked to this discussion is the widely debated issue of national power, which is commonly understood to be determined by natural and social elements or, alternatively, constant and dynamic elements.[8] This chapter gives special emphasis to natural resources such as hydrocarbons, and sees them as a constant element of national power distinct from, yet connected to, a nation's dynamic economic capacity. Natural resources can contribute to economic development and the overall economic capabilities of a country. They can be converted into national power as well as affect its foreign security and economic relations.[9]

In this context, energy security – namely, 'the uninterrupted availability of energy sources at an affordable price'[10] – is important in its own right because of the state's need to securely exploit and defend its natural resources, especially when contested or claimed by other states. Moreover, in geopolitically problematic cases energy could actually have a negative impact 'in raising the perceived stakes of interaction with other states either in a bilateral or multilateral context.'[11] As such, energy-related insecurities and threat perceptions are highly relevant to interstate cooperation and alliance formation in the eastern Mediterranean as well.

A 'comfortable' quasi-alliance

Though power, profit and threats could explain well the drivers behind the formation of an alliance, the Israel–Cyprus–Greece partnership does not fit exactly into the category of traditional or formal alliances, mainly because the three countries have not signed a formal military treaty. Therefore this paper proposes that the partnership in question should be seen as a 'comfortable' quasi-alliance.

In the literature, the term 'quasi-alliance' does not always mean the same thing. For example, whereas Victor Cha[12] defines it as 'two states that are unallied but share a third great power patron as a common ally,' Degang Sun[13] talks of a 'permanent or ad hoc informal security cooperation arrangement, based not only on formal collective defence pacts, but on tacit agreements between two or among more international regimes.' The latter definition seems more appropriate for the partnership under examination, especially when certain criteria are taken into account. Among other features, Sun argues that "the formation of a quasi-alliance hinges on the establishment of tacit agreement between and among the elites of different states," while its management "relies on mutual expectation based on communiques, joint declarations, memoranda, treaties of friendship and cooperation, declarations on the press conference, domestic laws … or even UN resolutions, instead of military treaties."[14]

Sun also suggests that, just like a formal alliance, a quasi-alliance is aimed at winning or deterring a common enemy, or a perceived common threat.[15] However, this paper argues that things may not be as clear cut when it comes to Israel, Cyprus and Greece. While the partnership fulfils the quasi-alliance criteria to a great extent, it remains informal and its military offensive character is underdeveloped and downplayed by the parties. This is due to a number of problems that could arise if the three states pursued a more offensive or military cooperation: they would upset Turkey further and deepen the geopolitical polarization of the eastern Mediterranean. Moreover, they would reduce the possibility for rapprochement or deeper relations between each of the states and Turkey. After all, Turkey, Israel, Cyprus and Greece are bound by geography to co-exist, thus any policy that would exclude the possibility of improved relationships would arguably prove not to be wise in the long term. The latter perception seems to be particularly salient in the case of Israel.[16] Hence, the partnership has developed into a 'comfortable' quasi-alliance – one that gives the three states geopolitical leverage vis-à-vis Turkey and accommodates their profit related interests even as it provides each state political flexibility in the medium or long term regarding relations with Turkey.

The level of analysis emphasized here is primarily the regional: the eastern Mediterranean. A number of authors have been calling for emphasis on the regional level, arguing that it has become increasingly important for international security since the end of the cold war.[17] Although the eastern Mediterranean is not commonly perceived or analysed as a distinct region, the discovery of hydrocarbons led analysts to pay unprecedented attention to the political, economic and security relations between the involved states within this limited geographical area. Proedrou[18] has, for example, called it an energy and security complex while Adamides and Christou argued that the Turkey–Israel–Cyprus triangle could be seen as a security sub-complex "at the edge of two RSCs [Regional Security Complexes – Europe and the Middle

East] and an insulator state [Turkey]."[19] Therefore the eastern Mediterranean and the quasi-alliance in question have been calling for a more region and subject specific enquiry, to which this chapter aims to contribute.

Furthermore, this regional focus is also in line with Walt's understanding of balancing behaviour. He notes that due to geographical proximity, "regional states are more sensitive to threats from other regional powers," and therefore threats from local actors are the primary driver of alliance formation by the states of a region.[20] Lastly, although penetration of the region by great powers (mostly the United States and Russia) is not absent, the geopolitical and geoeconomic dynamics in the eastern Mediterranean concern primarily the regional actors under examination. Therefore the chapter does not pay particular attention to the involvement or role of great powers in this specific phenomenon.

Quasi-alliance: background and motivations

As noted earlier, the quasi-alliance in question is looked at through the lens of two sets of individual and collective motivations: power/profit related and threat related. Under the first category are economic and defence/military motivations. Under the latter category are security threat perceptions. As is demonstrated below, Turkey is considered to be the primary actor perceived as a security threat by all three states of the quasi-alliance and the primary motivation that brought them together. The issue of natural resources or energy (in)security is included in both categories. As mentioned earlier, that is because energy can boost the economy and therefore the overall national power, while at the same time it could constitute a point of vulnerability for a nation; one that could generate (energy) insecurities and in turn (energy) security threat perceptions.

Lastly, natural resources are important for another reason: they can become the motivation for interstate cooperation because of the know-how and infrastructure other nations could provide for their exploitation, given that political relations between the concerned parties are positive.[21] That is the case with Cyprus and, to a lesser extent, Greece. These states do not have a tradition in the exploitation of natural resources. Israel has a relatively more developed energy sector and experience that could benefit Cyprus and Greece, despite the fact that only recently (2000s) it has itself become a resource abundant country.

Before moving on to the actual individual and collective motivations that brought Israel, Cyprus and Greece together, a look at the preexisting disputes – patterns of enmity and amity[22] – between each of these countries with Turkey is essential for understanding the background against which their cooperation and the security threat perceptions of each state emerged. At the same time, looking at the pre-existing and, later, the post 2011 dynamics will shed light on the continuity of certain alliance motivations and the introduction of new ones, particularly with regard to Israel. The selection of 2011 as a turning point is directly related to Israel's significant shift towards Cyprus and Greece and its role as the cornerstone of the quasi-alliance.

Preexisting problems with Turkey: The background of a perceived security threat

The formation of what has been called a 'geopolitical triangle,'[23] 'energy triangle'[24] or 'axis'[25] by Israel, Greece and Cyprus was favored because of the preexistence of outstanding bilateral issues with Turkey. Had these countries had good relations with Turkey, regional cooperation, be it in the energy sector or elsewhere, would have included Turkey as well. However, this is not the case rather patterns of enmity and amity have played a significant role.

First, as far as the RoC is concerned, the main problem has been the Turkish military occupation of the island's north since 1974 and everything that comes with it domestically and diplomatically. In this sense, Turkey is not only an external, international threat to the RoC but also a domestic one – coming from within the island – since Ankara maintains military forces in the northern part of Cyprus and the occupied territories are practically part of Turkey's geopolitical space of control and influence.[26] Thus, geographical proximity, Turkey's offensive capabilities and perceptions of Ankara's threatening intentions in the RoC constituted an already existing high level threat.[27] Furthermore, this perception is often expressed publicly as the official view of the RoC. For example, the website of the RoC's Foreign Ministry states: "A member state of the United Nations and the European Union today, Cyprus continues to be victim of unabashed international aggression by Turkey."[28]

Similarly, Greek–Turkish relations have been problematic for decades due to the bilateral dispute over the Aegean's maritime zones, airspace and other issues such as the treatment of the Greek and Turkish minorities in each country, respectively.[29] From a Greek perspective, Turkish claims over the Aegean Sea in particular and the often projected Turkish military offensive capabilities through Turkey's violations of Greek maritime and airspace are seen as a threat.[30] As pointed out repeatedly in the literature, the same factors of geographical proximity, offensive capabilities and perceived intentions affect the extent to which Greece sees Turkey as a threat.[31] Despite the threat perceptions that stem from the bilateral problems, it should be noted that Greece's official stance is that the two countries should focus on low politics by way of deescalating the tensions, and work their way up to more difficult disputes.[32]

When it comes to Israel, its relations with Turkey have been relatively positive between 2002 and 2010. However, although the two countries signed a series of strategic agreements in 1996, thus forming a highly important alliance, the state of affairs between them changed gradually after the AKP came to power in Turkey.[33] Since then the ideological and geopolitical shifts that occurred led Ankara to support the Palestinians like never before and harshly criticize Israel's policies towards them on a number of occasions.[34] Israel's case is different from those of Cyprus and Greece in that it does not have the same historical background of enmity with Turkey, though their relations have not always been stable.[35] However, Turkey's offensive capabilities and intentions, as projected through Turkish foreign policy behavior and threats, increased Israel's threat perception of Turkey.

Their relationship hit record low in May 2010 when Turkey downgraded its defence and diplomatic relations with Israel after Israeli soldiers raided the Turkish ship Mavi Marmara killing nine activists – eight Turkish and one Turkish-American – who were carrying humanitarian aid to Gaza. In September 2011, following the release of the United Nations' Palmer Report regarding the Mavi Marmara incident, Turkey, which found the report to be unfair, downgraded the bilateral relations further and announced that it would suspend all its military and commercial ties with Israel.[36] Eventually only defence ties were suspended. Commercial and economic ties continued and in fact boomed, hitting record high volumes in 2011 and 2014.[37] In March 2013, after mediation efforts from US President Barack Obama, Israel apologized to Turkey and agreed to compensate the families of the victims, as Turkey had demanded, in order for a rapprochement to be possible. The negotiations on the amount of compensation had reached a deadlock due to disagreements but they got back on track after Israel made a new offer in 2014.[38] The two countries fully restored their diplomatic relations in late June 2016.

Although deterioration in Turkish–Israeli relations started, most notably, with the Israeli war on Gaza in 2008-09 and Turkey's vigorous opposition to Israeli policies, it happens that the year when the Israel–Cyprus–Greece quasi-alliance started to emerge, 2011, was the year that Turkey–Israel relations took the final hit and their alliance essentially froze. It can be suggested that by the end of 2011 Israel perceived Turkey to be a threat for a number of reasons. First, the AKP's emergence as an avid supporter of the Palestinians was happening at the expense of Israel. The fact that Turkey, a traditional (western) ally, joined the pro-Palestinian and anti-Israeli Arab camp was at the very least alarming to Israel.

Not only that, but in 2011 Turkey announced sanctions against the Jewish state and also threatened the expansion of naval military operations in the eastern Mediterranean.[39] Lastly, the visits of then Turkish prime minister, currently president Recep Tayyıp Erdoğan, to Iran and his personal relationship with then Iranian President Mahmoud Ahmadinejad, worried Israel since it perceives Iran as one of the greatest security threats posed to it.[40] In Israel many actually believed that Ahmadinejad was dictating policies to Erdoğan regarding Israel and other matters and that Erdoğan was happy to implement them.[41] Of course Israel's threat perception of Turkey may not have been the equivalent to its threat perception of Hamas, for example.

However Ankara maintained a clearly hostile stance on a number of levels, which in conjunction with the frozen diplomatic and military Turkish–Israeli relations, contributed to Israel's turn towards Cyprus and Greece.

Post-2011 motivations and Turkey

Apart from the preexisting reasons that consolidated the security threat perceptions about Turkey (a collective motivation) by Cyprus, Greece and Israel, thereby favoring the emergence of the trilateral cooperation, the developments that took place between 2011 and 2015 rendered the partnership even more necessary for all three states. The efforts to discover hydrocarbons in the RoC's EEZ led to an angry reaction from Turkey from the summer of 2011 when it started threatening the island nation.[42] In this context, Turkey later announced illegal hydrocarbon explorations in the Cypriot occupied territories and in northern Cypriot waters which are controlled by the Turkish-Cypriot administration.[43] At the same time it had also illegally delimited its continental shelf with the de facto Turkish-Cypriot state, recognized only by Turkey.[44] For the same reasons, Turkey also threatened that it would freeze its relations with the European Union and the negotiations for the resolution of the Cyprus problem when the RoC would assume the presidency of the Council of the EU – and so it did.[45]

Moreover, Turkey's efforts to solidify its power on the island, by trying to upgrade the legal status of the Turkish-Cypriot administration, gave rise to multiple insecurities in the RoC as well.[46] Such Turkish efforts are evident, for example, in the maps decisions published by the journal of the Turkish Republic regarding the authorization of the Turkish Petroleum Corporation (TPAO) for the conduct of explorations outside of Turkish national waters and within Cypriot maritime space. These decisions ultimately aim at legitimizing illegal agreements between Turkey, TPAO and the Turkish-Cypriot administration, such as the delimitation of the continental shelf between Turkey and the Turkish-Cypriots as well as between the latter and TPAO.[47] Similarly, in 2014 Turkey illegally issued a Navigational Telex (NAVTEX) reserving maritime space in the RoC's EEZ, south of Cyprus, for seismic surveys and sent the seismic vessel Barbaros accompanied by warships to conduct the surveys.⁴⁸ These actions exacerbated the RoC's threat perceptions.

Also indicative of Turkey's goals in Cyprus were its efforts to capitalize on the Cypriot economic crisis, to communicatively downgrade the RoC and upgrade the Turkish-Cypriot administration.⁴⁹ Efforts such as Ankara's call upon Muslim states to develop bilateral relations with the Turkish-Cypriot administration, and by asking the EU to pressure the Greek-Cypriots for a quick settlement of the Cyprus problem testify to this.⁵⁰ It is worth noting that these Turkish policies reaffirm and exacerbate traditional threat perceptions of Turkey in the RoC. A long-standing fear in Cyprus is that Turkey will never leave the island and that it will always be trying to exert control over it in one way or the other.⁵¹ But this is not merely a Cypriot perception; some political and academic circles in Turkey concur that these are indeed Ankara's intentions in Cyprus.⁵²

In sum, it could be suggested that developments in the energy sector generated energy related insecurities and threat perceptions in the RoC which contributed to traditional security concerns and created the need for external support. From that perspective, its cooperation with Israel and Greece also provided material profits such as defence/deterrence capabilities and increased its overall relative power. Incidentally, potential profits from the exploitation of hydrocarbons acquired new significance when natural resources became the RoC's biggest economic hope in the midst of a collapsing economy, especially from March 2013 onwards.⁵³

As far as Greece is concerned, multiple factors led to the need for cooperation with regional actors. The economic and political crisis it has been going through; its own efforts for the discovery and exploitation of hydrocarbons in the Aegean; the need to delimitate its maritime zones; and the continuous violations of national waters and airspace by Turkey, according to the Greek perspective, created the need for an inter-state partnership that would provide security and deterrent capacity as well as economic and energy profits.⁵⁴ Turkey again has a central position in the decisions of Greece. At least from a Greek point of view, Ankara concentrates its efforts, among other things, on the issue of the Aegean where the abovementioned maps and movements of the Turkish government aim at indirectly projecting and solidifying its own vision of the Turkish continental shelf and EEZ by creating a politico-legal precedent, without taking into account the Greek islands – particularly of Rhodes and Kastelorizo – thus challenging the Greek sovereign rights over the eastern Aegean.[55]

Israel, on the other hand, in the midst of the Arab uprisings, the crisis with Iran and its nuclear programme, and its geopolitical position in between hostile (Arab) states, especially after the loss of Turkey as a regional ally, started searching for other partners.[56] An alliance would help it to counter-balance the regional power and threat of both Turkey and the Arab world, as well as increase its economic profits through cooperation in the energy domain. Like the motivations of Cyprus and Greece, Israel's were both power/profit and threat related. It is important to note that before Israel and Turkey got back on track to reconciliation, Turkish policies challenged Israel repeatedly, not only by cutting off diplomatic ties and using harsh anti-Israeli rhetoric but also by actions such as blocking it from participating in the NATO Chicago Summit of 2012.[57] In this light, Israel's cooperation with Cyprus and Greece remained important both because of Turkey's continuous hostile stance and the increasing regional instability.

At this point it should be mentioned that even after the 2013 Israeli apology to Turkey, Turkish–Israeli relations did not improve as quickly as one would expect. There were a lot of obstacles until their 2016 agreement that all but rendered the quasi-alliance obsolete.[58] Among other things, Turkey continued to harshly criticize Israel's policies vis-à-visa the Palestinians, thereby not leaving much room for constructive diplomacy,[59] while it accepted Israel's apology with great pride, presenting itself as the country that managed to make Israel bow.[60] The normalization of Turkey-Israel relations is certainly an important development, which may open up prospects for further cooperation between the two, even in the energy sector.[61] However, the mistrust will take some time to fade away. What is more, the Islamic authoritarian trajectory of Turkey's domestic political scene over the past years that deepened even further in the aftermath of the coup attempt against the AKP government on 15 July 2016, raises concerns in Israel.[62] Should the instability and high political risk in Turkey insist, Israel's commitment to Turkey on issues such as energy and military collaboration could potentially be affected.

Areas of cooperation and the 'comfortable' quasi-alliance

As argued, power/profit related and threat related motivations led Israel, Cyprus and Greece to co-operate in the form of a quasi-alliance. The importance of both sets of motivations has thus far been demonstrated with particular emphasis on the role of individual and collective traditional and contemporary security threat perceptions.

On the front of material and power related profits, the quasi-alliance consists of cooperation agreements on the political, economic, energy and military level. The start was essentially made in 2009 when Greece and Israel signed military and other agreements that were followed by a joint committee for strategic security cooperation on terrorism issues and a security cooperation agreement in 2011.[63] Another security cooperation agreement of a military nature was signed in 2015.[64]

Similarly, the RoC and Israel signed a military and defence cooperation agreement in 2012[65] and in the summer of 2015 they decided to 'engage in the creation of a Cooperation Committee and in strengthening the framework of bilateral agreements in the fields of defence and security'.[66] Indeed, in the case of Israel–Cyprus relations military cooperation followed energy cooperation as it was primarily aimed at defending the areas of extraction and exploitation of hydrocarbons, thus addressing or alleviating energy insecurities related to Turkish threats.[67] Moreover, the two countries have repeatedly reiterated their commitment to deepen energy, economic and security co-operation.[68]

The energy factor in particular is central to other examples of profit related cooperation as well,[69] which concern various agreements, projects in progress and negotiations for coexploitation of the natural gas reserves between Cyprus and Israel: namely, the Cypriot reserve 'Aphrodite' and the Israeli reserves 'Leviathan' and 'Tamar'.[70] The discussion also regards a host of options that Cyprus and Israel have to consider for the exportation of their natural gas – some of them concern Greece as well.[71] Furthermore, one of the most important joint ongoing projects is the 'EuroAsia Interconnector,' an unprecedentedly long submarine power cable that is to link Israel with Cyprus and Greece for the transfer of cheap electrical energy generated from Israeli and Cypriot natural gas to continental Europe. Lastly, the trilateral cooperation concerns joint crisis management operations with the potential participation of Romania and Bulgaria.[72] These are only a few examples, which demonstrate that cooperation between Israel, Cyprus and Greece goes beyond deterring or balancing threats. It is evidently profit driven as well and presupposes positive political relations.

Beyond the deepening Israel–Greece, Israel–Cyprus relations and the military or crisis management drills they conducted over past years on a bilateral level,[73] the three states have taken important collective steps as well. In 2013 they signed a memorandum of understanding and issued a joint communiqué.; they later held consultations on economic and security issues and announced that a tripartite summit is to be prepared.[74] The summit eventually took place on 28 January 2016. The joint declaration stated, among other things, that the three countries agreed to strengthen their cooperation 'in order to promote a trilateral partnership in different fields of common interest and to work together towards promoting peace, stability, security and prosperity in the Mediterranean and the wider region.'[75] This was an important step towards a closer cooperation between the three countries.

Against this background, and given the threat perceptions analyzed earlier, it can be suggested that apart from the individual motivations of each state the Turkish threat and the energy factor have been the two primary collective and interconnected motivations that led to the quasi-alliance. In addition, the abovementioned factors meet the basic criteria of a quasi-alliance in terms of motivations and methods of expressing mutual expectations and goals (e.g. communiques, joint statements, etc.). On the other hand, it is clear that Israel, Cyprus and Greece, despite their growing relations, have thus far fallen short of establishing a more formal and military oriented alliance. Thus the quasi-alliance lacks an offensive or strong military defensive character and in this sense remains rather politically 'comfortable' for the participating states. As suggested below, the main reason why this happens, has to do with Israel and less with Cyprus and Greece.

Prospects, challenges and the 'comfortable' component

It has been established that a common perception of Turkey as a threat and the role of natural resources have been the primary common motivations behind the co-operation of the three countries. It has also been observed that apart from these and other individual motivations, two factors triggered the Israel–Cyprus–Greece quasi-alliance: (i) the deterioration of Turkish–Israeli relations and (ii) the discovery of hydrocarbons by the RoC and Israel. Had Turkish–Israeli relations not deteriorated and their bilateral alliance remained strong, Israel might not have developed such ties with Cyprus and Greece, especially in the energy sector. It seems that the common energy related interests influenced Israel's calculations. Particular attention is paid to Israel as it is considered to be the cornerstone and the strongest party of the quasi-alliance. Greece and Cyprus have always been in close coordination and cooperation but it was not until Israel joined them that the game changed. Thus, although natural resources seem to be a constant variable, Israel's participation in or commitment to the quasi-alliance seems to be an alterable factor as it was initially based on its bad relations with Turkey. That is why the prospects and challenges of the partnership need to be examined in the light of Turkish–Israeli relations.[76]

One could argue that the quasi-alliance and the level of cooperation will largely depend on each party's commitment and relations with Turkey. Realistically, without the resolution of the Cyprus problem and of fundamental problems in Greek–Turkish relations, a close partnership between Cyprus and Greece with Turkey would be very unlikely; thus sustained cooperation with Israel would be beneficial for both of them. For Greece and Cyprus the quasi-alliance was a great and perhaps unique opportunity as Israel is a strong regional power. And although the Israeli apology and the possibility for improvements in Turkish–Israeli relations posed the first challenge, the partnership still made sense to all three states for reasons already mentioned, including Turkey's non-constructive stance towards Israel.

A first look at the Turkish–Israeli reconciliation process could lead one to believe that Greece and Cyprus were no longer seen by Israel as the best solution to its energy and security problems since Turkey re-entered the picture. A closer look would suggest that the reality was not that simple. Shortly after the Israeli apology Cyprus and Israel carried out a joint naval rescue drill. At around the same time then Israeli ambassador to Cyprus, Michael Harari, stated that developments in Turkish–Israeli relations will not affect Israel's relations with Cyprus.[77] Most importantly, after a visit of the RoC president, Nicos Anastasiades, to Israel, it was reported that Cyprus and Israel have entered a new period of strengthened ties while Israeli Prime Minister Benjamin Netanyahu "promised that Israel would continue to maintain good ties with Cyprus."[78] Also reassuring for the sustainability of the partnership were the military drills held by Israel with Greece and Cyprus, respectively. Those between Cyprus and Israel were particularly important as they came at around the same time Israel made its new compensation offer to Turkey and continued into the next year.[79]

In this context, although one could argue that after the apology Turkey was no longer seen by Israel as a security threat, the latter's cooperation with Cyprus and Greece did not seem to be particularly threatened. Apart from the apology, a number of issues on which Turkey and Israel have common interests could be seen as a second challenge. Among others, the wish to overthrow the Syrian regime and the management of the Islamic State crisis are two areas where Turkish and Israeli interests meet, at least partly. In particular, the further escalation of the Syrian crisis, the expansion of the Islamic State and the regional insecurity that comes with it, have contributed in bringing about the 2016 of Turkish-Israeli relations.[80] However, this development has not yet troubled the quasi-alliance.

On another note, the geopolitical realities have played an important role in shaping the nature of the quasi-alliance and therefore its future as well. To begin with, it has been argued that security relations between Turkey, Israel and Cyprus "have become intertwined and mutually exclusive as a result of the energy factor."[81] From this perspective, Israel can cooperate with either Turkey or Cyprus (and Greece). The possibility that Israel might choose one or the other highlights the reason why the Israel–Cyprus–Greece relationship has remained limited to its 'comfortable,' quasi character. For Israel, the stakes are too high and prevent it from investing too much in its relationship with Cyprus and Greece. After all, "Cyprus as well as Israel seem to avoid taking positions on sensitive political issues, while … they continue to reiterate that this relationship is not mutually exclusive and should not be considered as hostile towards the Arab states and Turkey respectively."[82] In this regard it is important for Cyprus, Israel and Greece to keep their options open.

In fact, at least at the political level, the quasi-alliance still endures mainly because its 'comfortable' and quasi character did not necessitate mutual exclusiveness with regard to Turkey–Israel and Israel–Cyprus–Greece relations. The 'comfortable' and quasi nature of the alliance allows the three states to manoeuvre politically so as not to exclude future parallel relations with Turkey. In the event of a settlement of the Cyprus problem, for example, Turkish–Cypriot relations will probably improve and, by extension, so will Greek–Turkish relations. Given Turkey's influence over Cyprus, it is only rational for the RoC not to push it too much. In addition, regardless of the bilateral problems, Athens would be reluctant to upset its profitable economic relations with Turkey.[83] This 'comfortable' approach also means that the transformation of the quasi-alliance into a more formal alliance is a rather unlikely scenario since none of the parties seems to be willing to engage in a formation with a more confrontational military character.

On a different level, the issue of energy cooperation remains difficult and is probably the only sector where, as things stand right now, Israel may have to pick either Turkey or Cyprus and Greece. From this perspective, a Turkey–Israel agreement for the transportation and exportation of Israeli natural gas to Europe through Turkey or even the supply of Israeli gas to Turkey could pose a third and more serious challenge to the quasi-alliance, particularly to its energy dimension. It might undermine the role Cyprus and Greece would have in the future energy plans of Israel and the broader energy architecture of the eastern Mediterranean. However, regardless of the normalization of Turkish-Israeli relations, an energy deal remains a complex issue for a number of reasons.[84]

Furthermore, given the domestic sociopolitical transformation of Turkey particularly after the coup attempt of July 2016, Israel, suspicious of what the future may bring, is likely to proceed with caution in its relations with Turkey. This might hinder the quick deepening of the Turkish-Israeli political relationship; and as noted earlier, it is nearly impossible for energy cooperation to precede with the full normalization of political relations. Therefore, the

Turkey–Israel reconciliation would be able to challenge the quasi-alliance not because of a Turkish–Israeli energy cooperation but because of the full restoration of political relations that would have to come first. By extension, the quasi-alliance could be affected in the energy sector and possibly other sectors as well. But as demonstrated thus far, political relations among the three parties have not been undermined. Turkey's debatable foreign policy orientation and growing anti-Western[85] stance have allowed the resilience of the quasi-alliance even after the Turkey-Israel accord. This was made clear when the RoC president, Nicos Anastasiades, visited Jerusalem in July 2016 and together with Israeli Prime Minister, Benjamin Netanyahu, vowed to increase cooperation while stressing "the importance of the trilateral framework between Israel, Cyprus, and Greece."[86] From this perspective, Turkey again occurs as a type of 'regulator' both of Turkish-Israeli relations and the quasi alliance. As long as Turkey is an unstable and unreliable partner, Israel will be keeping its options open and the quasi alliance will not lose its importance.

Israel–Cyprus–Greece: Conclusions and implications

This chapter has set three goals: to identify the individual and collective motivations behind the partnership in question; to look at its prospects and challenges; and to suggest that the Israel–Cyprus–Greece co-operation is a 'comfortable' quasi-alliance. Both the power/profit and threat related motivations have been identified. Individually, historical, energy, economic and security motivations have led to the emergence of the Israel–Cyprus–Greece partnership while collectively the Turkish threat and energy security played a primary role. Perhaps most importantly, the negative relations of Turkey with all three countries played a decisive role in leading to the quasi-alliance; a formation which to some extent played the role of balancing against the Turkish power and threat. In what followed, Israel and Turkey entered a period of rapprochement, which eventually led to a deal. Although this process briefly seemed to challenge the significance and resilience of the quasi-alliance a number of reasons mainly related with Turkish domestic and foreign affairs have not reversed the good and multi-leveled relations between Israel, Cyprus and Greece.

In terms of the nature of the partnership, it has been shown that it could be described as a 'comfortable' quasi-alliance. To one extent or another, it has some of the basic ingredients of a traditional alliance such as power, profit and deterrence considerations, cooperation on sectors such as military and defence, as well as the goal of balancing a common threat (Turkey). It has also served some 'identical' and some 'complementary' interests since 2011. However, from the very beginning, it has been lacking a more formal and substantive military-oriented character that would classify it as a formal alliance. It rather adopted a more 'comfortable' approach, falling short of a comprehensive military strategic agreement, and remained limited to military drills, declarations of security cooperation, joint communiques, memoranda of understanding, etc. It thus meets the criteria of a quasi-alliance instead of a formal alliance and points to the fact that although Turkey has been seen – to varying degrees – as a security threat by Israel, Cyprus and Greece, the three states are have not demonstrated the will to enhance their cooperation in any way that would be perceived by Ankara as confrontational.

In this light, the 'comfortable' and quasi character of the alliance might allow the three states to proceed with and profit from their cooperation, but their lack of commitment to pursuing a more formal alliance is evident and underlines the fact that this might be the farthest this alliance can get in terms of areas and degrees of cooperation. Moreover, through the reluctance of the three parties to advance their partnership, they demonstrate willingness – and a hope, one might add – for a positive change in the political and security dynamics of the eastern Mediterranean: for a geopolitical environment in which their cooperation with Turkey would not be impossible. As far as Israel is concerned, the issue at stake today is not the existence of diplomatic relations but a more meaningful, stable and strategic partnership with Turkey.

Lastly, the potential of a closer Turkish–Israeli relationship and energy cooperation could in the future create certain problems for Cyprus and Greece, not so much in terms of their political relations with Israel but with regard to their energy security policies. This might be one of the reasons why Cyprus and Greece are forming another quasi-alliance with Egypt.[87] For Cyprus and Greece it is only reasonable to step up their efforts towards widening their regional networks and coming up with contingency plans. No matter how good their relations are right now, relying solely on their cooperation with Israel would be irrational; the same applies for Israel as well. After all, it is widely known that alliances – and even more so quasi-alliances – are more often than not temporal.

Notes

1. This chapter is an updated version of Z. Tziarras, Israel-Cyprus-Greece: a 'Comfortable' Quasi-Alliance, Mediterranean Politics, January 2016, v.21, n.3, 402-427.
2. H. J. Morgenthau, *Politics among Nations: The Struggle for Power and Peace*, Brief ed., New York, McGraw-Hill Inc., 1993, 197.
3. K. Waltz, *Theory of International Politics*, Long Grove, IL, Waveland Press Inc., 2010, 118, 166.
4. R. Schweller, Bandwagoning for profit: Bringing the revisionist state back in, *International Security*, v.19, n.1, 1994, 82.
5. S. Waltz, *Theory of International Politics*, 166.
6. H. J. Morgenthau, *Politics among Nations*, 198.
7. Stephen Walt, *The Origins of Alliances*, Ithaca and London, Cornell University Press, 1987, 5.
8. A. Davutoğlu, Στρατηγικό Βάθος: Η Διεθνής Θέση της Τουρκίας [*Strategic Depth: Turkey's Place in the World*]. Athens, Poiotita, 2010, 48–65. David Jablonsky, National Power, in J. B. Bartholomees, Jr., ed.; *The US Army War College Guide to National Security Issues: Theory of War and Strategy*, v. 1, 4th ed., Carlisle, Strategic Studies Institute, 2010, 126–134; O. Christou and C. Adamides, Energy Securitization and Desecuritization in the New Middle East, *Security Dialogue*, v. 44, iss.5-6, 2013, 507-522. D. Jablonsky, *National Power*, 128–129.
9. Energy Security, International Energy Agency, 2013, available at http://www.iea.org/topics/energysecurity/.
10. C. Adamides and O. Christou, Energy security and the transformation of regional securitization relations in the Eastern Mediterranean, in S. Katsikides & Pavlos. I. Koktsidis, eds., *Societies in Transition: Economic, Political and Security Transformations in Contemporary Europe*, Cham, Heidelberg, New York, Dordrecht, London: Springer, 194; Constantinos Adamides and Odysseas Christou, Beyond Hegemony: Cyprus, energy Securitization and the emergence of new regional security complexes, in S. N. Litsas and A. Tziampiris, eds., *The Eastern Mediterranean in Transition: Multipolarity, Politics and Power*, Surrey, Ashgate,181.

[11] V. Cha, Abandonment, entrapment, and neoclassical realism in Asia: The United States, Japan and Korea, *International Studies Quarterly*, v. 44, n. 2, 2000,262.
[12] D. Sun, Brothers indeed: Syria-Iran quasi-alliance revisited, *Journal of Middle Eastern and Islamic Studies (in Asia)*, v.3, n.2, 2009, 68.
[13] Ibid.
[14] Op.cit.
[15] Z. Tziarras, The new geopolitical landscape in the Eastern Mediterranean: The Israeli perception, *Eastern Mediterranean Geopolitical Review*, v.1, 2015, 32-43..
[16] B. Buzan and O. Waever, *Regions and Powers: The Structure of International Security*. Cambridge, Cambridge University Press, 2003; D. Lake and P. Morgan, The new regionalism in security affairs, in David Lake and Patrick Morgan, *Regional Orders: Building Security in a New World*, Pennsylvania, Pennsylvania State University Press, 1997, 6.
[17] F. Proedrou, Re-conceptualizing the energy and security complex in the Eastern Mediterranean, *Cyprus Review*, v.24, n.2, 2012.
[18] C. Adamides and O. Christou, Beyond Hegemony, 182. See also, A. Kaliber, Re-imagining Cyprus: the rise of regionalism in Turkey's security Lexicon, in T. Diez and N. Tocci, *Cyprus: A Conflict at the Crossroads*, Manchester and New York, Manchester University Press, 2013, 105-123.
[19] S. M. Walt, *The Origins of Alliances*, 168.
[20] C. Adamides and O. Christou, Energy security and the transformation of regional securitization relations in the Eastern Mediterranean, *Societies in Transition*, New York, Springer International Publishing, 2015, 193–194; W. Khadduri, East Mediterranean Gas: Opportunities and challenges, *Mediterranean Politics*,v.17, n.1, 2012 111–117; Y. M. Zhukov, Trouble in the eastern Mediterranean: The Coming dash for gas, *Foreign Affairs*, 20 March 2012, https://www.foreignaffairs.com/articles/cyprus/2013-03-20/trouble-eastern-mediterranean-sea.
[21] A terminology often mentioned in the writings of B. Buzan. Patterns of enmity and amity (affected by historical factors) are said to define regional security complexes. See, B. Buzan, The Southeast Asian Security Complex, *Contemporary Southeast Asia*, 10, 1, 1988, 1–16; B. Buzan and O. Waever, Regions and Powers, 45.
[22] T. Ntokos,Ένταση στην Ανατολική Μεσόγειο: Το Γεωπολιτικό 'Τετράγωνο' Ελλάδας-Κύπρου-Ισραήλ-Τουρκίας [Tension in the Eastern Mediterranean: The geopolitical 'rectangle' of Greece-Cyprus-Israel-Turkey], *ELIAMEP, Working Paper No. 23*, 2011, http://www.eliamep.gr/wp-content/uploads/2011/10/23_2011__WORKING_PAPER___Thanos_Dokos.pdf.
[23] G. Stavris, The new energy triangle of Cyprus-Greece-Israel: Casting a net for Turkey?, *Turkish Policy Quarterly*, 2012, v.11, n.2 87–102.
[24] D. Huber and N. Tocci, Behind the scenes of the Turkish-Israeli breakthrough, Istituto Affari Internazionali, *IAI Working Paper No. 1315*, 2013, http://www.iai.it/pdf/DocIAI/iaiwp1315.pdf.

25 I. Mazis, Ο Γεωστρατηγικός Άξονας Ισραήλ-Κύπρου-Ελλάδος [The geostrategic axis Israel-Cyprus-Greece], *Foreign Affairs The Hellenic Edition*, 6 April 2012, http://foreignaffairs.gr/articles/68736/ioannis-th-mazis/o-geostratigikos-aksonas-israilkyproy-ellados?page=3; Interview with an anonymous Republic of Cyprus official, Nicosia, 22 October 2013.

26 P. Tank, Cyprus: a note on security guarantees and threat perceptions, *The Turkish Yearbook of International Relations*, XXXV, 2015, 169–176.

27 The Cyprus question: latest developments, Ministry of Foreign Affairs of the Republic of Cyprus, 29 May 2014, http://www.mfa.gov.cy/mfa/mfa2016.nsf/mfa58_en/mfa58_en?OpenDocument.

28 M. Aydın and K. Yfantis, eds., *Turkish-Greek Relations: The Security Dilemma in the Aegean*. London and New York, Routledge, 2004; A. Heraclides, *The Greek-Turkish Conflict in the Aegean: Imagined Enemies*. Basingstoke and New York, Palgrave Macmillan, 2010.

29 University in the Emirates, CEO of Strategy International Institute, Athens, 26 January 2014; Interview with Anonymous Greek official, Athens, 10 February 2014.

30 G. S. Ayman, Negotiation and deterrence in asymmetrical power situations: The Turkish-Greek case, in M. Aydın and K. Yfantis, eds. *Turkish-Greek Relations: The Security Dilemma in the Aegean*, London and New York, Routledge, 2004, 213–244; T. Dokos and P. J. Tsakonas, Greek-Turkish relations in the post-cold war era, in C. Kollias & G. Gulnuk-Senesen, eds, *Greece and Turkey in the 21st Century: Conflict or Cooperation*, New York, Nova Science Publications, 2016, 9–35.

31 E. Athanassopoulou, Turkey and Greece in Nicholas Kitchen, ed., *Turkey's Global Strategy*, London, LSE Ideas, 2011, 17-18, http://www.lse.ac.uk/IDEAS/publications/reports/pdf/SR007/greece.pdf.

32 S. Brom, The Israeli-Turkish relationship, in W. B. Quandt, ed., *Troubled Triangle: The United States, Turkey and Israel in the New Middle East*, Charlottesville, VA, Just World Books, 2011 57-64.

33 Ibid.

34 J. Abadi, Israel and Turkey: From overt to covert relations, *The Journal of Conflict Studies*, 15, 2, 1995, https://journals.lib.unb.ca/index.php/JCS/article/view/4548.

35 G. Palmer, et al., Report of the Secretary-General's Panel of Inquiry on the 31 May 2010 Flotilla Incident. United Nations, 2011; PM: Turkey to impose more sanctions on Israel, boost presence in east Med, *Today's Zaman*, 6 September 2011, http://www.todayszaman.com/news-255903-pm-turkey-to-impose-more-sanctions-on-israel-boost-presence-in-east-med.html.

36 S. Cağaptay and T. Evans, The unexpected vitality of Turkish-Israeli trade relations, *The Washington Institute for Near East Policy, Research Notes No. 16*, 2012, http://www.washingtoninstitute.org/uploads/Documents/pubs/ResearchNote16.pdf.

37 B. Ravid, Israel offers Turkey $20 m in compensation over Gaza Flotilla Raid, *Haaretz*, 3 February 2014, http://www.haaretz.com/news/diplomacy-defence/1.572069, accessed 20 February 2014.

38 PM: Turkey to impose more sanctions on Israel, boost presence in east Med,
39 Interview with O. B. Dinçer, Researcher at International Strategic Research Organization (USAK), Ankara, 19 July 2013; Interview with Dr. L. Fishman, Assistant Professor, Brooklyn College, City University of New York, 23 January 2014.
40 Interview with Dr. O. Tür, Associate Professor, International Relations in Middle East Technical University, Ankara, 17 July 2013.
41 C. Barber, Turkey threatens naval action over Cyprus drilling, *Famagusta Gazette*, 6 September 2011, http://famagusta-gazette.com/turkey-threatens-naval-actionover-cyprus-drilling-p12883-69.htm; W. Khadduri, *East Mediterranean Gas: Opportunities and Challenge*, 2012, 116.
42 H. Smith, Turkey natural gas search stokes tensions with Cyprus, *The Guardian*, 2 October 2011, http://www.theguardian.com/world/2011/oct/02/turkey-gassearch-tensions-cyprus.
43 Statement by Prime Minister Erdogan following the signing of continental shelf delimitation agreement between Turkey and the Turkish Republic of Northern Cyprus, Ministry of Foreign Affairs of the Republic of Turkey, 21 September 2011, http://www.mfa.gov.tr/statement-by-prime-minister-erdogan-following-the-signing-of-continental-shelf-delimitation-agreement-between-turkey-and-the-tur.en.mfa.
44 Jonathan Burch, Turkey to freeze EU ties if Cyprus gets EU presidency, *Reuters*, 18 September 2011, http://www.reuters.com/article/2011/09/18/us-turkeycyprus-idUSTRE78H20L20110918.
45 Interview with an anonymous Republic of Cyprus official, 22 October 2013.
46 C. Minagias, Οι Επίσημοι Τουρκικοί Χάρτες Αμφισβήτησης της Ελληνικής Α.Ο.Ζ. [The official Turkish maps which dispute the Greek EEZ], GeoStrategy, 28 April 2012, http://www.geostrategy.gr/pdf/20120428%20Official%20Turkish%20Maps.pdf.
47 Jonathan Sterns, Cyprus presses EU to warn Turkey over warship intrusion, Bloomberg, 28 October 2014, http://www.bloomberg.com/news/2014-10-23/cyprus-presseseu-to-warn-turkey-over-warship-intrusion.html, accessed 28 December 2014.
48 Z. Tziarras, Economic crisis in Cyprus: Repercussions, Turkey and the Turkish-Cypriots, e-International Relations, 3 January 2013, http://www.e-ir.info/2013/01/03/economic-crisis-in-cyprus-repercussions-turkey-and-the-turkish-cypriots/.
49 İ. Yezdani, Lift embargo, Turkish Cyprus calls on Muslims, Hurriyet Daily News, 18 December 2012, http://www.hurriyetdailynews.com/lift-embargo-turkishcyprus-calls-on-muslims.aspx?PageID=238&NID=37076&NewsCatID=359.
50 R. Bryant and C. Yakinthou, Cypriot perceptions of Turkey. Istanbul, TESEV Publications, 2012; Interview with an anonymous Republic of Cyprus official, 22 October 2013.

51 A. Davutoğlu, Strategic Depth, pp. 275, 279; Interview with retired Turkish Ambassador Prof. A. Engin Oba, Chair, Department of International Relations, Çağ Üniversitesi; Advisor to Chairman of Turkish Asian Centre for Strategic Studies, Ankara, 12 June 2013.
52 Natural gas proceeds can boost Cyprus economy says Noble, Famagusta Gazette, 09 April 2013, http://famagusta-gazette.com/natural-gas-proceeds-can-boost-cyprus-economy-says-noble-p18894-69.htm, accessed 1 April 2017.
53 I. Mazis, The geostrategic axis Israel-Cyprus-Greece; Interview with Dr. M. P. Efthymiopoulos, 26 January 2.
54 A. Heraclides, *The Greek-Turkish Conflict in the Aegean*, pp. 167–193; C. Minagias, The official Turkish maps which dispute the Greek EEZ.
55 E. Inbar, The strategic implications for Israel, in E. Inbar, ed., *The Arab Spring, Democracy and Security: Domestic and International Ramifications*, Oxon and New York, Routledge, 2013, 156.
56 S. Yanatma, Turkey blocks EU from NATO summit unless OIC also attends, Today's Zaman, 30 April 2012, http://www.atlanticcouncil.org/blogs/natosource/turkey-blocks-eu-from-nato-summit-unless-oic-also-attends.
57 Isabel Kershner, Israel and Turkey agree to Resume Full Diplomatic Ties, *The New York Times*, 26 June 2016, http://www.nytimes.com/2016/06/27/world/middleeast/israel-and-turkey-agree-to-resume-full-diplomatic-ties.html?_r=0.
58 Daniel Dombey, Erdogan slams Israel as Gaza conflict ends diplomatic thaw, Financial Times, 22 July 2014, http://www.ft.com/cms/s/0/2be8ee72-10fd-11e4-b116-00144feabdc0.html#axzz3PwLDDKnH; D. Dombey, Erdoğan lashes out at Israel over incursion into al-Aqsa in Jerusalem, Today's Zaman, 6 November 2014, http://www.todayszaman.com/national_erdogan-lashesout-at-israel-over-incursion-into-al-aqsa-in-jerusalem_363744.html; President Erdoğan slams 'advocates of Israel', Today's Zaman, 16 January 2015, http://www.todayszaman.com/diplomacy_president-erdogan-slams-advocates-ofisrael_370004.html.
59 Herb Keinon, Claim of Turkish sensitivity astonishes Israelis, *The Jerusalem Post*, 4 October 2013, http://www.jpost.com/Diplomacy-and-Politics/Kerrys-claim-of-Turkish-sensitivity-astonishes-Israelis-309038.
60 A. Ben Solomon and M. M. Grossman, Despite Turkey-Israel Accord, Gas Deal Complex, *The Jerusalem Post*, 28 June 2016, http://www.jpost.com/Israel-News/Politics-And-Diplomacy/Despite-Turkey-Israel-accord-gas-deal-complex-458002.
61 G. Mitchell, Will Turkey's Failed Coup impact Energy Cooperation with Israel?, *Mideast Insider*, 21 July 2016, http://mideastinsider.com/will-turkey-failed-coup-impact-energy-cooperation-israel/.
62 A. Midkiff, Shifting dynamics in the Eastern Mediterranean: The developing relationship between Greece and Israel, *Perspectives on Business and Economics*, v.30, 2012, 49.

63 n.a., Israel and Greece sign security cooperation agreement, *Middle East Monitor*, 20 July 2015, https://www.middleeastmonitor.com/news/europe/19913-israeland-greece-sign-security-cooperation-agreement.
64 Greek Cyprus ratifies military cooperation deal with Israel, *Today's Zaman*, 3 July 2012, http://www.todayszaman.com/newsDetail_getNewsById.action?newsId=285.
65 n.a., Cyprus-Israel agree to co-operate on defence and security, *SigmaLive*, 04 August 2015, http://www.s.com/en/news/local/133232/cyprusisrael-agree-tocooperate-on-defence-and-security#.dpuf.
66 Interview with an anonymous Republic of Cyprus official, 22 October 2013; Interview with Dr.M. P. Efthymiopoulos, 26 January 2014; Interview with an anonymous Greek official, 10 February 2014.
67 Cyprus and Israel agree to strengthen ties on energy, security, *Cyprus Mail*, 28 July 2015, http://cyprus-mail.com/2015/07/28/netanyahu-in-cyprus/.
68 C. Adamides and O. Christou, Energy security and the transformation of regional securitization relations in the Eastern Mediterranean,196.
69 J. Cohen, Greece, Israel sign pact on security cooperation, *Jewish Telegraphic Agency*, 05 September 2011, http://www.jta.org/2011/09/05/news-opinion/israel-middle-east/greece-israel-sign-pact-on-security-cooperation; A. Athanasopoulos, Προς συμφωνία Κύπρου - Ισραήλ για συνεκμετάλλευση του φυσικού αερίου [Towards a Cyprus-Israel agreement for the co exploitation of natural gas], *To Vima*, 17 February 2012, http://www.tovima.gr/politics/article/?aid=444083.
70 S. Evripidou, Experts agree that an LNG plant is best option for Cyprus, *Cyprus Mail*, 23 November 2013, http://cyprus-mail.com/2013/11/23/experts-agree-that-anlng-plant-is-best-option-for-cyprus/; S. Henderson, Natural gas export options for Israel and Cyprus, The German Marshall Fund of the United States, September 2013, http://www.gmfus.org/wp-content/blogs.dir/1/files_mf/1378838051Henderson_NatGasExportOptions_Sep13_web.pdd.
71 I. Fisher, Greece, Cyprus to advance Israeli power line to Europe, *Haaretz*, 27 April 2012, http://www.haaretz.com/business/greece-cyprus-to-advance-israelipower-line-to-europe-1.426816; Panagiotis Tsaggaris, "Μαρκουλλή: Η Άγκυρα προωθεί το Σχέδιο Β'" [Markoulli: Ankara Forwards the Plan B'], Kathimerini CY, 24 April 2012, http://www.kathimerini.com.cy/index.php?pageaction=kat&modid=1&artid=86623.
72 For a timeline of drills and agreements see, P. Nastos, Greek-Israeli-Cyprus military and security relations: A preview, *Research Institute for European and American Studies*, 15 December 2013, http://www. rieas.gr/research-areas/2014-07-30-08-58-27/greek-israel-studies/2077-greek-israelicyprus-military-and-security-relations-a-preview.
73 Cyprus, Israel and Greece sign MoU on cooperation in the fields of energy and water resources, 8.8.2013, Ministry of Energy, Commerce, Industry and Tourism of the Republic of Cyprus, 9 August 2013, http://www.mcit.gov.cy/mcit/mcit.nsf/All/66CE31A752AE27E8C2257BC2002A6F48?OpenDocument; Israel,

Greece and Cyprus hold trilateral consultations, I24News, 12 November 2014, http://www.i24news.tv/en/news/israel/diplomacy-defence/50742-141112-israel-greece-and-cyprus-hold-trilateral-consultations.

74 Cyprus – Israel - Greece Trilateral Summit Declaration – Nicosia, Ministry of Foreign Affairs of the Republic of Cyprus, 28 January 2016, http://www.mfa.gov.cy/mfa/mfa2006.nsf/All/9B0625444ED9A963C2257F480045A4AF?OpenDocment.

75 C. Adamides and O. Christou, *Beyond Hegemony*, 182.

76 n.a., 5 πολεμικά σκάφη του Ισραήλ στη Λεμεσό [5 Israeli Warships in Limassol], *SigmaLive*, 22 April 2013, available at http://www.sigmalive.com/news/local/41758; n.a., Η βελτίωση σχέσεων Τουρκίας-Ισραήλ, δεν επηρεάζουν την Κύπρο [The Improvement of Turkish-Israeli Relations does not affect Cyprus], SigmaLive, 2 May 2013, http://www.sigmalive.com/news/politics/43337.

77 D. Lev, PM: We will always be a friend to Cyprus, *Israel National News*, 5 June.2013, http://www.israelnationalnews.com/News/News.aspx/167772#.UY0dZrWG2_t.

78 G. Cohen, US to join largest aerial drill in Israel's history, along with Italy, Greece, *Haaretz*, 6 November 2013, http://www.haaretz.com/news/diplomacy-defence/.premium-1.556533; Cyprus and Israel mount joint military exercise, Cyprus Mail, 11 February 2014, http://cyprus-mail.com/2014/02/11/cyprus-and-israel-mount-joint-militaryexercise/.

79 S. Demirtaş, Israel calls on Turkey to stand united in anti-terror fight, *Hurriyet Daily News*, 12 October 2015, http://www.hurriyetdailynews.com/Default.aspx?PageID=238&NID=89723&NewsCatID=510.

80 C. Adamides and O. Christou, *Beyond Hegemony*,182.

81 C. Adamides and O. Christou, Energy security and the transformation of regional securitization relations in the Eastern Mediterranean, 197; Tziarras, The New Geopolitical Landscape in the Eastern Mediterranean, *Eastern Mediterranean Geopolitical Review*, fall 2015, 39–41.

82 E. Athanassopoulou, Turkey and Greece in Nicholas Kitchen, ed., *Turkey's Global Strategy*, London, LSE Ideas, 2011, 17-18, http://www.lse.ac.uk/IDEAS/publications/reports/pdf/SR007/greece.pdf..

83 A. Ben Solomon and M. M. Grossman, Despite Turkey-Israel Accord, Gas Deal Complex. S. Idiz, More than meets the eye in Turkish-Israeli ties, *Al-Monitor*, 22 February 2013, http://www.al-monitor.com/pulse/originals/2013/02/mavi-marmaraflotilla-turkey-israel-relations.html#; J. Mitnick, Israel and Turkey explore energy ties, The Wall Street Journal, 26 March 2013, http://online.wsj.com/news/articles/SB10001424127887324105204578382243773388484.

84 See e.g., Z. Tziarras, Turkey – the 'new Iran': Revolution and foreign policy, *Academy for Strategic Analyses, Working Paper No. 52*, July 2016, http://www.acastran.org/%CE%BA%CE%B5%CE%B9%CE%BC%CE%B5%CE%B
D%CE%B1https://www.academia.edu/27282972/Turkey_-_the_new_Iran_Revolution_and_Foreign_Policy.

[85] N. Keidar, Israel and Cyprus to increase cooperation, *Israel National News*, 25 July 2016, http://www.israelnationalnews.com/News/News.aspx/215458.
[86] Joint press release after the trilateral meeting of the Ministers of Foreign Affairs of the Republic of Cyprus, the Arab Republic of Egypt and the Hellenic Republic, Ministry of Foreign Affairs of the Republic of Cyprus, 30 September 2015, http://www.mfa.gov.cy/mfa/mfa2006.nsf/All/AA1E963BA7B3F03AC2257ED20032E77A?OpenDocument.

[7]
TURKEY AND THE TURKISH REPUBLIC OF NORTHERN CYPRUS: A THORNY RELATIONSHIP*

Kıvanç Ulusoy

Introduction

The Presidential elections which took place in Northern Cyprus in April 2015 brought a renewed dynamism to the United Nations' (UN) efforts to resolve the Cyprus conflict. The UN sponsored talks resumed on 15 May after a stalemate of eight month. The Greek and Turkish Cypriot leaders decided to adopt confidence building measures in a new drive to settle the conflict. The UN mediator Espen Barth Eide, a Norwegian political scientist, underlined that the Greek Cypriot leader Nicos Anastasiades and the newly-elected Turkish Cypriot counterpart Mustafa Akıncı share their vision for a united Cyprus. The collapse of the Cyprus Republic as a result of the interethnic clashes between Turkish and Greek Cypriots brought a decades old conflict on the island. The parties have been desperately searching for a unity of the two peoples living on the island despite the absence of a unifying identity. The peace has been maintained through permanent negotiations under the UN auspices since the eruption of the intercommunal strife in the early 1960s. The situation came to be more complex as a result of the division of the island after a Greek inspired coup and the following military intervention by Turkey in 1974. Today, Cyprus comprises a southern Greek Cypriot state, a member state of the European Union (EU), recognised worldwide, and a breakaway Turkish Cypriot state in the North, called Turkish Republic of Northern Cyprus (TRNC) recognised only by Turkey.

The negotiations for settlement aimed at balancing divergent interests of Greece, Turkey and the United Kingdom (the three guarantor powers of the Cyprus constitution) and the two communities on the island. They took place in an open ended time frame under the UN auspices. However, from the early

1980s onwards Greece's membership to the European Community (EC) and the membership applications of Turkey and the Cyprus Republic brought increased pressure over the parties. The expectation for an EU membership provided a time constraint for the parties to work for a settlement. Aiming to accept Cyprus as a unified entity, the EU had significant leverage over the membership applications of Cyprus and Turkey in the context of the Eastern enlargement. However, the rejection of the UN sponsored plan in 2004 shows that even the time leverage and the award of membership wasn't enough for the parties to unify the island.

Since the collapse of the so called Annan Plan in April 2004, the conflict turned to be even more complex as the Greek Cypriot side became an EU member. The UN efforts continued despite the slim chance of unification on the island. The latest presidential elections in Northern Cyprus gave a new lease of life to these efforts. The newly elected Turkish Cypriot president Mustafa Akıncı, the ex-mayor in Nicosia between 1976-1990, was welcomed by the Greek Cypriot side because of his prosolution attitude and his concrete promises in terms of progressing in the confidence building measures. In this context, this chapter focus on the political context that brought Mustafa Akıncı to power and the possible repercussions of his election as president on the resolution of the Cyprus conflict. I argue that the election of Akıncı could have serious effects in particular on the relations between Turkey and the TRNC, which would inevitably affect the peace efforts on the island. His election could bring more dignified relations between Turkey and the TRNC, which would pave the way to the consolidation of a more legitimate administration in the North of the island and a stronger hand for the Turkish Cypriots in the latest negotiations process for the settlement of the dispute.

A brief definition of the problem

Cyprus was split into two after the Turkish intervention in 1974 following a Greek inspired coup to topple the Makarios regime which had been in power since the foundation of the Republic. Archbishop Makarios was also *Ethnarch*, the national leader of the Greek Cypriot community. In fact, the roots of division and the conflict were sown before the independence of Cyprus from Britain in the late 1950s. The anti-colonial struggle brought Greeks and Turks against each other as the Turkish Cypriots were against *enosis* - the unification of the island with Greece - then defended by the Greek Cypriot nationalists as the ultimate destiny of the island. As a counterweight to the Greek ideal of *enosis* or union, the Turkish Cypriots began to float the idea of *Taksim* or partition. The struggle between Turkish and Greek Cypriots, the necessity of a balance of power between Greece and Turkey in the Eastern Mediterranean and the strategic calculations of the UK under the Cold War circumstances brought a rare form of solution to the issue of to whom the island belongs. The incomplete statehood of the Republic, which was a short-lived consensus model of the UK, Greece, and Turkey determines the essence of the conflict.[1] The Republic was founded in 1960 as a result of the agreements in Zurich (11 February 1959) and London (19 February 1959). Cyprus, Greece, Turkey and the UK signed the three treaties: the Treaty of Guarantee, the Treaty of Alliance, and the Treaty of Establishment. The treaties defined the basic political structure of the state and the Constitution of 16 August 1960. This situation, the limited sovereignty of the Republic to any domestic constitutional changes by the guaranteeing, is comparable to the four power status of Berlin after the World War II. The guarantors had the right to intervene either commonly or singularly to restore the constitutional order, institutionalizing power sharing between Turkish (constituting 18% of population) and Greek Cypriots (constituting 80% of population).[2] The UK kept its sovereign military bases, occupying 3% of the island.[3]

The mediation efforts started with the US President Johnson's attempt after the outbreak of violence between communities in 1963. The UK hosted a conference in London in January 1964, followed by the NATO proposal of stationing peacekeeping forces in March 1964. The UN Security Council passed Resolution 186 on March 4, calling for stationing peacekeeping force (UNFICYP) in Cyprus.[4] The conflict between the communities gained a new dimension with the involvement of the motherlands in the 1960s. Finally, the tensions brought the Greek coup on 15 July 1974 followed by Turkey's intervention on July 20. The island's division into two separate zones after the intervention changed the negotiations' ground in 1974. The efforts continued under the initiatives of various UN Secretary Generals such as Kurt Waldheim (1972-1981), Boutros Boutros-Ghali (1992-1996) and Kofi Annan (1997-2006). On the basis of previous agreements between the community leaders, a reunification deal would create a two-state federation, one Greek Cypriot and the other Turkish Cypriot.⁵ The settlement talks under the UN auspices have over the years foundered on the competencies of each, the redrawing of territorial boundaries and property claims by tens of thousands of internally displaced people.⁶

The conflict has gradually been Europeanized internalized by the European Community (EC)/European Union (EU) - as the conflicting parties deepened their relationship with the European integration process. The UK (1975), Greece (1981) and the Cyprus Republic (2004) became EU member states and Turkey is currently negotiating for accession. The relations between Cyprus and the EU was based on Association Agreement of 1973. Turkish Cypriots did not object to the Customs Union by 2001 as it was beneficial for all Cypriots and the agreement was signed by Greece and Turkey too. However, the relations entered a new phase when Greece became an EC member in 1981. Greece pursued a policy of linking the improvement in EU-Turkey relations to the settlement of its disputes with Turkey. The Greek policy was effective. It corresponded with the EU's policy of delaying Turkey's membership. In response to the proclamation of the TRNC in 1983, the EC foreign ministers made a statement underlining that they continued to regard the Kyprianou Government as the sole legitimate government and called upon all parties not to recognise this act.⁷ In a similar vein, the UN Security Council adopted a resolution in November 1983 stating that Northern Cyprus' declaration of independence was invalid.⁸ Condemning the declaration of the Turkish Cypriot leadership in establishing an independent state, the European Parliament (EP) declared that it did not recognise the TRNC and called upon Turkey to cooperate with the UN for a lasting solution.⁹ In response to Turkey's membership application in 1987, the EU required Turkey to solve its bilateral disputes with Greece, including the Cyprus problem.¹⁰ In April 1988, the European Council concluded that the "Cyprus problem affects EU-Turkey relations." At the Summit in Dublin in June 1990, the Council stressed its deep concern at the situation, firmly affirming its support for unity, independence, sovereignty and territorial integrity of Cyprus in accordance with the UN resolution.¹¹

Following Cyprus' membership application in 1990, the EU applied the conditionality framework as in other candidates. Asking for the reunification of the island before accession and supporting the UN's role as mediator, the EU argued membership would be an incentive for settlement. UN mediators benefited from the EU timetable applied to Cyprus and Turkey from the late 1990s onwards. The EU dimension was part of the latest settlement plan, called the Annan Plan which came to the table in 2002. However, it was not possible to synchronise the moments that left both sides under pressure. The EU accession negotiations with Cyprus and Turkey's slow progress towards membership had different dynamics. Facing with Greece's threat to hold the Eastern enlargement hostage to Cyprus' accession at the Helsinki Summit in 1999, the EU left the Turkish Cypriots with a bleak outlook of watching the Greek Cypriot progress in negotiations and Turkey's strategic calculations for its candidacy. This was reinforced by Turkey's decision, for its own EU prospect, to change the balance decisively in favor of the Plan.

After two years of negotiations under the UN auspices in 2004, Turkey proposed the formula of letting Annan "fill in the blanks" in the case of differences between parties. The Plan was revised a number of times before being put to a referendum on 24 April 2004, and receiving the support of Turkish Cypriots (65%), but rejected by the Greek Cypriots (75.38%). When the Greek Cypriots were under the greatest pressure up to March 2003, Turkey was reluctant to pressure the Turkish Cypriot leadership. When Turkey and Turkish Cypriots aimed for seriously negotiating the settlement from the late 2003 onwards, the EU pressures on the Greek Cypriots were already relaxed.[12] The Cyprus Republic became an EU member in 2004. As the period between 2002-2004 showed, politics and geopolitical calculations prevailed over the objective conditions of membership. The EU conditionality was not consistently applied in the Cyprus case. Greece prevented EU from implementing a different policy. Other members appeared reluctant to accept Turkey to the EU. Incorporating the whole territory of Cyprus, the EU accepted that the *acquis* would be applied only in areas controlled by the Greek Cypriot administration.

A thorny relationship

Left with a bleak outlook because of the Greek Cypriot leadership's expectation of their unilateral submission to the Republic of Cyprus which is the only internationally recognised political entity and now an EU member, and the EU's incapacity to end their isolation despite their "yes" vote to the Plan, the Turkish Cypriots approached Turkey's policies in regard to the Cyprus conflict. The passionate quest for a "solution and the EU" membership that was observed in their protests against the long-lasting Turkish Cypriot leader Rauf Denktaş' reluctance to negotiate the Plan in 2002 and 2003, melted as a result of the Greek Cypriots «blatant no» and the EU's incapacity to make a fair response. After Cyprus' EU membership in 2004, a series of intercommunal surveys demonstrates that the relations between Turkish and Greek Cypriots did not improve despite the opening of the border in 2003 and the subsequent openings of new cross points along the Green Line which divided the island into two sectors. A survey conducted a short time after the Annan Plan referendums underlined that Turkish Cypriots were disappointed by the Greek Cypriots' rejection of «common state» and the indifference of the international community to their plea inevitably sided with Turkey for their security. They (65%) regarded their special relations with Turkey could provide the necessary security and be an asset for them in case the TRNC one day became an EU member.[13] Another survey showed that the majority of Turkish Cypriots found the Plan's Security provisions, acknowledging the intervening role (though in the last resort), acceptable as they did not trust the Greek Cypriots.[14] A survey done by the UN in 2007 showed that Greek Cypriots (80%) and Turkish Cypriots (90%) crossing to the other side had almost no contact with the other community.[15] Another survey conducted in 2009 showed that Greek Cypriots (56%) and Turkish Cypriots (61.9%) as pessimistic about the peace negotiations and not expecting a solution in the short-term.[16]

However, the same survey showed that despite their lack of trust to the Greek Cypriots, Turkish Cypriots feelings towards Turkey evolved in time. They had a divided stance regarding Turkey's role in the conflict resolution. The survey showed that in response to the prospect of a continuation of the

Treaty of Guarantee, their support was far from enthusiastic with only 47% of Turkish Cypriots finding the continuation of the Treaty of Guarantee satisfactory or essential, 27% finding it merely tolerable and 26% finding it unacceptable.[17] On the other hand, another survey gives us credible clues regarding how relations would be between the communities. While neither community is expressing anxiety over a possible erosion of cultural/religious identity through a settlement (Greek Cypriots %35 and Turkish Cypriots 38%), both communities (Greek Cypriots 69% and Turkish Cypriots 56%) fear the prospect of renewed conflict between them in case a settlement is reached. Turkish Cypriots (53%) fear that the communities have grown too far apart and can no longer live together.[18] While the departure of foreign troops (mainly referring to almost 30 thousand Turkish troops stationed since the 1974 intervention) from the island is the Greek Cypriots' (98%) main security concern, Turkish Cypriots (25%) do not consider changes in security provisions as a motivating factor for a settlement.[19] The talks for reunification continued for years, leaving tens of thousands of Cypriots on both sides displaced. The Annan Plan suggesting the restructuring of the Republic as a «United Republic of Cyprus,» constituted by a federation of two states was put to referendum in 2004 and overwhelmingly rejected by the Greek Cypriots. Over the past decade, the negotiations continued under the changing leaderships: Papadopoulos-Talat (2006-2008), Talat-Hristofias (2008-2010), Eroğlu-Hristofias (2008-2013), Eroğlu-Anastasiadis (2013-2014). As the surveys showed despite the low expectations of a solution in short term, Turkish and Greek Cypriots, deeply divided in terms of security, have been unhappy with the *status quo* and do not believe that their leaders have been doing enough to change it.

More than a decade after the collapse of the Annan Plan, the election of the former leftist mayor of Nicosia Mustafa Akıncı as the President of the TRNC created an unexpected optimism on both sides.[20] The two-round presidential elections were held in April 2015. In the first round, held on 19 April, the incumbent president and independent candidate Eroğlu (28.4%) and independent candidate Akıncı (26.8%) progressed to the second round. Neither Akıncı nor Eroğlu managed to pass the 50% benchmark that would constitute a majority. The parliament speaker Sibel Siber (22.5%), the candidate of the governing Republican Turkish Party (CTP), and the ex-chief negotiator Kudret Özersay (21.2%), an independent candidate and academic, failed to pass to the second round. While Prime Minister Özkan Yorgancıoğlu announced that he would be stepping down in the upcoming party congress because of Siber's failure, Özersay's success surprised many. While Siber declared in her kick off presidential campaign that she would work hard for the recommencement of negotiations to aim for a federal solution based on political equality and to construct healthy relations with Turkey,[21] Özersay built his campaign on active diplomatic policy in the negotiations and for combatting the partisanship and nepotism in politics.[22] Eroğlu, supported by the National Unity Party (UBP) and the Democratic Party-National Forces (DP) in the first round, announced his withdrawal from political life following the election. The other candidates were Arif Kırdağ (Independent), Mustafa Ulaş (Independent) and Mustafa Onurer (Cyprus Socialist Party). The second round took place on 26 April 2015 and was won by Akıncı (60.3%). Akıncı's bid to win the two way run off against Eroğlu was boosted by support from socialist candidate Siber who came in third in the first round and other prosolution leftists groups in Northern Cyprus. Many in Cyprus and abroad thought the victory of Akıncı was a clear sign for a solution as he was considered as a candidate who could reach out to Greek Cypriots and make the necessary compromises to progress in the talks.[23]

Apart from being a prosettlement candidate, according to many Turkish Cypriots, there are several crucial things that made Akıncı's campaign different from the other candidates. First of all, many believed that he stood up against Turkey.[24] Indeed, Akıncı underlined that he wanted a "brotherly relationship" with Turkey, rather than a relationship hitherto described as "mother-daughter relationship." He wanted Turkish Cypriots to stand on their own feet and govern themselves. None of the other candidates mentioned this quest for independence from Turkey so explicitly. Akıncı actually wanted to 'change' the relationship of Northern Cyprus with Turkey.[25] This was the essence of his campaign slogan of "change," which corresponded with Turkish Cypriots' feelings of disenchantment towards

Turkey. The bitter feelings of Turkish Cypriots against Turkey showed itself in lately the mass rallies which took place in the first half of 2011 against the austerity measures. Akıncı was able to read the meaning and the significance of those rallies. The first protest which took place on 28 January 2011 had an average turnout of 50,000 people. Following these protests, the Turkish government replaced its ambassador to TRNC. The Justice and Development Party (AKP) government in Ankara appointed Halil Akça, Turkey's fiscal grant maker to northern Cyprus, as the ambassador. Akça was actually one of the major targets of the demonstrations due to drafting tight fiscal policies. Harsh reactions of Turkish Prime Minister Recep Tayyip Erdoğan against the protesters, stating that the Turkish Cypriots were receiving hand-outs from Turkey, pushed them to organize second and third rallies on 2 March and 7 April 2011 with an average turnout of 80,000 people.

The TRNC economy ($4 billion) mainly relies on $600 million of financial aid Ankara provides annually. Northern Cyprus had been under a trade embargo since the Turkish military intervention in 1974. In addition, living standards in Northern Cyprus, especially public sector wages and pensions, have been higher than those in Turkey, making Turkish Cypriots come under fire from Ankara for their spending levels. The protests in 2011 called as "demonstrations for existence and survival" were mainly organized by the syndical platform and civil society organizations. They were supported by the main opposition Republican Turkish Party (CTP), the Communal Democracy Party (TDP) and the Democrat Party (DP). Turkish Cypriots participating in the rallies were against their government's austerity measures imposed by Turkey to cut its budget deficit and rein in public finances, reducing the vast public sector, slashing salaries and selling loss-making state companies. The austerity package also included privatization and curbing the rights of trade unions, which often strike.[26] Despite President Eroğlu's and Prime Minister Küçük's call on protesters for common sense, the first rally on January 28 turned into an anti-Turkey protest. Turkish Cypriots, chanting anti-Turkey slogans, criticized Erdoğan's calling them a burden on Turkey's shoulders.[27] Some, carrying the Greek Cypriot flag, criticised the island's colonisation by Anatolians and raised complaints over the erosion of their cultural identity. They voiced opposition to perceived Islamization under the JDP in Turkey.[28] Erdoğan's criticism of protests sent shockwaves across the northern part of the island. Furthermore Turkish Cypriots protested what they saw as unfair economic policies; they had the sense that they were losing control of their own destiny.[29] Turkey, seeing demonstrations as insulting and anti-Turkish, accused organizers of the protest of having links with Greek Cyprus.[30] In this context, Akıncı's victory was a result of the accumulated feelings against Turkey.[31] Akıncı promised to "conduct relations in a self-respecting manner without being obdurate towards Ankara." His victory was a clear sign that Turkish Cypriots understood that the looming prospect for solution left them with the option of being absorbed into a Turkey that was turning its back on Europe and democratic standards under the AKP government.[32]

The other major issue of the election was the question of how to negotiate with the Greek Cypriots. A new round of the UN mediated talks had resumed in February 2014 and produced a joint declaration of "seven points" underlining the leaders' determination to resume structured negotiations in a results oriented manner.[33] In October 2014, the Greek Cypriots suspended the talks in response to Turkey's plans to search for gas in their territorial waters by seismic research vessel *Barbaros*. Turkey withdrew the ship in March 2015. Greek Cyprus argued that Turkey conducted exploration in its Exclusive Economic Zone (EEZ) to control the hydrocarbon reserves off the island. Turkey said the TRNC was entitled to the island's energy resources and aimed to defend its rights. Following a six month suspension amid this row over offshore gas reserves, the elections appeared crucial in choosing a candidate trusted to carry out negotiating with the Greek Cypriots. On the eve of elections, Akıncı said that he would work urgently to reach a satisfactory settlement. The incumbent President Eroğlu, considered as a hardliner, had already shown a tough stance in negotiations. Greek Cypriots did not trust him because of his past as a staunch follower of Denktaş' policies. During the elections, Eroğlu criticised his three main challengers (Akıncı, Siber and Özersay) saying that they would concede too much to Greek Cypriots. However, the cumulative vote of the three challengers, 70%, was a clear sign of voters' quest for a renewed effort for solution. In the second round, Siber's camp (CTP) and many Özersay supporters endorsed Akıncı.

Espen Barth Eide, the UN envoy to Cyprus, after meeting with leaders Eroğlu and Anastasiadis on 7 April, underlined that the "circumstances were now right" for the resumption of negotiation and for the stalled peace talks to resume within weeks following the presidential ballot. The two parties are now led by advocates of reunification. Many people remembered that as mayor of Turkish Nicosia, Akinci managed to cooperate with the Greek Cypriot mayor on the sewerage system and the Nicosia master plan, despite the opposition of Denktash. Anastasiades, then leader of the Democratic Rally party, supported the Annan Plan. Akıncı and Anastasiades were both born in the central-southern Limassol district while the nation was still under British rule. The Greek Cypriot leader Anastasiades was also happy with the election results. The stance taken by the leader of the Turkish Cypriots made a difference. However, as the earlier election of Talat and Hristofyas and their disappointing negotiations showed, previous administrations had prematurely welcomed the change on the opposite side. As the previous experience showed[34] hopes of reconciliation could easily be dashed.

During the elections another major point that made Akıncı different from the other candidates was his concrete proposal for confidence building measures. He pledged to return *Varosha*, a once-affluent suburb of Famagusta currently under the control of the Turkish Army, to its owners, the Greek Cypriots. For Eroglu and the other candidates, the return of *Varosha* to the Greek Cypriots could only be a part of a comprehensive settlement. Akıncı proposed to return the city as a part of the confidence building measures to pave the way for a settlement. He said "instead of living side by side of a corpse, let *Varosha* become a lively city where people live, contractors from both communities do business together and young people can find jobs."[35] In fact, no one previously proposed to take such a bold step in the 40 years since Turkey's intervention in 1974. The election of Akıncı, the Turkish Cypriot politician with the best track record in working with Greek Cypriots, actually puts pressure on Anastasiades. Returning *Varosha* was an effective challenge to his Greek counterpart to make an equivalent move. Allowing international flights to land at *Ercan* International Airport might be an option. The opening of *Varosha* and *Ercan* could trigger huge dynamics in the peace negotiations. Especially the opening Ercan could result in Turkey's move to open Turkish ports and airports to Greek Cypriot vessels and planes. This eventually would takes away the reason for EU, blocking Turkey's accession negotiations.[36] While it looks as if Akıncı and Anastasiades are the most prosolution leaders in Cyprus, Turkey remains a determining player for crafting a settlement of the Cyprus conflict.

Conclusion

On 27 April, a day after the elections, Akıncı had a public argument with the Turkish President Erdoğan. Akıncı stated that the status of the relationship between Turkey and TRNC should change. Akıncı claimed that the "mother-daughter" relationship between Turkey and Northern Cyprus should be replaced by a "fraternal" one. He said "it should be a relationship of brothers/sisters, not a relationship of a motherland and her child." Erdoğan slammed Akıncı's call for new relations on more equal terms, stating he "should mind what he says" and reminded him of Turkey's financial and military support, as well as the Turkish soldiers who fell in Cyprus in 1974.[37] He said "Do his ears hear what he says? Even working together as brothers has its conditions. We paid a price for northern Cyprus. We gave martyrs and we continue to pay a price... For Turkey, northern Cyprus is our baby. We will continue to look at it the way a mother looks at her baby." Rejecting Ankara's paternalistic approach and calling for respect for the sovereignty of Turkish Cypriots, Akıncı said he stood behind his words and could not understand why Erdoğan opposed a fraternal relationship. Saying that his policies were approved by the Turkish Cypriot people and asking if "Turkey [did] not want its daughter to grow." Aiming to end the Turkish Cypriots' subordinate position, Akıncı underlined Turkey should stop treating them as a "child," and asked for more mature relations. Soon the parties calmed down and the newly elected Turkish Cypriot President Akıncı paid the first official visit to Ankara on May 6, a little more than a week after this war of words with President Erdoğan.[38] Nevertheless, this initial row between Turkey and the TRNC might signal a potential fallout that could threaten the ongoing peace talks. It showed the limits of Akıncı's freedom of manoeuvre in the negotiations.

The resolution of the conflict in Cyprus requires the support of Greek Cypriots and the approval from Turkey which has stationed 30,000 troops on the island since the 1974 intervention. With Anastasiades' coming to power in the South in 2013 and the election of Akıncı in the North in 2015, the chances for resolutions were improved have never looked better.[39] The surveys and voting on both sides of the island where the majority of the people think they can agree on a solution but more importantly that they can mobilize their people to pass and implement it.[40] Both leaders seem to be against the excessive waste of "time" over the past decades with delaying tactics and fake negotiations. This time they seem to be aware of the disappointment of their peoples and the international community. With the election of Akıncı, after a decade of disenchantment, the hopes appear to be unfolding for a reunited homeland and a modern state guided by European values.[41] However, Akinci's election is a significant piece of, yet only a part of the Cypriot puzzle. At the moment, there is great anticipation that the reunification could give the Cypriot economy a much needed boost. After coming to power, Anastasiades negotiated for a 10 billion euro bailout from the IMF and Cyprus's European partners. The conditions included the imposition of a levy on depositors. Meanwhile, thought to be the architect of the latest resumption of talks in February 2014 with the active role of the UN envoy Lisa Buttenheim, the United States underlined its support to the UN led Cyprus negotiations.[42]

In this context, the EU's position looks puzzling and worth a brief comment in these concluding remarks. Despite Akıncı's desire that the EU should assist Turkish Cypriots in moving toward a solution, the EU has been silent over the recent conflict resolution efforts in Cyprus.[43] The EU decision to accept the Cyprus Republic as a member and the sole represener of the island had left the Turkish Cypriots outside and the *acquis* suspended in the north of the island. Its decision to start accession negotiations with Turkey with an accent on the open ended character of negotiations simply resulted in lifting the EU's leverage on Turkey for domestic reform and foreign policy change. A credible EU impact, a key variable to pressure the parties toward a solution no longer exists, leaving the strongholds of conditionality with regards to fundamental freedoms and good neighborliness violated. While talks about a settlement have begun, yet new ideas are needed. Greek and Turkish Cypriots have separate lives and languages. There is a fear that a unified new administration might be more threatening than the peaceful status quo. A recent study by the International Crisis Group shows that though imperfect, the Cypriots on both sides are getting used to the peaceful *status quo* which would lead to a permanent division of the island and different models such as *Taiwanization* of Cyprus.[44]

The EU has much to consider in Cyprus. The economic crisis in the south continues. Deprivation of property rights and obstacles in developing natural gas fields in their territorial waters will deepen their economic depression. The passing of time diminishes leverage over Turkey and furthers uncertainty for an indefinite period. EU membership would provide the guarantee to implement the confidence building measures such as: the return of the ghost beach resort near Famagusta, withdrawal of Turkish troops, give up the international guarantees, offer compensation in a deal on property, stability in the post-settlement period and maximize benefits of the energy resources in the south of the island. Without a settlement, the partition will continue, the relations between Turkey and the EU will stay in stalemate and NATO will passively witness diplomatic frictions between Cyprus and Turkey. Turkish Cypriots wish to be in the EU and govern themselves. Probably the most dramatic result will be that the Turkish Cypriots continue to face an unjustified isolation. Passage of time does not benefit either side for it clears the alternatives, and it consolidates the partition.

Notes

[*] This chapter was first published in *Journal of South Asian and Middle Eastern Studies* (2016, XI (1): 66-79).
[1] For a comprehensive study of the period, see T. Ehrlich, *Cyprus 1958-1967: International Crisis and the Role of Law*, London: Oxford University Press, 1974.
[2] The rest of the population was composed of minorities such as Maronites.

3   For the British bases on Cyprus, see, Costas Constantinou and Olivier Richmond, The Long Mile of Empire: Power, Legitimation and the UK Bases in Cyprus, *Mediterranean Politics*, 2005, v. 10, n. 1, 65-84; A. Stergiou, The Exceptional Case of the British Military Bases on Cyprus, *Middle Eastern Studies*, 2014, v.51, n.2, 285-300.
4   United Nations. Security Council Resolution No. 186, 4 March 1964, S/5575.
5   Makarios-Denktas Summit, 12 February 1977 and Denktas Kiprianu Summit, 19 February 1979.
6   For a detailed study of the UN efforts of settlement, see F. Hoffmeister, *Legal Aspects of the Cyprus Problem*, Leiden: Martinus Nijhoff Publishers, 2006.
7   European Union. Declaration of 17 November 1983, EC Bulletin 1983/11.
8   United Nations, Security Council Resolution No. 541, 18 November 1983, S/PV2597.
9   Resolution on Cyprus, *Official Journal*, C217, Brussels, 1983.
10 Commission's Opinion on Turkey's Request for Accession to the Community, SEC (89) 2290 Final, Brussels, 1989.
11 European Union, Presidency Conclusions, Dublin, 25-26 June 1990.
12 This period could be followed in the memoirs of a close observer and the British envoy for Cyprus, D. Hannay, *Cyprus: The Search for a Solution*, London: I.B. Tauris, 2005.
13 A. Gitmez, G. Yalman, K. Ulusoy and C. Ustun, METU, Change in Cyprus in the Context of Europeanization, survey and research funded by the Scientific and Technological Research Council of Turkey, Ankara: Center for European Studies, 2006.
14 A. Lordos, E. Kaymak, and N. Tocci, Is there a still hope for a comprehensive settlement?, *Friends of Cyprus Report No.48*, 5-20. 2004; A. Lordos, Rational Agent or Unthinking Follower? 2005, https://ecpr.eu/Filestore/PaperProposal/b67d4879-d016-4fa1-8a15-d3ac021a937b.pdf., accessed 4 April 2017.
15 UNFICYP. The UN in Cyprus: An Inter-Communal Survey of Public Opinion, 2007.
16 A. Lordos, E. Kaymak and N. Tocci, *A People's Peace in Cyprus*, Brussels: CEPS, 2009, 5.
17 Ibid, 30.
18 A. Sözen, S. Christou, A. Lordos, and E. Kaymak, Cyprus 2015: Solving the Cyprus Problem: Hopes and Fears, Interpeace / 'Cyprus 2015' Initiative, 2011, 85.
19 Ibid., 83.
20 M. Kambas, Cyprus peace talks resume with confidence-building measures, *Reuters*, 15 May 2015; H. Smith, Mustafa Akinci wins northern Cyprus Presidential Elections, *The Guardian*, 27 April 2015.
21 Siber event kicks off presidential campaign, *KP Daily News*, 24 February 2015.

[22] Özersay: Silent majority will bring real change, *KP Daily News*, 9 February 2015.
[23] Author's interview with Turkish Cypriot political analyst Mete Hatay, 10 June 2015.
[24] Author's interviews in Northern Cyprus with ordinary Turkish Cypriots, 10 June 2015.
[25] Akıncı Kıbrıs'ta denklemi degiştirebilir mi?, 27 April 2015, http://dw.com/p/1FFir.
[26] Thousands of Turkish Cypriots protest wage cuts, *Hürriyet Daily News*, 29 January 2011.
[27] AYŞE EVİNE DÖN!, *Milliyet*, 3 March 2011.
[28] KKTC'de Toplumsal Varoluş Mitingi Düzenlendi, *Yeni Şafak*, 2 March 2011.
[29] Hülya Özerkan, Turkish PM's tough words on protests stir up northern Cyprus, *Hürriyet Daily News*, 2 March 2011.
[30] KKTC government cautious as Turkish Cypriots hold new anti-austerity protest, *Today's Zaman*, 3 March 2011.
[31] Author's interview with the Turkish Cypriot academics Prof. Dr. Ahmet Sözen, 10 June 2015.
[32] Turkish Cypriots again defy Ankara, *Hürriyet Daily News*, 3 February 2011.
[33] Joint Declaration: Final version as agreed by two leaders, *Cyprus Mail*, 11 February 2014.
[34] The author's interview with the Turkish Cypriot academics Prof. Dr. Mehmet Hasgüler, 10 June 2015.
[35] Akıncı: Let Varosha become a lively town, *KP Daily News*, 8 February 2015.
[36] J. Mortimer, Turkish Cypriot presidential candidate brings hope for unity, *Al Monitor*, 23 April 2015.
[37] Erdoğan lambasts newly elected Turkish Cypriot President Akıncı for remarks over relationship with Turkey, *Today's Zaman*, 27 April 2015.
[38] Newly elected Turkish Cypriot president pays first visit to Turkey, *Hurriyet Daily News*, May 6, 2015.
[39] P. Tugwell and G. Georgiou, New Turkish-Cypriot Leader Fuels Cyprus Reunification Optimism, Bloomberg Business, 7 May 2015.
[40] The author's interviews in Cyprus with ordinary Cypriots from 9-12 June 2015.
[41] Editorial: The Guardian view on the prospect for a Cyprus settlement, *The Guardian*, 27 April 2015.
[42] A glimmering hope, *The Economist*, 15 February 2014; Cyprus peace talks resume after two-year break, *Deutsche Welle*, 23 February 2014.
[43] Akıncı: EU should prepare Turkish Cypriots for a solution, http://mfa.gov.ct.tr.
[44] Divided Cyprus: Coming to terms on an imperfect reality, *International Crisis Group, Europe Report No. 229*, 14 March 2014.

[8]
GREECE – ISRAEL – THE EAST-MEDITERRANEAN: WILL COMMON DENOMINATORS HELP THE THIRD STAGE?

Amikam Nachmani

A few years ago we witnessed a surprising initiative by two prime ministers: Benjamin Netanyahu of Israel and George Papandreou of Greece. Reportedly, the personal relationship and chemistry between Papandreou and Netanyahu – both American educated – helped to build the present unexpected and promising relationship between Greece and Israel. We should state at the outset that it is fitting that Greek-Israeli relations would have their own *raison d'être*, and not only as a result of a crisis in Turkish-Israeli relations, or because of a shared US educational background of future Israeli or Greek heads of state.

Greece and Israel, though so geographically close in the Mediterranean Basin, yet in the first forty years of Israel's existence as an independent state (i.e., the first stage, 1948–1990), the two states could not have been farther apart politically. Fear for the fate of the Greek communities in the Arab Middle East prevented Greece from opening an embassy in Israel until 1990. Even when the Greek diaspora, primarily in Alexandria, Egypt, was widely expelled and scattered in 1957 as a result of the Suez Crisis, no improvement occurred in the relations between the two countries. The Greek need for Arab votes in the Cypriot conflict, plus the emphasis placed in Israel on relations with Turkey, certainly did not help relations between Athens and Jerusalem.

A second chapter, an *entente cordiale* in Israel-Greek relations, lasted for about twenty years from 1990 to 2010. It opened with the establishment of full diplomatic relations between the two countries. The entrance of Greece into the European Union (1981) stressed the need for good relations between Israel and the

Hellenistic world. The collapse of communism and the end of the Cold War, the decreased impact of the Arab oil crisis and the 1990s open Egyptian and Jordanian détentes with Israel and the Palestinian-Israeli peace negotiations all added to the warming of relations between Israel and Greece. Starting in 2010, Israel and Greece passed through a third gateway into a period of enhanced relations that both countries hoped would make the most of the changing geopolitical opportunities. Their similarities and shared interests could only help them achieve this.

Greece and Israel: Common denominators

Analysis of history, culture, politics and societies in Greece and Israel points to the existence of various mutual aims and interests. These common denominators are likely to help Athens and Jerusalem to intensify their joint future and overcome disagreements and differences.

It is fair to say that in the twentieth century no other two peoples in the world were victimized more cruelly and suffered more profoundly, caught up in the grip of rising nationalism and the resurgent nation-state (one state for one nation) as were the Greeks and Israelis. One and a half million Greeks who lived for thousands of years in Asia Minor (Western Turkey today) were forced to leave the region in the early 1920s to the last one of them, in the well-known "Greek-Turkish Population Transfer Agreement." Theoretically, Turkey then became a state for Turks only. Following the 1956 Suez War, Greeks who lived for millennia in Egypt were expelled by President Gamal Abdel Nasser. Egypt became a country for Egyptians only. The expulsion of 250,000 Greek Cypriots from northern Cyprus is seen in Greece as another painful example of the inability of the modern nation-state to accommodate non-native ethnicities.

The destruction and extermination of the Jewish people in Europe in 1933–1945 turned many of the European states into countries of one nationality, in other words the embodiment of the pure nation-state concept. The elimination of the Jewish and Greek diasporas throughout the entire Middle East and North Africa is another reminder of the intolerance of the modern nation-state and of its inability or refusal to accept the "other." In short, Greece and Israel share this common denominator and occasionally relive its frequent painful reminders.

Greece, Cyprus and Israel push back attempts of external coercion to resolve the conflicts in which the three are involved. Such is the position of Israel in its conflict with the Palestinians, and that of the Greek side in the Cypriot conflict. Naturally, Greece and Israel reject attempts of foreign intervention in their internal affairs. For example, the European attempt of the 2010s – that of Germany in particular – to impose an economic recession and financial restrictions on the Greeks in return for loans and credits, brought about the following: "If you were asked to define in one sentence what it is to be Greek nowadays … then 'it means to be a subject of a small democracy that lives under foreign administration. All that is left to us is to boycott the foreign authorities and the foreign high commissioner, and to continue our struggle for democracy, independence and freedom, once and for all.'"[1]

Another common denominator shared by the three eastern Mediterranean neighbors is that Greece, Israel and Cyprus are small states surrounded by larger nations with stronger economies. Often the three recognize their limitations, which lead them to feel redundant and objects of condescension. The humiliating financial situation in which Athens has lately found itself vis-à-vis the economic giants of the European Union emphasizes Greek weakness and helplessness. The growing rifts between Greece and the EU's western wealthiest members (Germany and France) encourage Greece to look eastward and forge new relationships with countries of its own size, for example Israel.

The Greek Orthodox Church, Middle Eastern Christians: A crisis of cataclysmic magnitude

The Eastern Mediterranean region is traditionally not tolerant of minorities. Long before the misleadingly titled "Arab Spring" erupted, tolerance towards religious and ethnic minorities had sharply decreased. The Greek Orthodox Church is facing a growing demand to replace Greek clergy by Arab clergy; Arabization of the clergy is an often heard mantra nowadays among Middle Eastern Christians. One of the results of this controversy is continued cooperation between Middle Eastern Orthodox Christianity and Israel. In fact, this had already begun in the 1940s and 1950s. The intention then of the Catholic Church to achieve dominance in Jerusalem and hegemony over the Holy Places was perceived by Orthodox Christianity as an attempt to curb its influence. As a result a surprising accord developed then between the Greek Orthodox Patriarchates in the Holy Land and the newly established State of Israel, both of whom vehemently objected to the Vatican's policy that called for the internationalization of Jerusalem, Bethlehem and the Holy Places.

Today, the remaining Christians throughout the Middle East are poised on the edge of flight, or worse, extinction. Relatively recent surveys show that Christian communities amount to less than five percent of the entire Middle Eastern population and their numbers are expected to drop even further. A hundred years ago (1910) in the last census of the Ottoman era, Christians made up between 13.6 and 25 percent of the Middle East's population.[2] True, the Middle East is no exception: according to a PEW Research Centre report, in 2013 Christians faced harassment in 102 countries (Muslims suffered similar treatment in 99 nations and Jews in 77). Five of the 18 countries with "very high government restrictions on religion" were in the Middle East.[3]

Middle Eastern Christians represent less than one percent of the world's Christians, but their declining numbers is of particular concern for the Vatican, which does not want to see the birthplace of Christianity devoid of the faithful.[4] Analyzing Middle Eastern trends following the Arab Spring, *Time Magazine*'s Aryn Baker has recently concluded that if current demographic developments continue, the Middle East's population of 12 million Christians will be halved by 2020. While much of the decline is attributed to job search emigration and falling birth rates, political turmoil in the wake of the ill-fated Arab Spring has accelerated the trend: at least one in four Syrian Christians, who in 1992 made up eight percent of the country's population, have left since the Syrian civil war began in 2011. Also, an estimated 93,000 Copts have left Egypt in the years following the 2011 revolution that toppled President Mubarak.[5]

Middle Eastern Christians suffer from intermittent repression and persecution, in particular, since the post-World War II decolonization process and the rise of the Arab nation-states. The rise of radical Islam, the recent breakdown in law and order, the lack of economic security, and the political and ethnic strife across the Middle East and North Africa are all factors driving mass emigration. Another common denominator that characterizes the last seventy years of the encounter between the Muslim Arab world and its Christian communities is the perception of the latter as unpatriotic. Christians who have lived for centuries in Arab lands are suddenly branded as foreigners, disloyal to the Arab cause and as religious infidels, whose affiliations are to external if not enemy forces. As a consequence, apart from "regular" or "softer" crimes, like verbal and physical violence, Christians have endured violation of basic human rights and inequality before the law, the destruction and burning of their churches and cemeteries, property expropriations and compulsion to sell their homes and land, and coercion to wearing "proper" (Muslim) attire and abstinence from alcohol. Christian community leaders, clergy and political leaders were assassinated and kidnapped, (the Maronite Christian Gemayel family in Lebanon). Christian women and young girls raped, forced into unwanted marriages, enslaved and trafficked, and adults and children were compelled to convert.

In a clear reaction to the phenomena mentioned above, massive Christian emigration from Arab and Muslim countries took place. For example in 2013, 54,000 Christians resided in the Palestinian West Bank; in the early 2000s they had numbered some 75,000. In the Gaza Strip (population 1.816 million in 2014), Christians amounted to 4,500 in the year 2000; by 2013 fewer than 1,500 Christians lived there, less than one percent.[6] This decline of Eastern Christianity after two thousand years in the Middle East has not met with any substantial global protest or sympathy, certainly not in the magnitude of the solidarity expressed regarding other catastrophes, tsunamis, earthquakes or the plight of the Palestinians.[7]

Over all, about 16.5 million Christians currently live in the Arab countries, Turkey and Iran – a small minority, whose numbers are continuously dwindling, within a total population of around 286 million. Christians lived in Iraq for almost two millennia, and 1.4 million lived there before the American invasion in 2003 and the fall from power of President Saddam Hussein. In 2010, 1.4 percent of the Iraqis were Christians.[8] In 2015, only about 150,000 Christians remained in Iraq, mainly Christian Assyrians, whose ancestors began converting to Christianity within years of Jesus' death and have kept their faith despite the growth of Islam in their homeland and, most shockingly, the genocide of Christian Assyrians in the 1910s and early 1920s. Close to 300,000 Assyrians, half of the Assyrian population, were massacred then in Ottoman and Turkish genocide campaigns, assisted by Kurds, Arabs, Chechens, Persians and Circassians, against the Christian minorities of the Ottoman Empire, i.e., the Armenians, Greeks and Assyrians.[9]

Turning to Egypt, the nine million Copts there face harassment and molestation, in particular, after the fall of the Mubarak regime in early 2011. President Hosni Mubarak made a point of protecting Egypt's Christians during his 29 years in power as a way to gain legitimacy from the West.[10] In the year 1910, 18.7 percent of the Egyptians were Christians; by 2010 the number dropped to 10.1 percent.[11] Acute lack of security enables radical Muslim groups to attack Copts, burn their churches and property, kidnap Coptic girls and force their conversion and marriage to non-Copts. Since early August 2013 mobs attacked 63 churches and ransacked Christian orphanages and businesses across Egypt. Allegedly, supporters of the ousted Muslim Brothers Party President Muhammad Morsi, seeking to avenge Christian support of the July 2013 military coup that toppled the Ikhwan (Muslim Brothers), are held responsible. In many cases the Egyptian police did not intervene to stop the riots.[12] Female Christian students were asked to wear veils on some Egyptian university campuses, and churchgoers were forced to lower the volume of their services in predominantly Muslim neighbourhoods.[13] The Copts' situation further deteriorated because the new 2012 Egyptian constitution gave Sunni Muslim law priority in any future legal enactments (article 219). Another article reaffirms the inferior *dhimmi* status of Christians (and Jews) in Egypt. This and Egypt's deteriorating economy caused half a million Copts to leave Egypt in the last decade.[14]

In Lebanon the daily decreasing Christian population presently stands just above one million out of four. In 1910 Lebanese Christians were 77.5 percent of their country's population; in 2010 they were 34.3 percent, and now around 25 percent.[15] The history behind the steady decline recounts the civil war of the 1970s and 1980s, the wars since the 1970s with Palestinian armed organizations that moved to Lebanon from Jordan, intermittent clashes with Israel, the presence of millions of Muslim Syrians in Lebanon and Syria's practical subjugation of the country up to the Syrian army's retreat from Lebanon in 2005, the rise of the Shiite community and Hezbollah, and finally the bloody feuds within the Lebanese Christian camp. No wonder the country is hemorrhaging its Christians at an unprecedented rate.

Jordan's Christian community is in relatively good shape, and numbers about a quarter of a million people who enjoy the protection of King Abdullah's government and the armed forces. They benefit economically from global tourism to Jordan and the Christian pilgrims who visit the holy sites at the Jordan River, Mt. Nebo and Madaba.

Syria's Christians, who numbered 2.3 million before the eruption of the monstrous 2011 civil war there have dwindled to some 400,000 with further losses every day. In the northern Syrian town of Raqqa, now controlled by the rebels fighting the Assad regime (mainly the radical Sunni fighters of DAESH, i.e., ISIS, the Islamic State in Iraq and Syria), Christians may stay only if they pay a $650 poll tax, practice their religion in one church only, do not ring bells, do not evangelize and do not pray within earshot of Muslims. Christians in other parts of Syria were less fortunate. YouTube is full of horrific videos showing Christians being beheaded, attacked and in one gruesome case, even crucified. Little wonder that many Christians have fled the war along with the close to three million Syrian refugees.[16]

Iran's over 220,000 established Christians, mainly Armenians and Assyrians, enjoy a stable life under the Islamic Republic authorities and are even represented in parliament. However, the 10,000-strong *new* Christian community, Muslims who have converted to Christianity, is severely persecuted by officials, so much so that their Christian worship takes place clandestinely.[17]

Israel's Christians numbered around 158,000 in 2012, about two percent of the population; in 2008 they were a community of 123,000. Despite this rare increase in a Middle East country, the overall percentage of Christians in Israel has decreased by almost one percentage point since World War II (three percent now down to two). Past active, even vibrant Christian churches are presently empty and gradually becoming museums. Israel's Christian fertility rate is 2.17 children per woman, the Israeli Muslim rate is 3.5 children and in 2013 Jewish women bore 3.05 children. Accordingly, the Christian community's annual growth rate at 1.9 percent is the lowest in Israel, as opposed to the Muslims' just fewer than three percent. Cities like Nazareth that previously had a Christian majority are now overwhelmingly Muslim, that is, presently 70 percent Muslim and 30 percent Christian, the diametric opposite of the post-World War II Nazareth ratio. In pre-June 1967 Six Day War Jerusalem, Christians were 4.1 percent of the city's population of some 267,000 people (East and West Jerusalem combined). In December 2012 Jerusalem's 14,700-strong Christian community was less than two percent of the city's population. Particularly indicatory of the current situation is the fact that Christians are a *minority* in Jerusalem's Old City *Christian Quarter*.[18] It bears pointing out that Jerusalem's Christians are not just feeling the heat from Islamic extremists; suspected radical right-wing and Orthodox Israeli Jews are responsible with some regularity for defacing Christian churches and seminaries in Jerusalem, often with slurs maligning Jesus. In the years 2009 to 2015, 44 mosques and churches were set ablaze, most probably by extremist Jews. The latest incident of such vandalism was the slogan "Death to the heathen Christians, the enemies of Israel," scrawled on the walls of Jerusalem's Dormition Abbey at Mt. Zion on 17 January 2016.[19]

Greece and Israel: Illegal immigration

The difficulty in dealing with foreign migrants is another shared Greek and Israeli challenge. Since the early 1990s with the collapse of communism, the strife in the former communist Balkan countries and the upheavals that are ravaging the Middle East and North Africa in the wake of the Arab Spring, Greece has to cope with hundreds of thousands of immigrants, refugees, jobless migrants and asylum seekers. The Greek media openly blame Turkey for diverting this human traffic and for smuggling the immigrants – Iraqis, Syrians, Kurds, Afghans, Pakistanis, Somalis, Sudanese, Algerians, Libyans and others – directly into its territory. Geography also contributes to the demographic catastrophe because the thousands of Greek islands and thus Greece's lengthy shoreline (eleventh longest in the world) make inspection and control of this illegal immigration a hopeless, practically impossible task. The result is that

80 percent of all illegal immigration into the EU passes through Greece.[20] Greece is merely a stepping stone for the majority of immigrants; their aim is to quickly leave Greece for richer northwestern EU destinations. It is estimated that of the eleven million Greeks, a tenth are immigrants, one third of them illegal. A quarter of Greek school children are immigrants, mainly from Albania and Middle Eastern and Asian countries.

The Greek refugee/illegal immigrant syndrome finds a parallel in the tens of thousands of African immigrants seeking sanctuary in Israel via the Sinai Peninsula. To stem this recent tide of drifting humanity, Israel has just finished constructing a 230-kilometer (143 miles) long, seven-meter high fence (23 feet), even higher at some points, along the Sinai Desert international boundary, the south-western border with Egypt, from Rafah in north to Eilat in the south. Greece, too, is in the midst of building a fence along its Turkish border to intercept illegal immigrants attempting to invade its territory. (The sharp criticism of the Greek media and public opinion reduced the length of the planned fence from 206 kilometers [128 miles] to a meagre 12.6 kilometers [7.8 miles].[21]). Already hundreds of EU armed troops from 25 EU member states patrol the Greek-Turkish border, attempting to check the flow of immigrants into Greece. In a recent (2016) EU-Turkey agreement, Ankara agreed to curtail the traffic of immigrants from its territory into Greece, and to re-absorb immigrants that are already in Greece.

For economic and political reasons, Greece has been a country of emigration. Meanwhile, negative population growth and the aging Greek people have caused Greece to accept immigration from countries sending young, low-paid job seekers. Between the 1880s and the 1950s about 12 percent of Greeks emigrated to North America, Australia and Africa. Alternatively, in the 1920s about 1.3 million Greeks living in Asia Minor returned to Greece while 150,000 Muslims in Greece left for Turkey, which became known as the Greek-Turkish Population Exchange or Transfer.

Conflicts between indigenous Greeks and immigrants are not rare. Immigrant squatters reportedly supported by local anarchists invaded buildings in Athens, from where they are difficult to evict. A courthouse in central Athens was likewise invaded by squatters who refused to vacate it. The area around Omonia Square in southern Athens has become a sort of no-go zone where even local police are reluctant to patrol. According to reports some Greek hospitals refuse to treat immigrants. The European Social Survey graded Greece as the No. 1 (!) xenophobic country in Europe. Human Rights Watch documented dozens of attacks on immigrants and complained that immigrants were labelled "cockroaches" in the Greek parliament. A Council of Europe report drawn up by European Commission against Racism and Intolerance states that racial prejudice and violence against migrants persists in Greece despite an anti-racism law effective since 2014.[22]

Greece and Israel: No effective political leadership

Both Greece and Israel have been subjected to over influence and intervention by the military in civil and political life. Also, in both countries the founding fathers minimized important chapters in the histories of their nations and glorified others: David Ben-Gurion belittled the 2,000 years of Jewish exile and Diaspora and made a direct link between the Jewish Biblical past and the modern era's (19th and 20th centuries) Jewish settlement in the Holy Land. The Greek state links Modern Greece to its Hellenic and Byzantine past and belittles the long chapters in between – for example, 400 years of Ottoman rule.

The inability of both societies – the Greek and the Israeli – to produce effective political leaderships that would lead their countries in times of crisis is a crucial common feature that characterizes life in both nations. The Greek case of paucity in leadership is described in the following quotation; the gap between the highly successful performance of diaspora Greeks in comparison with the miserable and poor achievements at home is clearly discernible, in particular when "the Greek character" is evaluated. The recent negotiations between Athens and the EU about the financial support that Greece would receive from Brussels brought about the following non-flattering assessment:

> The Greeks are lazy, they hate work, time is not time and one's word is not a word. Most of them work as civil servants, earn a lot of money and practically do nothing until they retire at age

50. The coasts and islands are indeed beautiful, but the cities are neglected, crowded, [and] too popular. [...]

Whoever perceives the Greeks like this is convinced that he is much more European than them, more developed, more efficient, more improved and wiser than them, partly because he enjoys a thriving independent economy. [...]

Indeed, the Greek composition includes a rotten and corrupt political system, an inflated bureaucracy, side by side with magnificent views, wonderful language and wonderful cultural legacy, megalomaniac linkage to ancient history and ambivalent belonging to the Balkans and Europe.

This mixture is characterized by quick thinking and wit; by initiatives and diligence as evidenced by the success of Greek businessmen and entrepreneurs in the US, Australia, and New Zealand and in many European countries. *It is so sad that in spite of all this the Greek society cannot produce proper leaders that would rescue it from what strangles it.*[23]

Similarly, a repeated question is asked whether Israel or Judaism could produce exceptional political leaders. Diaspora Jewish history of 2000 years records very few Jewish political figures and leaders, apparently the reason why the Jews of the twentieth century were left without a tradition of political leadership. Given the pressing realities of the world around them, the traditional business ("expertise") of Jewish spiritual and communal leaders – lobbying, begging and the secretive payment of ransom and bribery to ameliorate the inferior situation of their communities or rescue them from captivity and extermination – should have spawned top-notch statesmen and political leadership. The question asked and answered, "Where is the 'Jewish mind?' In Israel we suffer from intelligent but primitive [*sic*] political-security thinking that cannot deal with challenges,"[24] embodies the sad conclusion alluded to above, namely, that the 2,000 years of Diaspora experience of a nation without a state has denied contemporary Israel the benefit of a fully-fledged Jewish tradition of political leadership.

Professor Yehezkel Dror of the Hebrew University of Jerusalem, an eminent Israeli political scientist, has examined the absence of the "Jewish mind": Israel seems to lack impressive leaders. It probably takes ages, certainly more than three generations (from the 1948 independence of modern Israel) to produce a tradition of political leadership. Dror pinpointed the lacuna in the annals of the Jewish people. Israel faces fateful decisions, but the inability of its political and security echelons to produce outstanding leadership qualities ("The[ir] primitiveness [*sic*] is expressed in the failings of Israeli political security thinking") cannot be dismissed as mere hiccups to be overcome. The present day issues are too crucial to wait for future solutions. Many studies have proven unusual success by Jews, since the Emancipation, in the areas of science, medicine and technology. The survival of the Jewish people and indeed its flourishing in exile apparently prove the existence of a collective "Jewish mind," or an abundance of gifted people. In Israel there are many areas that reflect highly successful creativity in the economic sphere, civil society and among several governmental bodies. However, this norm does not exist in the area of political thinking, where the question "Where is the Jewish mind?" repeats itself.

Hypotheses about the nature of the successful "Jewish mind" in the Diaspora contain explanations for its absence in the political security arenas in contemporary Israel. According to some of these hypotheses, the difficult conditions of the Diaspora led to the development of talents that fit the circumstances, either as cultural traits or as individual, quasi-genetic traits. Some of the hypotheses emphasize the role of demanding, elitist Torah and Talmud study and the world of learning in general. But these processes did not apply to diplomacy, an area in which the Jewish people were not involved in during the exilic period. The Jewish minorities' methods of dealing with the ruling government were mainly through go-betweens, because in circumstances when they were second class citizens only a few Jews attained positions of political leadership. In other words, Israelis lack a tradition of statesmanship, of educational institutions aimed at developing leadership, and of a "quasi-aristocracy" out of which democratic leadership grows. The years of the state's existence are too few to fill this gap.[25]

As noted, Jews focused on the world of Jewish religious and legal (*Halacha*) learning until the Emancipation and Enlightenment (*Haskalah*), which enabled some Jews to contribute to their wider societies. Hence, today of all Nobel laureates, ca. 22 percent are Jews or people descended from Jews (at least 193 out of 855, as of 2014). This is rather astonishing as Jews number less than one quarter of one per cent of the world's population, meaning that the number of Jewish Nobel Prize laureates is one hundred times more than their actual numbers (population) could be expected to produce. One of the explanations for this impressive phenomenon is linked to the unique history of the Jews. Persecutions, anxieties, expulsions, wanderings and flight caused Jews to gravitate to *professions focusing on knowledge* – an asset that could be carried with them from one place to another – like Jewish studies, medicine, science, law, literature, business, trade, diamond cutting, watch making, etc.[26]

Israeli scientist Aaron Ciechanover, the 2004 Nobel Prize chemistry laureate (shared with the Israeli Avram Hershko and the American Irwin Rose), stated his thoughts about the apparent feeling of stability and the cessation of constant wandering that the establishment of the State of Israel has produced, and the resulting (detrimental) impact of these changes on Israeli education and learning, certainly on potential Israeli Nobel Prize laureates. The frequent expulsions, instability and wandering throughout the two millennia of the Diaspora caused Jews to focus on learning. The seeming stability and security that the State of Israel bestows on Israel's Jews has caused the majority to lose the habit of learning. Half of world Jewry lives in Israel, yet Israelis have not contributed half of the Jewish Nobel laureates, laments Ciechanover.

> The share of Israeli scientists among the Nobel winners is less than one fifth in comparison to world Jewish scientists. This is particularly so if you bear in mind that almost half of the Jewish people live in Israel [...] The establishment of the State of Israel has changed the direction [of learning and excellence that produced Nobel laureates in the Jewish Diaspora].
>
> The existence of a stable land, the feeling of security, and perhaps also haughtiness, undermined the pillars of learning. This,

together with the death of the generation and of the leaders that established the State, gradually caused a decrease in the value of education and learning. Israeli society and leadership find it difficult to recognise the huge contribution of education, learning and research, and that of teachers and scientists, and on turning of Israel into an economic power, as the cradle of Jewish culture. They have not yet decided the place [of learning, education, etc.] among Israel's social and national values.[27]

Greece and Israel: Economic aspects

The hundreds of thousands of Israeli tourists who favored Turkey over Greece as a vacation destination until the breakdown in Israeli-Turkish relations in 2010 have put back on track the common economic Greco-Israeli interests and emphasized the economic potential to be found in the third phase of relations between Athens and Jerusalem. Around 77,000 Israelis visited Greece in 2009; the number rose to 200,000 in 2010, 350,000 in 2013, and close to 450,000 in 2015. Energy explorations in the Eastern Mediterranean Basin in the Israeli and Cypriot EEZs (Exclusive Economic Zones) have discovered a vast undersea gas reserve. The facilities that Greece could supply to this new gas industry with a transit hub or the construction of liquidizing installations (that transform gas into liquid) could serve a huge number of potential European energy consumers. This and other business and trade components emphasize the economic prosperity that can cement healthy Greco-Israeli-Cypriot relations.

Much has been said about the Cypriot and Israeli gas explorations and even more predicted about the potential economic boom that these discoveries hold for the Jerusalem-Athens-Nicosia triangle. It is about time that this potential be translated into solid projects, rich earnings and savings in utility costs for all three peoples. Israel, Greece and Cyprus, the sole three non-Muslim countries in the Eastern Mediterranean, must not miss this third opportunity. Now is the time. Israelis have learned, and more than once, from bitter experience that special relationships and strategic alliances are built slowly, but their collapse is rapid.

The Jewish and Israeli Mediterranean image: How to perceive Greece

Historically speaking, Jews and Israelis viewed Greece as an extension of their perception of the Mediterranean Sea. Alas, the Med has long been seen as a menace, a natural adversary, which modern Israel has treated with caution and awe. Whenever possible, Jews who lived in Ottoman Palestine strove to skip over the Mediterranean and land instead in Paris, London or Berlin, and to avoid the urban centers along the Eastern Mediterranean.

Greece was perceived as part of the Eastern Mediterranean Basin and of the Levant, and not of Europe. Incidentally, up to a generation or so ago, Greece and Europe were not seen as one; indeed, middle-aged Greeks, when boarding a plane in Athens on its way to London, Paris or Berlin used to say, *"Sa pao styn Evropi."* – I go to Europe. In January–February 2012, during the demonstrations in Athens against the humiliating conditions that the EU imposed on Greece before advancing it financial support, the demonstrators shouted, *"Pame!"* Let's go ahead and leave Europe!

Ruth Almog, who regularly writes for *Tarboot VeSifroot*, the cultural and literary weekend supplement of the Israeli *Haaretz* newspaper, describes Israeli intellectuals who wish to be connected to the Mediterranean world and who perceived Greece to be part and parcel of Mediterranean culture. Between the 1960s and 1990s there was a genuine yearning for the Mediterranean culture, particularly Greece, writes Almog. In her seminal article, "Who Will Stand in the Shadow of the Olive Tree and in the Company of the Cricket?" Almog reviewed the Hebrew anthology of the renowned Greek poet Yannis Ritzos.[28] Almog describes the days when the charm of Greek culture was perceived as a cultural option for Israelis. She differentiated between Europe and Greece: the Mediterranean and Greek ideas were ideal substitutes for the geographically distant Europe. The continent is culturally different, it is threatening and deterring and likewise are its values. This is Europe that frequently exterminated its Jews, culminating in the Holocaust. Unlike Europe, the Mediterranean was not estranged from Israeli intellectuals: its flora and fauna were known to Palestinian Jews and to Israelis. The same olive tree, the same food, climate, sun, scenery and landscape are to be found in Israel as in Greece:

> [In approaching the Mediterranean and Greece] I think that we looked for a larger identity in comparison to the young Israeli one that was not yet solidified and matured [Israel was established in 1948]. Also, geographically Western Europe was far away and not easily reachable as it is today.
>
> Retrospectively, we looked for a Mediterranean identity. It expressed the connection that we had towards the olive tree – that symbol of a sunny entity that we can find in the Greek islands and in the area [the stretches] between us and Greece.
>
> The Mediterranean Sea offered us the option to belong to a [larger] geographic culture [...] When we considered ourselves as part of the Mediterranean Sea, our past and present worlds became bigger. True, we yearned for Greece – that cradle of the Western culture, a place in which secular literature was first written and Western philosophy was created. The entire Western philosophy is no more than footnotes to Plato.
>
> [...] The yearning for Greece expressed longing for something primordial, more naïve, less urban, less spoiled.[29]

Haaretz's essayist Avirama Golan is even clearer and more precise pertaining to the Greek culture that attracts Israelis to Greece. Israelis imagine that "good things are Greek things": it is the Greek scenery and human nature, it is Greek simplicity, the pleasure embodied in Greek singing and dancing, the healthy Greek food, the easy-going mood, the live-and-let-live atmosphere, and so on. Seemingly, Greece is a mirror image of the modernized, vibrant, sophisticated, westernized Israel. Superficial knowledge about Greece and Greeks attracts the Israelis, laments Golan:

> It is interesting to examine the image of Greece in Israel. Part of it is based on the idealization Hollywood does to the noble savage: the Greeks live in picturesque houses on magnificent islands, they drink *ouzu*, they eat simple but healthy food, they

live and let live, they grow mustaches, they sing in the *tavernas*, they do plate-smashing, they dance the *sirtaki* [...] and they joyfully shout *yasu*!³⁰

But at the other end of the spectrum, all bad things came from the Mediterranean, "The Great Sea" [הים הגדול]. The upshot of this attitude was an ambivalent perception of the Med that was reflected in Israeli urban culture, architecture, even in railways and train services. Tel-Aviv, a relatively modern city established in 1909, knowingly and intentionally turned its back on the Mediterranean Sea. A string of high-rise hotels along Tel-Aviv's shoreline apparently acts as a partition or barrier between the city and the Sea. ("Let the tourists come between us and the tsunami.") Tel Aviv's main streets and boulevards run *parallel* to the Sea, that is north-south, rather than perpendicular or east-west, which would have inserted and introduced the Sea into the city. Barcelona, for example, is the opposite. The 1.2-kilometer Ramblas Promenade that connects the city center's Plaça de Catalunya and the Christopher Columbus monument at the city's port directly brings the Mediterranean Sea deep into the city's center. Even the Promenade's paving stones are in the shape of waves. In a recent *Haaretz* article the author mentioned that, "...Tel Aviv has discovered quite late in the day that it is a coastal town – see the sharp turn that Allenby Road makes towards its end: suddenly those who built the road discovered the [Mediterranean] Sea; and suddenly they were haunted and attacked by the strongest of passions: to come closer to the Sea."³¹ Turning away from the Sea and the havoc this causes to urban architecture is the gist of the protest of Ami Shinar, an Israeli architect who was hired to reconnect the Israel's northern city of Haifa and its eponymous port on the Mediterranean Sea.³² The City of Haifa, a Mediterranean city, was also separated from the Sea. To separate Haifa from the Mediterranean, neither hotels nor boulevards (as in Tel Aviv) were used; instead, the culprit here was the north-south running railway line that functioned as a barrier, separating the city from the port and seashore. One has to read Shinar's cry to understand what he protests and complains about – the incomprehensible separation of Jews and Israelis from the Mediterranean Sea.

> This is an unbelievable phenomenon. I really fail to comprehend it. Why? Why to run away from the Sea when you could adhere to it like in every other normal Mediterranean town?[33]

Shinar calls himself an "urban rectifier" or "urban repairer" who mends and fixes what was ruined, destroyed and so poorly designed and planned in Israeli new urban architecture for the past more than 60 years, sustaining the separation of the people from the Mediterranean Sea. The following is an incredible interview with Shinar that describes the poor and broken connection between Israeli towns and the Mediterranean:

> The first thing [in the re-planning of Haifa's waterfront and connecting the town to the port] was to persuade the railroad authorities to build a sunken railway instead of the ground-level tracks that separates the town from the port. A train that goes [from Tel Aviv] to Jerusalem – will somebody dare to cut through and level out mountains instead of digging a tunnel through them and laying the tracks inside it? Surely, nobody will dare to do so, and this is the reason why [presently] an almost 30-kilometer long tunnel is built for the use of the train that goes [from Tel Aviv] to Jerusalem. However, in Haifa – a city of 300,000 people – the rail tracks separate the water from the city and everybody accepts this abnormality. In the new plan [to connect Haifa to the Sea] we left a middle option: to build bridges over the train tracks, because we knew that building sunken rail tracks was an option which could not be taken lightly. So I am glad that we managed to persuade them to build a sunken railway. [...]
>
> According to Shinar the situation that presently prevails in Haifa is not greatly different from what exists in other towns in Israel; the *last thing* that you could say about these towns is that they are Mediterranean towns. Haifa, really, does not look like

Piraeus, or at least for the moment doesn't resemble it. "Where are we and where is the Mediterranean Sea?" asks Shinar. "We are so much separated from the Mediterranean atmosphere, and it is particularly so in our towns. Apart from Tel Aviv that somehow only just reaches the Sea, *none of our towns reaches the Sea*. This is an unbelievable phenomenon. I really fail to comprehend it. *Why? Why run away from the Sea when you could cling to it like in every other normal Mediterranean town?*" [...]

Towns were planned and designed here [in Israel] that are [...] separated from the Sea. Take for example Ashkelon: it is a nice place, but it, too, turns its back on the Sea, as if the Sea is unimportant. In Ashdod the situation is even worse [...] In Israel a town engineer [or a town planner] is actually an urban mender and repairer. He has to repair what was spoiled for 60 years.[34]

The Dakar was an Israeli submarine that sank on its maiden voyage in the Mediterranean in January 1968. None of its crew of sixty-nine survived. In 1999 the sub's wreckage was found on the seabed at a depth of 3,000 meters, south of Crete. The loss of the Dakar triggered a national trauma in Israel. Painful associations of Israel, Jews, the Mediterranean and the submarine Dakar blended together to create fearful reaction to the Sea being a source for threats and disasters. The very relations and symbiosis between Jews, Israelis and the Sea were questioned. "20 years ago [in 1948 when the State of Israel was established], when the founders of the State of Israel opened an outlet to the Great Sea, it was already then a defiance to mother nature, a defiance to the very Creation. [...] The most puzzling procurement acquired by the Jewish nation, which later became Israel, was the [Mediterranean] Sea," wrote the journalist Uri Kesari in an obituary to the sailors of the Dakar.[35]

Fifty years earlier (1919), when Tel Aviv was ten years old, its first Lord Mayor Meir Dizengoff, declared that "Jews do not like to bathe in the Sea," and "ordered" that the people of Tel Aviv should not bathe in the Sea.[36]

The first municipal beach where people were allowed to bathe and the first municipal lifeguard services appeared in Tel Aviv in ca. 1928. The Israeli singer Shlomo Artzi in his song "Under the Mediterranean Sky," emphasized that "half the world already sings [in] Greek," alluding to half of the pop music broadcast in Israel being Greek songs, which constitute the leading foreign-language pop music heard on local radio stations. However, Artzi placed his "Greek statement" between a line about the Oriental music programs on Israeli radio, and a line describing an unexplained shivering, either from *terror* or from love, that shakes his very existence.

> Now it's time for oriental [music]/
> Half of the world already sings in Greek/
> My body trembles … from terror and love/
> Half of the world hates the other half/
> My body trembles/
> Who is foe and who is friend are jumbled.

> עכשיו יש את הזמן במזרחית/
> חצי עולם כבר שר יוון/
> בגוף שלי צמרמורת ... מטרור ואהבה/
> חצי עולם שונא חצי/
> בגוף שלי צמרמורת/
> מתערב מי אויב ומי ידיד.

Israeli Painting and the Mediterranean

Traditionally Israeli painting practically ignores the Sea. For example, Tel Aviv's most famous artist in the 1930s, Joseph Zaritzki (1891–1985), who lived in Tel Aviv — a reminder: a Mediterranean city — and who painted hundreds of cityscapes of his surroundings, hardly ever showed the Mediterranean. "A guest who comes from Mars to the galleries and studios of our contemporary art will not be able to guess that he's landed in a Mediterranean country."³⁷ David Ben-Gurion, the founding father of modern Israel, ridiculed the naval adventures and "achievements" of the ancient Hebrews and their attempts to become seafarers. These ancient Jews titled the Mediterranean – comparatively speaking a closed lake, certainly small in comparison to the earth's oceans – the "Great Sea" (though relative to the Sea of Galilee and the Dead and Red Seas it was immeasurably huge). If they called the Med the "Great Sea," it shows that the Hebrew seafarers had very limited naval experience and that they did not reach the oceans beyond the Pillars of Hercules (Gibraltar) and certainly did not cross them, wrote Ben Gurion.³⁸ Indeed, in ancient times the Sea was a barrier, a frontier, a threatening, hazardous and mysterious huge mass of water. Every possible evil and invasion came from the Great Sea. The dreaded Philistines (one of the Peoples of the Sea, גויי הים) who invaded southern Canaan came from the Sea, as did the Greek-speaking peoples of the Eastern Mediterranean.³⁹

The Arab World and the Mediterranean Sea = The Middle White Sea

Perceiving the Mediterranean as a threat was not confined to the Jews. For the Arab world, in fact for all Middle Easterners, save perhaps the Maronite Christians in Lebanon, who consider themselves as descendants of the ancient Phoenicians, the Sea is a constant disaster waiting to happen. The modern Arabic and Turkish names of the Mediterranean Sea is *The Middle White Sea*, white being a reference to the color white associated with the West and Western peoples. In Turkish, the Sea is known as *Akdeniz,* meaning the "White Sea", to distinguish it from the Black Sea, *Karadeniz*. Eyal Zisser observes the way Middle Eastern Arabs view the Mediterranean.

> Pan Arabism [...] viewed the Mediterranean Sea as a hostile, even as a border that had to be converted into a fortified wall separating 'them' form 'us'. Everything coming from beyond this Sea was considered a threat. After all, it was from there – in the distant as well as the recent past – that the invader had come.

> Moreover, the Mediterranean Sea, and all that it symbolized, contained an ideological threat as well. The Mediterranean idea was considered cosmopolitan, an epithet in the Arab lexicon [...] Thus the Sea was meant not to connect but to separate the Arabs on one side, from the West and Europe on the other.[40]

Napoleon, France, Great Britain, the British-French 1956 Suez Crisis against Egypt, the 5 June 1967 Israeli air force attack on Egypt's airfields and air force, the frequent US interventions in Arab countries, even the latest military operation in Libya that toppled Muammar Ghaddafi's regime – all foreigners invaded the Arab Middle East via the Mediterranean. All initiatives that brought about the disintegration of the Arab Middle East came from the Sea.

Moreover, the Mediterranean Sea has often been described as a core feature of the Levant. The Levantine East-Mediterranean is portrayed in derogative terms – it is sentimental, it lacks depth, it is superficial, crowded, vulgar, decadent, and vociferous; it evokes the negative traits that diminish and weaken Europe, it is the backyard of Europe and it is the reason why the Levant is inferior and Western Europe is superior. See the following from a 1914 American book about how the West perceived Turkey, the epitome of the Levant. Western contempt and arrogance as well as contemporary third-world descriptions suit these perceptions. Here the vibrant West is compared to the phlegmatic Levant; neither science nor development should be produced by human beings:

> Our modern methods of criticism are foreign to the East. It is our liberation from dogmatism, our freedom to criticize, to disagree, to find fault, which produces the wonderful fruits of European civilization. Investigation must always precede scientific discovery, and the East never investigates. It has no understanding of the relation between cause and effect.
>
> A scholar who was collecting economic data once wrote to a Mohammedan merchant in an interior Turkish town, asking him for information as to the population of the town, the number of caravans entering it, etc. The Mohammedan wrote

back in indignation, saying that it was blasphemous to inquire into such things. If Allah had wanted these facts to be known he would have informed his people.[41]

Uncertainties and concerns: The Turkish element

The uncertainties aroused by Turkey's policies and intentions in the region are another common issue shared by Israelis, Greeks and Cypriots. Among other things it leads to frequent Greek-Israeli-Cypriot meetings and greater military and intelligence cooperation, where attempts are made to understand, analyze and decipher the Turkish maritime agenda. Also, both Israel and Greece have active diasporic lobbies in North America whose goal is to bring their respective mother countries into closer relations, using the Turkish issue as a reason for further cooperation.

Warmer Greek-Israeli relations should not be seen as an anti-Turkey alliance. There is no intention, neither in Athens nor in Jerusalem, to create an anti-Turkish axis in the Eastern Mediterranean arena. What concerns Athens are various moves that are perceived as Neo-Ottomanism or Pax-Ottomanism, both in the Middle East and in the Balkans. Yet, alienating Turkey is *not* in Greece's interest and neither in Israel's. Up to 2010 and before the financial crisis in Greece, the Turkish – Greek trade was booming. Turkey has emerged as a major trading partner for Greece, with excellent prospects of further increasing bilateral Turkish-Greek trade and commercial relations. This is a market of more than $3 billion annually (2009) and Turkey has become Greece's fifth largest export destination, while Turkey is the fourteenth largest supplier of commodities to Greek markets. Greek investments in Turkey are expected to reach over one-fifth, closer to a quarter, of direct foreign investments in Turkey.

Turkey's relations with the US are close. The US needs a partner in Turkey on almost every Middle East issue, namely, in Syria, Iraq, Iran, and in Afghanistan and Pakistan, as well as in Central Asia and the Caucasus. Still, it was Matthew Bryza, the US Deputy Assistant Secretary of State for European and Eurasian Affairs, who defined the change in the status of Turkey and the implications of this change for the Eastern Mediterranean nations. Turkey, he said, has become a superpower in its region and the US cannot ignore nor pressure Turkey. Bryza refers to Cyprus, but his words bare relevance for the entire Near East:

> When Greek Cypriot administration Parliament Speaker Marios Karoyan asked Bryza to put pressure on Turkey on the issue, Bryza replied, "The US can't do it [...] If this were the '70s, '80s or '90s, it could, but the US putting pressure on Turkey now is out of the question."[42]

The deteriorating relations between Turkey and Israel and the current crisis in the relations between Turkey and Syria against the backdrop of the latter's smoldering civil war are two subjects of intensive media interest. However, these are only some of the developments currently occurring in the Eastern Mediterranean. From the Turkish standpoint, the events in our region also reflect what is happening throughout the global system: Europe is ageing, the US is suffering from an economic slow-down, and both are in decline. As a rising power, Turkey is demarcating the borders of its influence: Central Asia, the Caucasus and the Balkans, on the one hand and on the other, black Africa, North Africa and the Middle East.

Relations between Israel and Turkey first began to deteriorate in 2004/2005 following growing hesitation among American Jewish lobbies to "explain" the Turkish policy vis-à-vis the Armenian genocide. The Turkish reactions to the ensuing Jewish lobbies' reluctance to support Ankara on this issue should be considered as the crossroad in Turkey-Israel relations. It was as if a sigh of relief was heard in Turkey: at long last Turkey could get shot of this Israeli lobbying! No need any more to be helped by these lobbies; no need to have good relations with Israel (that in return "explains" Turkey in Washington); no need to pursue a policy of good relations with Israel which is clearly *not* in Turkey's best interest; no need to be *blackmailed* anymore by these lobbies – were the rationales given in Ankara. That is to say, for years Turkish interests called for anti-Israeli policies, but the need to be helped by the Israeli and Jewish lobbies – which was the blackmail – forced Turkey to restrict and curtail its anti-Israeli policies.

Will the Obama administration declare Turkey a "committer of genocide" this April 24 (the anniversary of the Armenian genocide)? I don't know.

At a certain point in Turkey's Middle East policy, those who are pushing the government to turn against Israel might welcome this development, in order to say "we told you so." Personally, I wouldn't care. On the contrary, I would just thank God and be glad that the blackmail which has been imposed on us for so many years had ended.

We were blackmailed to have good relations with Israel. We were repeatedly told that Israel would help us in Washington to thwart attempts to define World War I killings of Armenians as genocide. True, the Turkish-Armenian rapprochement is only in its early stages but it finally has the potential to reduce the importance of Israeli lobbying in the US on behalf of Turkey. *Finally we might be independent of the need of Israeli lobbying on our behalf in Washington. It is so good to get rid of this blackmailing!*[43]

Despite the political tension between Ankara and Jerusalem, trade between the two countries has not been substantially affected. It reached a peak of $3.8 billion in 2008. It dropped to less than $2.5 billion in 2010 and again rose to $3.7 billion in 2011. In 2015 it was $4.1 billion.[44] The following memo-style report describes an extremely interesting side of the Turkey-Israel bilateral trade that thrived even when politically the two nations were at loggerheads because of the *MS Mavi Marmara* crisis (a Turkish protest ship en route to Gaza boarded by Israeli troops in June 2010). Notwithstanding the mutual Turkish-Israeli diplomatic wrangling over the affair, with the Syrian civil war raging, the export and import of goods to and from Turkey to the Gulf States, Jordan, Iraq and Saudi Arabia, previously facilitated overland via Syria, was rerouted through Israel's Mediterranean ports, Haifa and Ashdod, as reported in the following (partly paraphrased) article by Daniel Shmil:

The Economic Peace Rolls in Trucks from Turkey and Jordan

Trucks with license plate numbers from Jordan and Turkey [go] from Haifa to Jordan and back. [The trucks are] transporting Jordanian and Iraqi goods to Turkey and returning with Turkish goods for Jordan and Iraq. Because of the civil war in Syria, Israel has become the trade corridor [for Turkey]. Initially, Turkish trucks asked permission to carry medical oxygen for hospitals in Jordan. Jordanian trucks enter Israel at the Jordan River Terminal (Sheikh Hussein), go directly to Haifa Port (80km). Security: The trucks are carefully examined including X-rayed, go in convoys of 10 trucks, escorted by police.

Turkish trucks: come to Haifa on ferries (RORO = Roll On, Roll Off); in each ferry there are 50–150 loaded trucks, driven by Turkish drivers.

In the year 2011: 3,500 trucks going and coming from and to Jordan. (First by Israeli trucks only: unloading and loading goods onto Jordanian trucks at the Jordan River border-crossing facility, because there was no permission for Jordanian trucks to enter Israel.) In 2012: permission was given to Jordanian trucks to enter Israel, hence 6,400 trucks going and coming from and to Jordan. In January–March 2013: 2,600 trucks in both directions (Jordan-Haifa; Haifa-Jordan). Jordan to Turkey: trucks carry agriculture, textile, light industry. Turkey to Jordan: trucks carry raw materials for industry, packing materials, dry food, etc.

Jordanian drivers' passports are not stamped when entering or leaving Israel.

For the future, Israel expects 200 million NIS [New Israel Shekel] income (US$50–60 million) from port taxes, gas and petrol for the trucks, insurance and various other payments.

Average Monthly Trucks: Year 2011: Jordan River-Haifa Port, 292 trucks (transportation was done by Israeli trucks only). Year 2012 (when permission was given to Jordanian trucks to enter Israel): 533 trucks. January–March 2013: 867 trucks.[45]

In spite of the *Mavi Marmara* crisis and the disagreements following the Jewish lobbies' stand vis-à-vis Turkey and the Armenian genocide, important similarities also exist between Turkey and Israel. In June 2010 following the *Mavi Marmara* event, Aluf Benn (nowadays the *Haaretz* editor), specified these similarities and other common denominators in his article titled:

What a Loss!

- Both Ben-Gurion and Ataturk established secular states that aspired to become Western countries.
- Both countries are criticized for the way they treat their minorities.
- Both countries have suffered from the intervention and overinfluence of the military on civilian life.
- In both countries the influence of religion has greatly increased.
- In both Turkey and Israel the present governments are actively doing away with Kemalism (also called Atatürkism) and Ben-Gurion's heritage and ideology, respectively.
- In both countries the executive branches work to weaken the courts and legal systems.
- One of the results of Erdogan's active and intervening policies is greater [Israeli] cooperation on the military and intelligence fronts with several countries in the Balkans and Eastern Mediterranean.[46]

Another possible addition to Benn's list is that Israel's and Turkey's founding leaders minimized important chapters in their respective nation's past while glorifying more modern chapters. As previously pointed out, Ben-Gurion all but erased 2,000 years of Jewish exile and Diaspora and made a direct link between the Jewish Biblical past and the modern Jewish settlement in the Holy Land and the State of Israel. Mustafa Kemal linked modern Turkey to its Hittite Empire era, while canceling out the Muslim and Ottoman periods in the life of the Turkish people.

Epilogue

To sum up the common denominators and similarities that Greece and Israel share as common values, I end with a few excerpts from Benny Zipper's "Their Holocaust" (Haaretz, 12 October 2012). Zipper, the newspaper's editor of culture and literary affairs, who covered German Chancellor Angela Merkel's visit to Athens during which Greek demonstrators welcomed her with Nazi regalia and swastikas, spotted some similarities between Greeks and Israelis. Both use historical precedents to clarify and explain contemporary issues. Zipper also mentions important differences that color the two countries' relations with international actors. Occasionally Zipper is humorous; behind his humor the reader will find a few insights and home truths typical of Greece and Israel – typical of their relations with each other as well as with the world beyond the Mediterranean Sea.

> Something in the stormy Greek temperament woke up this week when the German Chancellor Angela Merkel visited Greece. It reminds me of the Israeli temperament. Something in the [...] appearance of the Greek demonstrators in brown shirts and swastika wanted to remind the Chancellor that the economic recession imposed on Greece [as a quid pro quo for receipt of EU financial aid] resembled the Nazi occupation of Greece. It was reminiscent of Israelis wide-spread inclination to use similar tactics.
>
> In right-wing demonstrations in Israel, when the demonstrators carry [derogatory] banners with pictures of leaders of the Israeli Left, these leaders were dressed in Nazi uniform. [One example of this was Yitzhak Rabin just before his assassination in

November 1995.] [...] Such is also the wide use of the yellow star badge in Israeli demonstrations. [The Nazi yellow Star of David badge identified Jews during World War II.]

Why in France, for example, do demonstrators not wear Nazi uniforms when they protest? [...] I have a feeling that it is the hot temperament of the Greeks and Israelis that produces senseless vulgar behavior like the use of Nazi regalia. [...] This is because the Greeks, like the Israelis, are convinced that they are the chosen peoples [!] who invented beauty and literature and philosophy [...] The successors of these two ancient cultures gave the world Homer, Sophocles and Plato; Moses, Isaiah and Jeremiah. [So you don't dare to teach them anything.] [...]

The modern Greeks [...] are proud as if each of them had written The Odyssey; this pride is baseless. Similarly, Israelis [...] are proud as if each of them had written the Bible; this pride too is baseless.

Another important similarity shared by the two peoples is that both are convinced that they are charged with the historical mission to be a bastion defending the West against Islam and barbarity. [...]

It is hard to find fronting the Mediterranean coasts two other countries [apart from Greece and Israel], who live in imaginary worlds. And even if somebody attempts to shake them and to wake them up from their sweet dreams, the reaction of both is to continue sleeping. In Greece it is Angela Merkel who attempts to wake the Greeks up from their economic dream. The US and the European countries repeatedly attempt to wake Israel up from its territorial dream, but to no avail. [Both] turn over on the other side and continue snoring.

[But there is a difference between Israel and Greece.] We [Israelis] get a huge foreign aid package and nobody asks us to lower our standard of living. [In return for EU aid, Greece is required to lower its standard of living]. Nobody dares attach conditions to the aid given to Israel such as demanding that Israelis lower their standard of living. If so, such a donor would immediately be called anti-Semitic and an enemy of the Jews. American Jewry would not vote for such a person in the next elections. Germany in particular would not dare to attach any pre-conditions to foreign aid to Israel.

Unlike Israel, and in spite of the huge Greek diaspora, Greece has failed to create an aura that intimates it is risky to hurt Greek feelings, and whoever dares to do so is an enemy. [...]

Now, for the first time Greece is attempting to adopt this strategy. Greece tries to copy us [Israel]! Shame on her: how come she is not ashamed to take from us the exclusive asset that compares everything to the Nazis![47]

Notes

[1] L. Peretz, The expulsion from Mount Olympus, *Musaf Haaretz*, 7 August 2015 (trans. from Hebrew).
[2] G. Botelho, Amid killings and kidnappings, can Christianity survive in the Middle East?, *CNN*, 27 February 2015, http://edition.cnn.com/2015/02/27/middleeast/christianity-middle-east/, accessed 1 April 2017.
[3] Ibid., quoted in Botelho, PEW Research Center Report.
[4] A. Baker, Unholy choices: Christians in the Middle East find themselves at crossroads in a region Rocked by war and revolution, *Time*, 21 April 2014, 25.
[5] Ibid.
[6] Israel Ministry of Foreign Affairs, Information Department (Middle East, Religious Affairs, Political Research Center), *Christian Communities in the Middle East*, 2013, 17 March (Hebrew).
[7] Bat Ye'or, a historian of the Middle East, said the following regarding the West's mild reaction to the massacre of Middle Eastern Christians: "Maybe it is one more sign of Western decadence, of a deliberate policy of deleting Christian identity by choosing globalization and Islamization – a policy based on the rejection of Judeo-Christian values rooted in our actual Western culture of execration of Israel. [...] Europe has desisted from defending itself, how would it defend others?" quoted in Giulio Meotti, (an Italian journalist with Il Foglio), The extinction of Eastern Christianity may figure Europe's own future, *Israel National News*, 5

April 2015, http://www.israelnationalnews.com/Articles/Article.aspx/16737#.VSKP05t02pp, accessed 16 August 2016.
8. Botelho.
9. Ibid.
10. Baker, *Unholy Choices*, 25–26.
11. Botelho.
12. Lauren E. Bohn, In Egypt, Christians Caught in Cross Fire, *Time*, 9 September 2013, 8; Baker, *Unholy Choices*, 26.
1. Baker, *Unholy Choices*, 27.
14. Israel Ministry of Foreign Affairs.
15. Botelho.
16. Baker, *Unholy Choices*, 24, 27.
17. Israel Ministry of Foreign Affairs.
18. Ibid.
19. T. Pileggi, Jerusalem Church Defaced with Anti-Christian Graffiti, *The Times of Israel*, 17 January 2016, http://www.timesofisrael.com/jerusalem-church-defaced-with-anti-christian-graffiti/, accessed 9 August 2016.
20. H. Smith, Greece tackles its image as a state of racists, *The Guardian*, 11 November 2003.
21. *Haaretz*, 4 January 2011; *The Economist*, 14 May 2009.
22. Judith Sunderland and Hugh Williamson, Xenophobia in Greece, *Suddeutsche Zeitung*, 13 May 2013; Smith, Greece tackles its image.
2. A. Golan, We are the Greeks, *Haaretz*, 9 November 2011 (emphasis added).
24. Y. Dror, Where is the 'Jewish Mind'?, *Haaretz*, 30 July 2010.
25. Ibid.
26. The Israeli scientist Aaron Ciechanover: Nobel Laureate in Chemistry, 2004, *Haaretz*, 13 October 2009.
27. Ibid.
28. R. Almog, Who will stand in the shadow of the olive tree and in the company of the cricket?, *Haaretz* Cultural and Literary Supplement, 30 May 2014. Almog reviewed the Hebrew translation of the anthology of Yannis Ritzos' poetry, Ikar Ha'Ikarim (Hebrew: The Essence of Essence, in Greek: *To Pio Arketo*), translated from the Greek by R. Sa'ari, Tel Aviv, Rimonim, 2014. Yiannis Ritzos (1909–1990) is considered among twentieth-century Greece's greatest poets.
29. Almog, Who will stand in the shadow?
30. Golan, We Are the Greeks.
31. A. Balaban, Tel Aviv Notes: Tel Aviv and the Stevedores, *Haaretz* Cultural and Literary Supplement, 22 August 2014.
32. A. Kril, Mediterranean character: Israel with its back to the Sea, Mussaf Haaretz, *Haaretz* Weekend Edition, 12 December 2014, 52. Interview with architect Ami Shinar, designer of Haifa's urban sea front.
33. Ibid.
34. Ibid, emphasis added..

35 U. Kesari, *Haaretz*, 25 January 1968, reprinted in *Haaretz*, 25 January 2010.
36 Reprinted in *Haaretz*, 17 March 2010.
37 H. Hever, *Toward the Longed-for Shore: The Sea in Hebrew Culture and Modern Hebrew Literature*. Jerusalem, Van Leer and Hakibbutz Hameuchad Publishers, 2007, 11 (Hebrew), quoting Gideon Ofrat, *Turning a Back on the Sea: Images of the Place in Israeli Art and Literature*. Tel Aviv, Amanut Israel, 1990, 148 (Hebrew).
38 Hever, *Toward the Longed-for Shore*, 17.
39 Rosen, People of the Book, People of the Sea: Mirror Images of the Soul, 36–39, in M. Rosen, ed., *Homelands and Diasporas: Greeks, Jews and their Migrations*. London, I. B. Tauris, 2008, 35–81.
40 E. Zisser, The Mediterranean Idea in Syria and Lebanon: Between Territorial Nationalism and Pan-Arabism, *Mediterranean Historical Review*, v.18, n.1, June 2003, 85.
41 S. Cobb, The Real Turk. Boston, *The Pilgrim Press*, 1914, 35.
42 M. Bryza, The US can't pressure on [sic] Turkey over Cyprus, *Milliyet*, 1 July 2009. https://www.google.co.il/webhp?sourceid=chrome-instant&ion=1&espv=2&ie=UTF-8#q=Mattthew+Bryza%2C+%E2%80%9CThe+US+Can%E2%80%99t+Pressure+on+Turkey+over+Cyprus%2C%E2%80%9D.
43 A. Zenturk, Will the US turn its back on Turkey?, *Star*, 2 March 2009, emphasis added.
44 O. Koren, The impact of the agreement with Turkey on Israeli export will be limited, *Haaretz, TheMarker*, 28 June 2016, 10.
45 D. Shmil, The economic peace rolls in trucks from Turkey and Jordan, *Haaretz, TheMarker*, 25 April 2013, 11.
46 Aluf Benn, What a Loss!, *Haaretz*, 9 June 2010.
47 B. Zipper, Their Holocaust, *Haaretz*, 12 October 2012.

[9]
EGYPT CAN REVERSE ITS DISMAL ENERGY PICTURE

Sohbet Karbuz

Introduction

Multiple challenges facing Egypt since the removal of President Mubarak from office on 11 February 2011 have not ended. Egypt has suffered a lot from a combination of socio-political turmoil and economic instability. Energy is not an exception. Arguably the country has experienced its most serious energy crisis.

Growing population, rising household incomes, a growing economy as well as increasing living standards and human development indicators have driven energy demand in Egypt higher over the past decades. However, despite meeting domestic energy demand has been a priority, to be able to supply affordable energy to all and to sustain rapid economic growth has become a major challenge.

While the delayed subsidy reform, rising population, inefficient use and waste of energy have caused a boom in energy demand in the country, production could not meet the expectations. Egypt has been looking to boost production to meet rising domestic demand, albeit with limited success.

Oil and gas production in Egypt has exhibited enormous growth since the start of the commercial petroleum activity early in the 20th century. Until 1975, oil was the only target for all exploration activities. That changed with the first commercial gas discovery in 1975. The period between 1975 and 2003 was Egypt's oil and gas era, dominated by oil; whereas since 2004 it has been and will continue to be the gas and oil era, dominated by gas.

A rising trend in oil production first made Egypt self-sufficient and then an exporter. However, oil production has stagnated for a long time and shows no sign of increasing. Demand for oil, on the other hand, has continued to climb. Fast growing domestic oil demand, stimulated by subsidized prices, in combination with declining production were principal factors that challenged Egypt's status as a net oil exporter. As a result, the country has become a net oil importer. More importantly, natural gas production in the country has been declining since 2010. This has been quite worrying because, with a population of 90 million, Egypt today is the largest gas consumer in Africa.

Natural gas is a main energy source for electricity generation and industrial production, and is also used for increasing reservoir pressure in oil fields. Increase in gas use has forced the government first to divert production that was contractually allocated to foreign companies involved in their extraction, and then to halt gas exports, and finally to import gas. In 2015, Egypt has become a net importer of both oil and gas, two crucial energy resources that make up 95% of the country's primary energy demand.

The aim of this chapter is multiple. It first gives an overview of challenges facing Egypt's economy and energy sector. It then focuses on natural gas, the backbone of Egypt's energy sector, and shows why Egypt has become a gas importing country. Finally it argues that Egypt will become a gas exporter again. While doing this it demonstrates that the reason of the recent decline in gas production is not due to the lack of gas resources because Egypt has a very large resource base. It is mainly due to not being able to convert resources fast enough into production capacity. The article also discusses a possible way forward for the Egyptian energy sector in general, and natural gas industry in particular.

The Egyptian economy is facing a paramount challenges

The economy has several problems. These include the dollar crunch, the growing income gap, liquidity shortage, a persistent budget deficit, mounting debt, double digit inflation, melting currency reserves which is contributing the rapid devaluation of the Egyptian pound, low growth rates, increasing (high youth) unemployment, growing role of the Armed Forces Engineering Authority in infrastructure projects and in the economy,[1] ineffective bureaucracy, and endemic corruption. It is not surprising that an article in Al-Ahram described the current location of the Egyptian economy as "between a rock and a hard place."[2]

Real gross domestic production (GDP) growth in 2015/16 has slowed down to an estimated 3.2% due mainly to declines in tourism. Tourism revenues which contribute around 12% of GDP have declined to $6.1 billion in 2015 from $7.3 billion in 2014.[3] Moreover, Suez Canal revenues declined to $5.17 billion in 2015, compared to $5.46 billion in 2014.[4] Egypt's budget deficit fell to almost 11% of its GDP in the fiscal year (FY) 2014/15,[5] compared to over 12% recorded in the previous year. Assuming that the government continues to implement its wide ranging reforms, the future prospects suggest a steady recovery.

Oil and natural gas are among the most important and strategic sectors in the country, accounting for 16% of GDP in fiscal year 2014/15. When the Suez Canal revenues are included, the total share of petroleum-related activities in national GDP is more than 29%.

In May 2015, Egypt hold "Egypt the Future" Economic Development Conference in Sharm El-Sheikh. Nearly $100 bn worth of MoUs were signed but the foreign direct investment in FY 2015/16 slightly increased to $3.1 bn from $2.6 bn the year before. Macroeconomic figures point to some improvement but the economy is still in dire straits.

Despite a significant stream of money flow to Egypt from the GCC (Gulf Cooperation Council) countries in cash deposits, loans and petroleum shipments[6] the economy is still in dire straits. Besides, the drastic fall in oil prices continues to harm the Egyptian economy in two ways. First, low oil prices have hampered the ability of GCC countries to continue providing Egypt with the financial aid. Second, since foreign direct investment in Egypt has historically been focused on extractive industries, mainly oil and gas, the decline in oil prices has led to a contraction of foreign investment in the oil and gas sector.[7]

The energy sector has not been better either. While production remained stagnant, delayed subsidy reform, rising population, inefficient use and waste of energy have caused a boom in energy demand in the country. The country is currently a net oil and gas importer. The supply-demand imbalance in the country therefore has also exacerbated the foreign currency crisis.[8]

This dismal situation was the result of decades-long failure to diversify Egypt's economy and energy. The country's economy and industrial structure has relied on inefficient and costly energy subsidy system,[9] which accounts for a large part of this budget deficit and public spending.

Subsidies has long been a painful economic burden

When fuel subsidies were instituted in Egypt a long time ago, the idea was that citizens should benefit from the hydrocarbons resources of the country. This entailed both financial subsidies to energy producer and consumers, and significant opportunity costs in terms of foregone foreign and government revenues.[10] The problem is that energy prices in Egypt have generally been priced below economic costs. The cost of these implicit subsidies (i.e. keeping prices below cost) have increased in time. Problems, however, started to arise when demand soared while oil production declined. Subsidies have become an ongoing controversy and concern when they are on the public finances.

This is why restructuring energy subsidies and adjustments to domestic fuel prices have been a key objective of government reforms since 2004. However, due to its sensitive nature it was not possible to carry out reforms in this issue. Gradual removal of these subsidies seemed also not possible to implement. The main concerns were drastic price increases and limited mitigating measures.

In July 2014 (start of the 2014/15 fiscal year), the Egyptian government introduced a five-year plan to phase out almost all fuel subsides by 2019.[11] With this reform the government wished to trim more than three-quarters of its subsidy bill. The fuel subsidy bill amounted to E£73.9 bn ($10.1 bn) in FY 2014/15 compared to E£126.2 bn ($18.1 bn) in FY 2013/14, due partly to fall in oil prices since the mid-2014. The most significant step of this reform was the 64% hike in diesel prices (to E£1.8 per liter).[12]

However, this reform has attracted increased public opposition. Consequently, in December 2015, Cairo backed away from its plan to eliminate energy subsidies. The current goal is to reduce fuel subsidies by 30% compared to July 2014. This is intended to be achieved in steps, to

E£61 bn ($8.3 bn) for the FY 2015/16 and to E£35 bn for the FY 2016/17. Although declining oil prices contributed significantly to falling petroleum subsidies, spending on electricity subsidies has been rising rapidly. In order to avert this situation, the government plans to double electricity tariffs across all consumer groups by FY 2018/19.

If higher gas prices agreed to operators are not passed through end users, it will bring additional financial strains to the government and hence the problem of energy subsidies will get worse. A subsidy reform can help to correct some market distortions but not sufficient to eliminate the imbalance in the energy supply and demand.

The country's energy sector — Egypt's pressing energy challenges

Egypt's primary energy mix is dominated by natural gas (50%) and oil (45%). They provide almost all of the country's primary energy to meet today's demands for economic activities and human needs. Oil and gas are expected to remain the driving force of Egypt's energy sector in the future, even if their combined share in primary energy demand declines. The problem is that oil production has been declining since its peak in 1993 and natural gas production has been declining in the past few years. More alarmingly, Egypt has become is a net importer of both oil and natural gas in 2015.

Overall energy demand in Egypt is expected to more than double and electricity demand to multiply by a factor of 3 in 2030.[13] To provide such incremental volumes of energy will be very challenging.

Egypt's electricity sector has also faced a number of pressing challenges. The most important ones include obtaining sufficient base and peak load capacity; ensuring the availability of natural gas for power production, at price levels that can be absorbed by the retail electricity tariff; implementing the government's ambitious renewable energy agenda; improving energy efficiency; and advancing reform of tariffs and subsidies. While Egyptians have been plugging in more and more, meeting peak load has become an immediate challenge. The problem is that natural gas sparks most of the kilowatts in the country.

More than 75% of electricity generation in Egypt is based on natural gas, the remainder being met mostly by oil and hydroelectricity.[14] The Nile River is the mainstay of Egypt's hydropower base. The share of gas has increased substantially since the late 1990s following significant discoveries of indigenous natural gas, declining oil production and the gas for oil substitution policy. Today, power plants consume more than half of the domestic natural gas supply.

Egypt has plans to further expand electricity capacity by using the country's vast wind and solar resources. Both resource development and policy preferences have led to an enormous increase of gas use in electricity production. Egypt is richly endowed with renewable energy resources from solar insolation in the vast western desert, hydropower from the Nile River to world-class wind resources along the Gulf of Suez. There is enormous potential for renewable energy development in Egypt. Yet, today the contribution of renewable energy sources to total primary energy supply is fairly limited. In other words, natural gas is and will remain the backbone of the power generation system in the country. This means that there will be more and more pressure on increasing domestic gas production. This will not be easy.

A greater emphasis is already being placed on renewable energy sources with a particular focus on developing 4.3 GW of wind and solar photovoltaic power capacity by 2027,[15] and having a larger share in its energy mix in an attempt to diversify the country's energy mix. Despite the political will, attractive feed-in-tariffs, and a flurry of MoUs signed for renewable projects since March 2015 development conference, tangible progress so far in terms of solid development contracts are meager. Despite that will, however, natural gas will continue to be the fuel of choice as the project to build the three largest combined cycle gas power plants in the world[16] clearly demonstrates.

Since 2015, Egypt has also been negotiating with the Russian Rosatom to fund and to construct a nuclear power plant in Dabaa. The project is planned to be completed by 2022 following the approval of the $25 bn Russian loan to Egypt issued in May 2016. However, it is rather unlikely to be completed by then.

The growing importance of natural gas in Egypt's energy sector

Oil production in Egypt peaked in 1993 at close to one million barrels per day. Since then production has been declining gradually despite discoveries and advanced production techniques at mature fields. This decline is unlikely to be reversed for a sustained period.

In the early stage of Egypt's gas industry, natural gas associated with oil production was flared because there was no network to collect gas from producing fields or a local market for the gas. A series of large gas discoveries between 1967 and 1971, changed the landscape. The first commercial natural gas discovery in Egypt was made in the Nile Delta in 1967 but the field was put on stream in 1975.

Since 1976 a series of non-associated gas discoveries were made but real attention turned to natural gas after Egypt's oil production reached its peak and large gas discoveries were put into production in the first decade of the 21st century.

A modest local natural gas market emerged with the start of commercial gas production in 1975. Construction of a 40 kilometer pipeline brought gas produced from the Abu Madi field to the Talkha area to fuel a power station, fertilizer and textile factories. This was the start of the National Gas Grid. Today natural gas is transmitted and distributed through over 7000 km long National Gas Grid.

The Egyptian government encouraged the use of natural gas in the domestic market. In the mid-1980s, the government actively promoted natural gas use as a substitute for oil and began to develop a network to use the gas for power generation, as well as in the end use sectors. Energy intensive industries, especially cement and steel factories and fertilizer plants have made a transition from oil to natural gas. Also, the government has encouraged the commercialization of compressed natural gas as a transportation fuel.

The gas-for-oil substitution policy was to make use of Egypt's abundant gas reserves and to free up oil for export. Towards those aims, policy shifted to allow private companies to apply for franchise areas throughout the country to build, own and operate gas distribution systems in joint ventures with government entities. Subsequently, the natural gas sector developed in an integrated way including field development, gas processing and treatment, transportation, distribution and marketing both for local and export markets. This stimulated more exploration, discoveries and production.

Egypt's natural gas policy played a major role in this achievement especially after 1993 when modifications allowed companies (in joint ventures with the government) to own the gas, which made commercial development more attractive. With more favorable conditions, the gas sector started to grow. The discovery of additional gas reserves combined with stagnant or declining oil production has led to large-scale integration of gas into national energy policy.

Over the past decade Egypt has climbed several rungs of the ladder towards the world's top natural gas producers as well as exporters. Marketed natural gas production increased from just 0.03 bcm in 1975 to more than 60 bcm in 2009. After staying above 60 bcm for a while, production has started to decline and remained below 50 bcm since 2014.

Once a major exporter, Egypt has now become a gas importer in 2015

Egypt began exporting natural gas by pipeline in 2003 at less than 1 bcm, which expanded to 19.5 bcm in 2008, but dropped later on due to booming gas demand.

Egypt has two gas export pipelines - the Arab Gas Pipeline (AGP) and the East Mediterranean Pipeline (also knows an El Arish-Ashkelon pipeline). The former connects the country with neighboring countries, Jordan, Syria and Lebanon. The subsea gas pipeline, the El Arish-Ashkelon, connects the AGP with Israel.

Natural gas exports by pipeline commenced through the AGP to Jordan in 2003. Egyptian gas via the AGP reached Syria in 2008 and Lebanon in 2009. Gas transportation on the AGP, however, remained less than half of its design capacity of 10 bcm/year. In January 2008, Turkey and Syria signed an agreement to construct a 63 kilometer pipeline as the first segment of a Syria-Turkey connection with the AGP. From Turkey, gas could reach Europe through the Kilis-Türkoglu interconnection and the Turkish national transmission grid. The connection was expected to be completed by 2011 but it has not materialized due to the lack of gas and changes in political environments in the region. There were also talks between 2008 and 2010 about bringing Iraqi gas or Iranian gas to AGP via Iraq and Syria with no tangible progress.

The Arab Gas Pipeline (AGP) infrastructure has been sabotaged several times, exports to Israel were halted in April 2012 and only small volumes of gas reached Jordan for some time.

Figure 1: Natural Gas Export Infrastructure.

The East Mediterranean Pipeline (El Arish–Ashkelon) is a 90 kilometer, 7 bcm capacity submarine pipeline from the AGP in Egypt to Israel. Although it is not officially a part of the AGP project, it branches off from it in Egypt. The pipeline is built, owned and operated by the East Mediterranean Gas Company, a joint stock company between Egyptian and Israeli interests organized in 2000 in accordance with the Egyptian Special Free Zones system. After becoming operational since May 2008, the East Mediterranean Gas Company bought Egyptian gas for resale in Israel. Deliveries from the pipeline stopped in 2013.

Egypt used to exports also liquefied natural gas (LNG) from two complexes (in Damietta and Idku)[17] to international markets. LNG exports started in 2004 at 2.3 bcm and risen to more than 15 bcm in 2008 but stopped in 2013.

The Damietta liquefaction plant was the first LNG facility in Egypt.[18] It was the world's largest LNG facility when completed in November 2004. First shipment from the plant was made in January 2005. It has one train with total capacity of 4.8 Mt/yr of LNG.

The Idku liquefaction plant has two trains with a total capacity of 7.2 Mt/yr.[19] The structure was designed for a multi-train site, so there is plenty of space for expansion, if needed. The first cargo from train-1 was lifted in May 2005. The first cargo from train-2 was shipped in September 2005.

When domestic gas production could not keep up with the pace of gas demand growth in 2008, concerns started to arise on how to balance increasing domestic demand for natural gas with export commitments. The booming demand for gas has forced the government first to freeze new gas export projects and then shift gas meant for LNG plants to feed the domestic market. This is despite the fact that domestic consumption declined from almost 53 bcm in 2012 to 48 bcm in 2014 and stabilized in 2015 at about the same level.

Diversion of gas away from industry to power generation meant that some energy intensive industrial plants had to run at below capacity particularly during the summer months when electricity demand peaks, so also the peak for gas demand. The inability of the government to provide natural gas to several industrial companies (such as cement mills, fertilizer plants and chemical industries which have been fueled almost entirely by natural gas) forced companies to cut their production substantially. In some cases (e.g., EMethanex methanol plant at Damietta)[20] some plants were often closed due to gas supply restrictions. Some others operated at reduced rates on an intermittent basis and even shut down during summer months. In order to help overcome the shortage on the domestic market the Egyptian government has allowed the private sector to import natural gas and to utilize state-owned infrastructure for that purpose in May 2015.

As a result, there have been no exports from the LNG plant in Damietta[21] since February 2013 and the second LNG plant in Idku operated at only 4% of its capacity on average in 2014. No LNG was exported in 2015. Contrary, Egypt turned into one of the world's newest LNG importers in 2015. Hence, Egypt has become a net importer of both oil and natural gas for the first time in its history.

EGAS has signed several LNG Sales and Purchase Agreements (SPAs) to import 191 LNG cargoes until 2020.[22] Egypt imported about 4 bcm of gas as LNG in 2015 and 10 bcm in 2016.[23]

Two Floating Storage and Regasification Unit (FSRU), both located in the port of Ain Sokhna in the Gulf of Suez, started operating respectively in April and October 2015.[24] Their combined capacity is 13.4 bcm/yr.[25] Egypt had plans to install a third FSRU with a capacity of 7.7 bcm/yr at the Red Sea port of Safaga in 2017, but no concrete action has taken place.

The main culprit: Not being able to convert resources into production capacity

Egypt's gas production has been declining since 2010 largely due to political instability. Important field development projects in particular in the North Alexandria and the West Nile Delta were delayed while no new exploration and production agreements were signed between 2010 and 2013. Moreover, increasing field development costs in the deep waters of the Mediterranean added additional challenges to already fragile investment climate and caused growing imbalance between supply and demand.

In fact, the reason for declining gas production has never been the lack of reserves or resources. Today remaining natural gas reserves in Egypt are estimated at around 1800 bcm, according to the Oil and Gas Journal. Almost 90% of these are non-associated gas, mostly in the Nile Delta and Mediterranean Sea areas. The yet-to-be discovered natural gas potential has been a much speculated issue, but recent estimates indicate a bright future.

In 2010, the US Geological Survey (USGS) has assessed the undiscovered oil and gas resource potential of the Nile Delta Basin Province (which corresponds to the Nile Delta and Mediterranean) to identify potentially extractable resources.[26] According to the USGS assessment, the Nile Delta contains an estimated (mean) 6321 bcm (223 tcf) of undiscovered, technically recoverable natural gas, 1.7 Gb of oil and 5.9 Gb of Natural Gas Liquids.

Egypt has potential for additional hydrocarbon discoveries, as the country is still relatively under-explored. There are plenty of sedimentary basins which are still in the early stage of exploration or not yet explored. The discovery of supergiant Zohr field offshore Egypt in August 2015 has confirmed once again the substantial hydrocarbons potential of the deep offshore areas in the Mediterranean Sea. There is little doubt that other areas will eventually be discovered. Some other major discoveries are possible recognizing the deeper knowledge of the geology, use of advanced technology such as improved mapping of subsalt plays and increased interest of foreign companies.

Moreover, according to the Cairo University's Mining Studies and Research Center shale oil could add 4.6 billion barrels of oil and shale gas also contribute another 2800 bcm to the country's reserves.[27] In addition, there is vast amount of stranded gas[28] in Egypt. Some estimates put it around 450 bcm.[29] Lack of infrastructure and other above the ground barriers currently make them difficult to utilize.

Egypt has a long and successful record of attracting international companies to participate in hydrocarbons exploration and production activities. Despite the political turbulence, Cairo has maintained a sustained level of exploration activity, with positive and encouraging results.

The Egyptian General Petroleum Corp's (EGPC) latest International Bid Round (with a closing date of August 31, 2016) offers 11 blocks to explore/exploit for oil and gas in the Gulf of Suez and Western Desert under the Production Sharing Agreement model. Ganoub El-Wadi Holding Company (Ganope)'s latest international tender (closing deadline is 30 November 2016) offers 10 blocks in the south of Gulf of Suez and in the Western Dessert. Egyptian Natural Gas Holding Company (Egas) is also expected to launch a tender including the areas in the Western part of the Mediterranean.

To date, exploration in the Western part of the Mediterranean has been limited - only two exploration wells have been drilled, and both were dry. Therefore, the petroleum systems are currently not well understood. In June 2015, EGAS commissioned the Norwegian firm PGS to carry out a 2-D and 3-D seismic survey over the western part of Egypt's Mediterranean offshore, which represents around 50% of its Exclusive Economic Zone (EEZ). New seismic data acquisition and reprocessing of the existing geophysical data will further enhance the geological understanding of the area and will form the basis for a future licensing round.

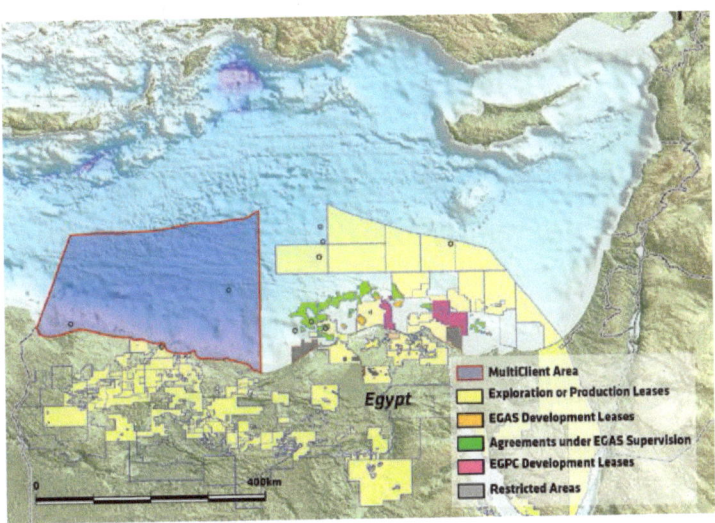

Figure 2: Location map of Egypt's Mediterranean Sea area showing licensed acreage together with the frontier area west of the Nile Delta. Source: GeoExpo, February 2016.

In August 2015, ENI discovered the super-giant Zohr field offshore Egypt, in the Shorouk block, with 850 bcm of estimated gas in place.[30] This largest discovery of its kind in the Mediterranean Sea, is a game changer at least from an exploration perspective. Zohr is a completely new reservoir structure, Miocene reef carbonates, contrary to conventional sandstone formations observed in the discoveries so far made in the region.[31] This has proven once again that oil and gas industry is an industry that is used to make impossible operations a routine.

Besides Zohr, numerous other significant oil and gas discoveries have been made recently in Egypt. For instance, in September 2015, Eni announced an important gas discovery in the Nooros exploration prospect in the Nile Delta,[32] a new oil discovery within the Meleiha concession in the Western Desert. BP made three discoveries in its North Damietta Offshore Concession[33] in the East Nile Delta, which is along the same trend of the Nooros field. The first discovery in the license was the Salamat discovery, the most important oil and gas discovery in 2013. The second one was Atoll field. In June 2016 BP announced its third discovery in the Baltim South Development Lease in the East Nile Delta. Further appraisal activities will be required to underpin the full resource potential of these discoveries but according to BP, the potential estimated in the concession goes beyond 140 bcm.

So, the availability of gas was not in question. Egypt has substantial reserves and undiscovered resource potential but the challenge is to convert reserves and resources into production capacity. The problem is that political unrest, debts owed to foreign partners, the price paid for gas, delays in the commissioning of several new projects have exacerbated investor confidence and slowed down developments in upstream sector.

Meanwhile, in response to the declining gas production, the government was aiming to offer new oil and gas exploration blocks for international bidding, sign new agreements with foreign companies, accelerate the process of putting discoveries into production (especially deep offshore projects) and increase production from the existing gas fields. However, investors were not quite confident that they would be paid and that they would make a positive return on their investment. More needed to be done to attract investments and encourage investors to invest.

Indeed, investments climate in upstream oil and gas sector have worsened due to two main challenges: Arrears owed to oil and gas companies; and low gas prices paid to the foreign partners. The government has been aware of these issues and has been trying to address them for a long time, albeit not very successfully. But things have started to change when the government proactively engaged with international companies and reformed several of the country's laws for improving the environment for investors.

Payments to foreign partners

Arrears owed to foreign companies have not only negatively affected new exploration and field development activities, but also delayed the implementation of major projects that could increase production. These arrears has been accumulating since 2008 when the EGPC was facing difficulties to pay for oil and gas debt to upstream operators. The situation deteriorated after 2011. Debts to foreign companies peaked at $7bn in 2013.

This amount was reduced to as low as $2.7 bn in October 2015, with the help of the Gulf States, but rose again to $3.2 bn in March 2016. These figures point out two issues: First, the objective of a reduction of the debt to foreign operators to $2.5 billion by the end of 2015 was not met. Second, it seems that the whole balance to be paid off by the end of 2016 sounds optimistic.

Overdue payments to foreign operators are still a major issue and a priority for the government but lack of foreign currency and depleting foreign reserves constitute a big constraint. Bringing the dollars that are on the street into the banks is still a major issue because of the imposed deposit ceiling and unfavorable return on investment.

In an attempt to reduce the burden that Egypt is facing with regard to lacking foreign currency reserves, the government has been negotiating with foreign partners on payments in local currency. EGPC reached an agreement with Eni to pay its $650 receivables (representing Eni's production share from JV's Agiba, Petrobel and Pharaonic) in Egyptian pounds.[34] It is possible that similar agreements may be reached with other partners.

Low gas prices paid to the foreign companies

Egyptian gas market prices for producers are set by the government. The obligation to sell the produced gas to state companies along with the low price paid for it by them have been deterring foreign companies from investing in upstream activities.[35]

In order to increase investor confidence, encourage more investment and attract investors into its upstream sector, Cairo had to improve pricing terms, i.e., the price Egypt pays for natural gas that foreign operators produce in the country. In 2013, EGAS increased the low price threshold in order to compensate for the high cost of drilling offshore, particularly in the deep-water blocks. In the new pricing guidelines introduced by EGAS, purchasing price of gas in new deals (i.e., production from new discoveries) ranges from $3.95 to $5.88/MMBtu, instead of $2.65/MMBtu.[36]

The new prices, negotiated on a case by case basis, are designed to reflect various criteria for each company, such as whether the gas produced comes from shallow or deeper waters and whether the company concerned intends to build a gas processing plant or not. Separate gas prices are now agreed on a case-by-case basis after the discovery, and the agreements are submitted for the approval of the Cabinet, and then Parliament, to permit the promulgation of the corresponding law.[37] Moreover, modifications to existing agreements have also been made.[38] Increasing the amount Egypt pays for gas to IOCs at a time of falling oil and gas prices worldwide has naturally caused a surge in Egypt's upstream sector. In the current environment of low gas prices worldwide[39] the offer from the Egyptian government is indeed very attractive.

Bright prospects for future gas production and exports

Marketed natural gas production in Egypt experienced a tremendous increase in the 2000s. But since 2009, it has been stagnant or declining steadily as a result of the depletion of mature fields (mostly offshore)[40], delays in new field development projects and the political unrest. In 2015, marketed production was 45.6 bcm, according to BP. Majority of it comes from the fields in the Mediterranean Sea.

The insistent policy of Cairo to attract foreign investments, the intensity of the exploration activities, promising new discoveries, and increasing number of field development project signal a booming gas production ahead.

Several gas fields have started producing recently.[41] The country has currently over a dozen of ongoing natural gas field development projects, many of which are expected to be finalized in the next five years: Zohr, North Alexandria,[42] Atoll, Salamat and West Delta Deep Marine (WDDM). According to the Ministry of Petroleum,[43] those five projects could add about 62 bcm/yr to Egypt's gross gas output.[44] Those extra volumes of gas will help offset the decline in mature fields and fill the gap between supply and demand. It will also present an opportunity for resuming gas export.

At the Egyptian Economic Development Conference in Sharm El Sheikh in March 2015, BP and DEA Egypt signed a deal with the Oil Ministry to invest $12 bn over the next four years in the WND project.[45] Final Investment Decision (FID) was taken in March 2015. The initial phase will involve the development of an estimated 141 bcm of gas reserves, together with 55 Mb of associated condensate. BP expects its 34 mcm/d of gas production from the WND project to start in 2017.[46] The EGPC will purchase all production at a price of $4.1/MMBtu.[47] All produced gas will feed the country's national gas grid.

WDDM gas fields,[48] also called the Magnificent Seven, contain Scarab/Saffron, Simian/Sienna, Sapphire, Sequoia, Senpad, Serpent, Saurus fields. The project was put on production in 2003 (with Scarab/Saffron) and is currently producing from Kafr El Sheikh, and El-Wastani from 28 wells. The output from Scarab/Saffron was initially directed to domestic market and Damietta LNG facility. Production from Simian/Sienna and Sapphire started in 2005 and their output was initially directed to the Egyptian LNG gas liquefaction plant (ELNG) at Idku.[49] The last phases of development of WDDM were designed to maintain the production rate. But due to delays, they only partly offset the decline in production from the concession.[50] Phase 9a, including 15 additional infill wells and development wells, started only in July 2014 due to the political unrest in the country. Production from Phase 9b was expected to start in 2016 with a production capacity of 3.6-4 bcm/yr by 2017 and a completion by 2020.

However, in March 2016, BG Group (now Shell) has stopped working at phases 9a and 9b after failure to reach an agreement on the price to be paid for extracted gas, and it withdrew rigs working on the 9a wells.[51] The joint venture between BG and the Egyptian government was also struggling to justify additional investment of $4 bn for the expansion Phase 9b. BG had announced in December 2015 that it was delaying developments bringing the Phase 9b wells on stream to mid-2016 at the earliest as receivables from Egypt continued to increase. According to the Egyptian media, BG demands government to raise price of gas to $7/MMBtu in the 9b concession area or pay $1 bn of arrears immediately.[52] The agreement reached with the government foresees BG's dues estimated at $1 bn to be paid by the end of 2016 and BG to complete the 9b phase of the project in the second half of 2018.[53]

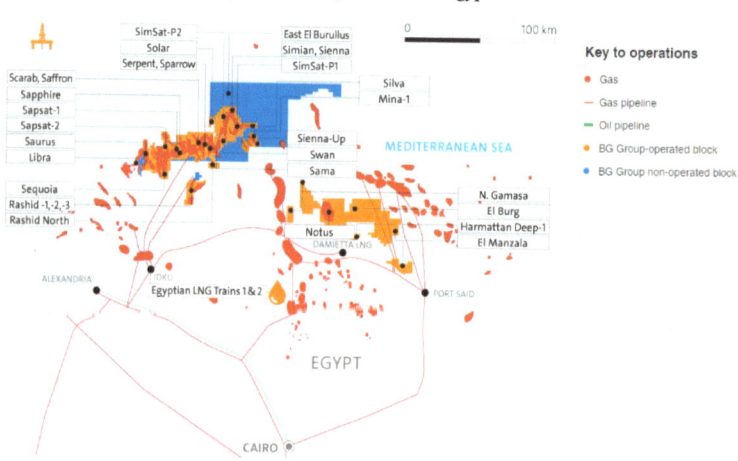

Figure 3: BG operations in Egypt / Source: BG.

The start of the gas production from recent ENI's Zohr discovery is envisaged by the end of 2017 at a rate of 10 bcm/yr (from 6 wells), with a progressive ramp up to around 28 bcm/yr by 2019 (with the drilling of 14 additional wells).[54] Peak production is expected to be achieved by 2026 at a rate of over 30 bcm/yr. Moreover, construction has already started on an onshore treatment plant to process gas produced from Zohr. Eni is expected to invest $12 bn, drilling 20 wells in the Zohr field. All the production will be provided to the domestic market.

Although a price for the gas has yet to be agreed, it will be based on EGAS' pricing formula, between $4-5.88/MMBtu. The Shorouk concession agreement signed between Eni and the Egyptian government will see 40% of revenues from Zohr go toward covering the investment in the field. Eni's repayment value will cover some $7bn worth of investment in Zohr over the next three years. The remaining revenues will be split, with Egypt receiving 65%, and Eni receiving 35%.[55]

BP also aims to accelerate the development of its March 2015 Atoll and Salamat discoveries in offshore North Damietta permit in East Nile Delta that are relatively close to existing BP-operated infrastructure. Gas production from the Atoll field, which contains an estimated 42 bcm of gas and 31 million barrels of condensates, will target the domestic market and is expected to begin in 2018. Its development will consist of two phases. In the first phase, in which existing exploration well in addition to two new development wells will tie back to existing infrastructure,[56] the field will produce some 8 mcm/d, from three wells.

The new gas field startups will help reverse the decline in currently producing fields but by how much and when is a matter of debate. So, is the future gas production in Egypt. According to OME, marketed natural gas production in Egypt will increase in the future and approach 120 bcm per year at around 2035. Afterwards, it is expected to fall fast. According to Cedigaz,[57] however, Egypt's marketed gas production will rise to approximately 65 bcm by the end of 2020 and 85 bcm by 2035.

A growing part of the additional output will likely earmark for domestic market. Nevertheless, Egypt is expected to regain its net gas exporter status in the early 2020s. In the meantime, Egypt is likely to export some LNG cargos irregular basis. Already in March 2016, an Egyptian LNG cargo was sent to India. The second one was sent to Japan in June 2016.

A Possible Way Forward

After years of underinvestment in upstream sector due to debt owed to foreign partners, low gas prices paid to them, as well as rampant consumption by a growing population and industry benefiting from generous energy subsidies, Egypt has become a net hydrocarbons importer.

Several years of unrest, a high degree of bureaucracy, frequent change of ministers and state company heads, delays to permit approvals, and slow decision making process have also played a role in severely deteriorating foreign investors' confidence.

Recently, the Egyptian government has taken active steps to attempt to reverse this situation and foster an attractive investment climate for potential investors. Paying down its debt to foreign operators whenever possible, announcing a settlement program for debt, reforming its subsidy program which will lead a substantial reduction in the level of energy subsidies, adjusting gas prices for new deep water projects have been amongst the biggest challenges to attract foreign investment to Egypt's upstream oil and gas sector. These efforts combined with engaging in open dialogue with foreign companies have helped restore investor confidence.

The Egyptian government has also modified other terms in its contracts with foreign partners. For instance, upstream companies are now able to offset signature bonuses against any arrears they are still owed by the government for their output. Moreover, contractual terms for unconventional hydrocarbons exploration are being amended to reflect the high cost of developing those technically difficult resources and make their development attractive to investors.

With all these changes, upstream oil and gas industry found a new impetus which may push the entire energy industry in the country forward. But some other obstacles must also be overcome.

One of them is the poor infrastructures,[58] especially in the Western Desert, which will entail significant investments in aboveground facilities. In addition there is the absence of a clear legal framework in the case of the development of unconventional resources. About the latter, the amount of water needed in fracking technique is obviously an issue in a country which falls below the United Nations threshold for water poverty.

Terms of the concession agreements can be further amended. For instance, a modification to the current system based on whether the gas in question is conventional, unconventional, stranded or deep offshore would make the country gas sector more attractive to invest.

Another important point is the gas flaring. Currently the amount of gas flared from oil fields still reaches 1.7 bcm/yr. Introducing new clauses in (existing) agreements, for instance, would perhaps help reduce gas flaring in the country.[59]

Domestic natural gas prices need to be further reformed to limit the burden of subsidies on the economy. Lower fuel and electricity subsidies as well as the implementation of the VAT would make energy prices a more expensive commodity and hence put pressure on demand growth. Ongoing liberalization process, tax reforms, increasing electricity prices for households and eliminating power subsidies entirely over the next few years is a right direction.

Egypt's petroleum policy in the next decades will have to address three important issues: formulation of adequate demand management policies; further development of oil and natural gas resources, specifically by stimulating exploratory efforts and accelerating the development of known fields; diversify and upgrade the use of natural gas within the economy, so that it could release relatively higher-value hydrocarbons for export, and diversify the electricity generation.

Egyptian government will need to pursue aggressive demand management policies and encourage investment in all the steps of the gas chain. A clear bet for energy efficiency, changing energy consumption habits of business and citizens and a thorough reform of energy tariffs (to align them to costs or international standards) and subsidies seem necessary to prevent excess demand growth. Improving energy efficiency is a key energy policy challenge. While there is great potential in all sectors, in a country where private vehicles are rapidly becoming more common and where significant new construction is foreseen, transport and buildings merit particular attention from policymakers. The combination of an energy efficiency plan and a sound renewable energy program could be the most effective policy to cope with the energy challenge in the medium and long-term.

The loss of experienced work force or human capital is another challenge that is becoming a major issue to be solved in Egypt's oil and gas sector. While capping the age of retirement at 60 leads to the loss of experienced people, recent arrangements about leveling and capping the salaries of senior staff including the CEO's is causing a flow of workforce from the public to the private sector. Before these issues create a vacuum in the availability of experienced people, the government must take radical actions.

Another radical step that would potentially increase the efficiency in energy sector, facilitate the functioning of the system and speed up decision making process is to combine Ministry of Petroleum and Ministry of Electricity and Renewable Energy under an umbrella, such as Ministry of Energy, and also create an independent energy regulator.

Last but not least, its geographic position at the crossroads of three continents provides Egypt great potential to have a larger share in international trade of oil and natural gas and be part of a wider electricity grid network. With its strategic location, existing infrastructure and many assets, Egypt is a good candidate to become a strategic gathering and dispatching as well as an economic center for inter-regional energy trade.

Concluding Remarks

More than five years after the overthrow of then president Hosni Mubarak, the socio-political turmoil and volatility in Egypt still remain in place.

Addressing the challenges mentioned in previous sections and seizing the opportunities in the energy sector will require a comprehensive strategy, enhanced cooperation with stakeholders, use of advanced technology, improved data management, and interactions with other sectors of the economy. An integrated national energy strategy that takes into account the characteristics and requirements of the different energy subsectors is a necessity.

The future of Egypt's energy sector will depend on the depth, timing and implementation of government policies as well as the ability of Cairo to meet its commitments. Decisions and choices made today will shape the country's energy future and the ability of the government to convert challenges into opportunities.

There is no doubt that gas production will match increasing domestic demand in the future, provided that right policies are developed and implemented. There are plenty of good perspectives for new discoveries. The government actions for fostering an attractive investment climate for potential investors will be crucial. Accelerating payments to foreign partners, issuing new bidding rounds, signing new agreements, intensifying field development projects, revising energy prices, and developing unconventional resources combined with an adequate framework and aggressive push for demand side energy management need to be among those actions. Otherwise the current momentum could fade out and the country's energy sector may enter into a twilight zone.

Notes

[1] M. Elmeshad, Egypt's Ad Hoc Economy, *Carnegie Endowment*, 20 July 2016, http://carnegieendowment.org/sada/64140, accessed 3 April 2017.
[2] *Al-Ahram*, 25 February 2016, 10.
[3] Two major incidents have put the tourism industry back on the brink. In September 2015, 10 Mexican tourists were mistakenly killed by the army, who had confused them for terrorists, in the Western Desert. In October 2015, a plane carrying Russian tourists crashed in Sinai, killing all its 224 passengers.
[4] This is despite the official opening in August 2015 of $8 billion new stretch of the canal.
[5] Egypt's fiscal year runs from July 1 to June 30. It refers to the start of the fiscal year, e.g., data in 2014 refer to Fiscal Year 2014/2015 (from 1 July 2014 to 30 June 2015).
[6] The loans from Saudi Arabia, Kuwait and the UAE helped to repay more than $2 billion to international players in 2015.
[7] Amr Adly, Egypt's Oil Dependency and Political Discontent, *Carnegie Endowment for International Peace*, 2 August 2016, http://carnegieendowment.org/2016/08/02/egypt-s-oil-dependency-and-political-discontent-pub-64224.
[8] Egypt currently is spending almost $400 million every month on energy imports to meet domestic demand, according to foreign trade statistics.
[9] Fuel subsidies generated large profits for the cement, fertilizer, iron and steel, glass, and aluminum industries but their capacity to create large numbers of jobs was limited.
[10] David Pearce and Ronald Edwards, Energy policy in a price-regulated developing economy: A study of Egypt, *Journal of Economic Studies*, 1984, v.11, n.1, 3 – 26.
[11] Heavily subsidized LPG was excluded.
[12] Diesel fuel is used by most of public transport of Egypt and trucks.
[13] OME (2011), MEP Egypt, *Observatoire Méditerranéen de l'Energie*, Paris.
[14] *EEHC Annual Report*, various years.
[15] *MEES*, 3 June 2016.

16 With a total capacity of 14.4 GW, these plants will be constructed at three different locations by Siemens by 2018 with a total cost of $6.6 bn. See, *African Energy*, iss. 322, 28 April 2016.
17 Both LNG complexes are tolling facilities. The contractor constructs, owns and operates the plant in return for a processing tariff from which it recovers its costs and makes a return. The upstream supply partners retain ownership of the gas and the LNG.
18 It is owned and operated by SEGAS (80% share - Union Fenosa Gas, 10% - EGAS and 10% - EGPC).
19 Beheira Natural Gas Liquefaction Company owns one liquefaction train with a design capacity of 3.6 Mt/yr. Shareholders are EGAS (12%), EGPC (12%), BG (35.5%), Petronas (35.5%) and GDF (5%). Idku Natural Gas Liquefaction Company owns the second train with a design capacity of 3.6 Mt/yr. The shareholders are EGAS (12%), EGPC (12%), BG (38%) and Petronas (38%).
20 *MEES*, 3 June 2016, 3.
21 The Government is in arbitration with Union Fenosa Gas, operator of the Damietta LNG plant, over the lack of feed gas.
22 *MEES*, 3 June 2016.
23 Imports come from various origins (Qatar, reloads from Europe, etc.) as well as from the excess gas capacity from the FSRU moored in Aqaba, Jordan.
24 The government signed a 5-year deal with Norway's Hoegh LNG for a floating LNG import terminal. The Gallant FSRU is moored at the port of Ain Sokhna.
25 The first one was chartered from Norway's Hoegh with a capacity of 5.7 bcm/yr and the second one from BW Group with 7.7 bcm/yr.
26 USGS, Assessment of Undiscovered Oil and Gas Resources of the Nile Delta Basin Province, Eastern Mediterranean, *Fact Sheet 2010-3027*, May 2010.
27 *Egypt Oil & Gas Newsletter*, 4 July 2015, 22.
28 A reserve of gas that has been discovered but remains undeveloped due to commercial, technological or logistical reasons,
29 *Egypt Oil and Gas Newsletter*, December 2014, 27.
30 Following the fourth drilling operation, the resource estimate is revised upwards to 906 bcm (32 Tcf) in mid-2016. How much of the estimated gas in place amount is recoverable is not yet made publicly available.
31 More specifically it is a lower-middle Miocene carbonate build-up, potentially charged by biogenic gas from Tertiary source rock.
32 The field is estimated to hold 70-80 bcm of gas in place. In September 2015, Eni (in partnership with BP) has begun production from its Nooros discovery in the Nile Delta. It is currently producing 8.6 mcm of gas, 3000 barrels of condensate and 1500 barrels of NGL per day from four wells (Egypt Oil and Gas, June 2016, 5). Production is expected to reach a capacity of around 3.5 bcm/yr by mid-2016. MEES, 59, 9, 4 March 2016.
33 BP holds a 50% stake in the Lease, and Eni, through its subsidiary IEOC, holds 50%.
34 *Egypt Oil and Gas Newsletter*, 4 July 2015.

35 When gas prices failed to keep up with increasing upstream costs driven largely by oil prices almost a decade from 2005 to 2014, the resulting squeeze on margins caused operators to cease or delay field development activities due to inadequate returns.
36 For years foreign companies operating in Egypt received no more than $2.65/MMBtu for the gas they produced. This fixed price became a major obstacle to develop natural gas projects in the country as it made some of the projects economically unviable.
37 For more details, see *Arab Oil & Gas, No 1027*, 1 July 2014.
38 In March 2015, the Ministry of Petroleum and BP agreed that the company would be paid $3 to $4.1/MMBtu for the gas produced from its West Nile Delta project. The project was delayed for several years partly because of the lack of agreement between the two parties about a gas price. The same month the government increased the price of gas RWE DEA Egypt will receive for the gas produced at the Disouq fields to $3.5/MMBtu, and to $3.95/MMBtu for the gas produced by BG from new developments. In order to encourage and speed up its upstream activities the Ministry of Petroleum signed in July 2015 an agreement with Eni that revised up the price of gas Eni would receive to a maximum of $5.88/MMBtu and a minimum of $4/MMBtu, depending on the volumes produced. In June 2016, the Ministry agreed with Shell and Apache on $4.6/MMtu instead of $2.9 for the price of gas at the Apollonia field in the Western Desert.
39 Global gas prices have been affected partially by the fall in oil prices, weak gas demand in key gas markets such as Europe and Asia, and excess LNG capacity.
40 Today, the majority of natural gas produced in Egypt comes from the fields in the Mediterranean Sea. Many of those fields suffer from steep decline rates. The decline rate at currently producing fields is argued to be more than 10%.
41 These include the Apollonia field in the Western Desert (Shell-Apache), the Nooros field (Eni) etc.
42 The North Alexandria project was scheduled to come into production by mid-2014, producing up to 25.5 mcm/d but it was halted in November 2011 due to the unstable political situation. Environmental and local community concerns prevented access to onshore facilities, which in turn forced to move it to another location. The project resumed in July 2014.
43 Press release, 12 January 2016.
44 It remains unclear whether those volumes refer to gross production or marketed production.
45 The two offshore concessions North Alexandria and West Mediterranean Deepwater are also referred as the West Nile Delta (WND) project. BP operates it with its associate RWE Dea holding.
46 Various press releases, BP. First gas output will be around 15 mcm/d rising to the 34 mcm/d plateau by the end of 2019.

⁴⁷ Latest Development of the Egyptian Gas Industry, *Cedigaz*, 15 June 2015. http://blog.cedigaz.org/latest-developments-egyptian-gas-industry/#more-1429

⁴⁸ The project is operated by Burullus Gas Company, the joint venture between British Gas (25%), Petronas (25%) and EGPC (50%).

⁴⁹ Almost all output has been dedicated to the domestic market since 2013.

⁵⁰ About 2.5 bcm/yr on average in 2015; MEES, 59, 3, 22 January 2016.

⁵¹ Reuters, BG Egypt suspends some development wells after price disagreement, 22 March 2016.

⁵² *Daily News Egypt*, 23 March 2016.

⁵³ *Egypt Oil and Gas Newsletter*, 5 June 2016. .

⁵⁴ The field is located in deep water adjacent to the Cypriot maritime border and is the first deep water Miocene carbonate discovery in the basin. Eni will receive 40% for cost recovery, while the remaining 60% will be divided 69%-31% between Egas and Eni respectively. Once Eni recovers all incurred cost, Egas' percentage will move to 40% of total production. (Zohr's financial agreement & seismic data, *Egypt Oil and Gas Newsletter*, 27 October 2015).

⁵⁵ MEES, 59, 1, 8 January 2016.

⁵⁶ BP sees early gas in 2018 from Egyptian Atoll field, Naturalgaseurope.com, 20 June 2016.

⁵⁷ Latest Development of the Egyptian Gas Industry, *Cediguz*, 15 June 2015. http://blog.cedigaz.org/latest-developments-egyptian-gas-industry/#more-1429

⁵⁸ For instance, in 2014, Apache had 35 rigs operating in its concessions in the Western Desert, which was equivalent to 50% of the existent rigs at that time in the Egyptian market, *Daily News Egypt*, 31 May 2014.

⁵⁹ Regarding flaring, possible bottlenecks in the network may exist. Recovered gases from the fields cannot be connected because of the high pressure (the network is 70 bar).

Bibliography

Abadi, J. 1995. Israel and Turkey: From overt to covert relations, *The Journal of Conflict Studies*, v.15, n.2, https://journals.lib.unb.ca/index.php/JCS/article/view/4548.

Adamides, C. and O. Christou 2015. Beyond Hegemony: Cyprus, energy securitization and the emergence of new regional security complexes, in S. N. Litsas and.A. Tziampiris, eds. *The Eastern Mediterranean in Transition: Multipolarity, Politics and Power*. Surrey: Routledge Publishing Co., 179-190.

Adamides, C. and O. Christou. 2015. Energy security and the transformation of regional securitization relations in the Eastern Mediterranean, in S. Katsikides & Pavlos. I. Koktsidis, eds. *Societies in Transition: Economic, Political and Security Transformations in Contemporary Europe*. London: Springer, pp. 189-205.

Adly, A. 2016. Egypt's Oil Dependency and Political Discontent, Carnegie Endowment for International Peace, 2 August, http://carnegieendowment.org/2016/08/02/egypt-s-oil-dependency-and-political-discontent-pub-64224.

Ajami, F. 2012. *The Syrian Rebellion*, Stanford: Hoover Institution Press.

Alvarez-Ossaro, I. Spring 2012. "Syrian Struggling Civil Society", *Middle East Quarterly*, pp. 23-32.

Andoura, S. and C. d'Oultremont. 2013. The role of gas in the external dimension of the EU energy transition, Notre Europe. Jacques Delors Institute Policy Paper v. 79.

Athanassopoulou, E. (2011). Turkey and Greece in Nicholas Kitchen, ed., *Turkey's Global Strategy*. London: LSE Ideas, 17-18, http://www.lse.ac.uk/IDEAS/publications/reports/pdf/SR007/greece.pdf.

Aydın, M. and K. Yfantis (eds.) 2004. *Turkish-Greek Relations: The Security Dilemma in the Aegean*. London and New York: Routledge.

Ayman, G. S. 2004. Negotiation and deterrence in asymmetrical power situations: The Turkish-Greek case, in M. Aydın and K. Yfantis, eds. *Turkish-Greek Relations: The Security Dilemma in the Aegean*. London and New York: Routledge, 213–244.

Bartholomees, J. B., Jr., ed. 2010. *The US Army War College Guide to National Security Issues: Theory of War and Strategy*, v.1, 4th ed. Carlisle: Strategic Studies Institute, 126-134.

Brom, S. 2011. The Israeli-Turkish relationship, in W. B. Quandt, ed., *Troubled Triangle: The United States, Turkey and Israel in the New Middle East*. Charlottesville, VA: Just World Books, 1-160.

Bruneton, A., Konophagos, E., and A. Foscolos, A. 2011. Economic and Geopolitical Importance of Eastern Mediterranean gas fields for Greece and the EU Emphasis on the Probable Natural Gas Deposits Occurring in the Libyan Sea within the Exclusive Economic Zone of Greece. *Mineral Wealth*, v.160, 7-22.

Bruneton, A., Konofagos, E. and A. Foscolos. 2012. Cretan gas fields: A new perspective for Greece's hydrocarbon resources, Pytheas Market Focus, 2012, http://images.derstandard.at/2013/08/21/greece_crete.pdf.

Bryant, R. and C. Yakinthou. 2012. *Cypriot Perceptions of Turkey*. Istanbul: TESEV Publications.

Buzan, B. 1988. The Southeast Asian Security Complex, *Contemporary Southeast Asia*, v. 10, n. 1, 1–16.

Buzan, B. 1991. *People, States & Fear: An Agenda for International Security Studies in the Post-Cold War Era*, 2nd edition, Hemel Hempstead: Harvester Wheatsheaf.

Buzan, B. and O. Waever. 2003. *Regions and Powers: The Structure of International Security*. Cambridge, Cambridge: University Press, 1-598.

Cağaptay, S. and T. Evans. 2012. The unexpected vitality of Turkish-Israeli trade relations, The Washington Institute for Near East Policy, *Research Notes No. 16*, http://www.washingtoninstitute.org/uploads/Documents/pubs/ResearchNote16.pdf.

Central Bank of Cyprus, Monetary Policy Report, 2002. http://www.centralbank.gov.cy/nqcontent.cfm?a_id=10364&lang=en.

Central Bank of Cyprus, Monetary Policy Reports 2002 and 2010, http://www.centralbank.gov.cy/nqcontent.cfm?a_id=9837&lang=en.

Cha, V. 2000. Abandonment, entrapment, and neoclassical realism in Asia: The United States, Japan and Korea, *International Studies Quarterly*, v. 44, n. 2, 262.

Cobb, S. 1914. *The Real Turk*. Boston: The Pilgrim Press.

Cohen, A. and K. DeCorla-Souza. 2011. *Eurasian Energy and Israeli Choices*. Jerusalem: The Begin-Sadat Center for Strategic Studies, Mideast Security and Policy Studies, n. 88, 32-34.

Conant, M. 1981. Resources and conflict: Oil-the likely contingencies, *The Adelphi Papers*, v.21, n.167, 45-50.

Constantinou, C. and Olivier Richmond. 2005. *The Long Mile of Empire: Power, Legitimation and the UK Bases in Cyprus, Mediterranean Politics*, v.10, n.1, 65-84.

Christou, O. and C. Adamides. 2013. Energy securitization and desecuritization in the new Middle East, *Security Dialogue*, CA: Sage Publishing Journals. v. 44, n.5-6, 507-522.

Cropsey, S. and E. Brown. 2014. Energy: The West's Strategic Opportunity in the Eastern Mediterranean, *Hudson Institute Paper No. 20*, 1-47, https://hudson.org/content/researchattachments/attachment/1443/2014_12_02_hudson_report_eastern_med_final_single_pages.pdf.

Davis, B. 1982. Geopolitics, world resources, and survival: A role playing game, *Geopolitics*, v. 81, n. 2, 56-61.

Davutoğlu, A. 2010. Στρατηγικό Βάθος: Η Διεθνής Θέση της Τουρκίας [*Strategic Depth: Turkey's Place in the World*]. Athens, Poiotita.

Dennison, S. and D. Pardijs, 2016. The world according to Europe's insurgent parties: Putin, migration and people power, European Council on Foreign Relations, 27 June: 1-3, 19-20, http://www.ecfr.eu/publications/summary/the_world_according_to_europes_insurgent_parties7055.

Dokos, T. and P. J. Tsakonas. 2016. Greek-Turkish relations in the post-cold war era, in C. Kollias & G. Gulnuk-Senesen, eds, *Greece and Turkey in the 21st Century: Conflict or Cooperation*. New York: Nova Science Publications, 9–35.

Eaton, R. 1987. Soviet Relations with Greece and Turkey, Hellenic Foundation for Defence and Foreign Policy, Occasional Papers, No. 2.

EIA (Energy Information Administration). 2013. Overview of oil and gas in the Eastern Mediterranean region, 1-29, https://www.eia.gov/beta/international/analysis_includes/regions_of_interest/Eastern_Mediterranean/eastern-mediterranean.pdf.

Ehrlich, T. 1974. *Cyprus 1958-1967: International Crisis and the Role of Law*. London: Oxford University Press.

Eksi, M. 2010. The role of energy in Turkish Foreign Policy, *The Turkish Yearbook of International Relations*, v. 41, 62-65.

Energy Security, International Energy Agency, 2013. http://www.iea.org/topics/energysecurity/.

Esposito, J. L. & Voll, J. O. 1996. *Islam and Democracy*, New York: Oxford University Press.

European Union. Declaration of 17 November, EC Bulletin 1983/11.

Fabry, N. and S. Zeghni. 2002. Foreign direct investment in Russia: How the investment Climate matters, *Communist and Post-Communist Studies*, v.35, n.3, September, 293-294.

Faustmann, H. 2001. The United Nations and the Internationalisation of the Cyprus Conflict 1949-1958, in J. Ker-Lindsay/Oliver Richmond, eds., *Promoting Peace and Development in Cyprus over Four Decades*. Houndmills, NY: Palgrave, 3-49.

Foscolos, A. 2014. Implementation of the Greek Exclusive Zone and its financial and geopolitical benefits, http://probeinternational.org/library/wp-content/uploads/2011/10/19052011_Foscolos_NEW1.pdf.

Foscolos, A. E., Konophagos, E., and A. Bruneton. 2012. The occurrence of converging plates, mud flow volcanoes and accretionary prism complexes in the Mediterranean Ridge. Their relationship to possible hydrocarbon accumulation offshore Crete. A new prospective for Greece's oil and natural resources. *Mineral Wealth*, v.165, 7-26.

Fouskas, V. 2003. US Foreign Policy in the Greater Middle East during the Cold War and the Position of Cyprus, in H. Richter and V. Fouskas, eds., *Cyprus and Europe: The Long Way Back*, Mannheim and Möhnesee: Bibliopolis, 73-88.

Giannakopoulos, A. 2016. The Eastern Mediterranean in the Light of Recent Energy Developments and Their Impact, in *Energy Cooperation and Security in the Eastern Mediterranean; A Seismic Shift towards Peace or Conflict?*, Research Paper No.8, 11 (February). Tel Aviv University, https://dacenter.tau.ac.il/publications.

Gitmez, A., Yalman, G., Ulusoy, K. and C. Ustun. 2006. METU. Change in Cyprus in the Context of Europeanization, survey and research funded by The Scientific and Technological Research Council of Turkey, Ankara: METU Center for European Studies, http://ces.metu.edu.tr/research-and-publications/completed-projects/cyprus.

Goodwin, J. 2011. Why we were surprised (again) by the Arab Spring, *Swiss Political Science Review*, 2011, v.17, n.4, 452-456.

Gressel, G. 2015. Russia's quiet military revolution and what it means for Europe. The European Council on Foreign Relations Policy Brief, October.

Günaydın, E. B. 2014. Can South-Eastern Mediterranean Gas be a supply for the EU?, Istituto Affari Internazionali, IAI Working Papers 14/17.

Hamatsou, A. 1999. The Russian Presence in Cyprus, (In Greek), *Sygchrona Themata*, vols.68-69-70, July 1998 – Mars 1999, 262-275.

Hannah, J. 1989. At arms length: Soviet-Syrian relations in the Gorbachev era, The Washington Institute for Near East Policy Paper No. 18, 5-8.

Hannay, D. 2005. *Cyprus, The Search for a Solution.* London: I.B. Tauris.

Hatina, M. & Kupferschmidt, U. M. (eds.). 2012. *The Muslim Brothers* (Hebrew), Tel Aviv: HaKibutz HaMeuhad.

Henderson, S. 2013. Natural gas export options for Israel and Cyprus, The German Marshall Fund of the United States, September, http://www.gmfus.org/wp-content/blogs.dir/1/files_mf/1378838051Henderson_NatGasExportOptions_Sep13_web.pdf.

Heraclides, A. 2010. *The Greek-Turkish Conflict in the Aegean: Imagined Enemies.* Basingstoke and New York: Palgrave Macmillan, 167-193.

Hever, H. 2007. *Toward the Longed-for Shore: The Sea in Hebrew Culture and Modern Hebrew Literature.* Jerusalem: Van Leer and Hakibbutz Hameuchad Publishers, 2007, 11 (Hebrew).

Hoffmeister, F. 2006. *Legal Aspects of the Cyprus Problem.* Leiden: Martinus Nijhoff Publishers.

Huber, D. and N. Tocci. 2013. Behind the scenes of the Turkish-Israeli breakthrough, Istituto Affari Internazionali, IAI Working Paper No. 13/15, http://www.iai.it/pdf/DocIAI/iaiwp1315.pdf.

Huysmans, J. 1998. The Question of the Limit: Desecuritisation and the Aesthetics of Horror in Political Realism, *Millennium*, v.27, n.3, 569-589.

Inan, Y. and M. Pınar Gözen. 2009. Turkey's maritime boundary relations, in: M. Kibaroglu, ed., *Eastern Mediterranean Countries and Issues.* Ankara: Foreign Policy Institute, 153-211.

Inbar, E. 2013. The strategic implications for Israel, in E. Inbar, ed., *The Arab Spring, Democracy and Security: Domestic and International Ramifications.* Oxon and New York: Routledge, 145-165.

Israel Ministry of Foreign Affairs, Information Department (Middle East, Religious Affairs, Political Research Center), Christian Communities in the Middle East, 2013, 17 March (Hebrew).

Jarosiewicz, A. 2015. The Southern Gas Corridor. The Azerbaijani-Turkish project becomes part of the game between Russia and the EU, Centre for Eastern Studies, n.53, 9-10.

Kaliber, A. 2013. Re-imagining Cyprus: the rise of regionalism in Turkey's security Lexicon, in T. Diez and N. Tocci, *Cyprus: A Conflict at the Crossroads.* Manchester and New York: Manchester University Press, 105-123.

Kamenopoulos, S., Agioutantis, Z. and K. Komnitsas. 2015. A framework for sustainable mining of Rare Earth Elements, in Borges De Lima and W. Leal Filho, eds., *Rare Earths Industry: Technological, Economic, and Environmental Implications*. Amsterdam, Elsevier Publication, 111-120.

Katz, M. 2004. Exploiting rivalries: Putin's foreign policy. *Current History*, v.103, n.675, October, 337-341.

Khadduri, W. 2012. East Mediterranean Gas: Opportunities and Challenge, *Mediterranean Politics*, v.17, n.1, 111-117.

Klapsis, A. 2015. An unholy alliance, the European far-right and Putin's Russia, *Wilfried Martens Centre for European Studies*, 1-74, https://www.martenscentre.eu/sites/default/files/publication-files/far-right-political-parties-in-europe-and-putins-russia.pdf.

Kim, Y. and S. Blank. 2016. The new great game of Caspian energy in 2013-14: 'Turk stream', Russia and Turkey, *Journal of Balkan and Near Eastern Studies*, v.18, n.1,1-19.

Klare, M. 2001. The new geography of conflict, *Foreign Affairs*, May/June, 49-61.

Lahoud, N. 2005. *Political Thought in Islam*, London & New York: Routledge.

Lake, D. and P. Morgan. 1997. The new regionalism in security affairs, in David Lake and Patrick Morgan, *Regional Orders: Building Security in a New World*. University Park, PA: Pennsylvania State University Press.

Le Billon, P. 2004. The geopolitics economy of resource wars, *Geopolitics*, 2004, v.9, n.1, 1-28.

Lederer, I. 1974. Historical Introduction, in Ivo Lederer and Wayne Vucinich, eds. *The Soviet Union and the Middle East. The Post-World War II Era*. Stanford University, Stanford, CA: Hoover Institute Publications, 2-3.

Lijphart, A. 1971. Comparative politics and the comparative method, *The American Political Science Review*, v.65, n.3, September, 682-693.

Liuhto, K. 2001. Russian Gas and Oil Giants Conquer Markets in the West: Evidence on the Internationalization of Gazprom and LUKoil, *Journal of East-West Business*, v.7, n.3, 31-72.

Liuhto, K. T. and S. S. Majuri, 2014. Outward foreign direct investment from Russia: A literature review, *Journal of East-West Business*, v.20, n.4, 198-224.

Lordos, A., Kaymak, E. and N. Tocci. 2004. Is there a still hope for a comprehensive settlement? Friends of Cyprus Report No.48, 5-20.

Lordos, A. 2005. Rational agent or unthinking follower? , https://ecpr.eu/Filestore/PaperProposal/b67d4879-d016-4fa1-8a15-d3ac021a937b.pdf.

Lordos, A. Kaymak, E. and N. Tocci. 2009. A People's Peace in Cyprus. Brussels: Centre for European Policy Studies (CEPS), issue 2, 21-118.

Makarychev, A.S. 2009. Russia in the Mediterranean region:(Re)sources of influence, *The Yearbook of the European Institute of the Mediterranean (IEMed)*,169-172.

Mann, S. 2001 March. The Greek-Turkish Dispute in the Aegean Sea: Its ramifications for NATO and the Prospects for Resolution, M.A. Thesis, National Security Affairs, U.S Naval Postgraduate School, Monterey, California, https://www.hsdl.org/?view&did=450238.

Ma'oz, M. 1989. *Asad – The Sphinx of Damascus*, London & New York: Grove Press.

Ma'oz, M. 2016. Strategic Upheavals in the Mediterranean and Middle Eastern countries since the "Arab Spring"; *Journal of Balkan and Near Eastern Studies*, vol. 18, No. 4, pp. 352-350.

Mazis, I. 2012. Ο Γεωστρατηγικός Άξονας Ισραήλ-Κύπρου-Ελλάδος [The geostrategic axis Israel-Cyprus-Greece], *Foreign Affairs*, The Hellenic Edition, 6 April, http://foreignaffairs.gr/articles/68736/ioannis-th-mazis/o-geostratigikos-aksonas-israilkyproy-ellados?page=3

Mekel, A. 2016. A new geopolitical bloc is born in the Eastern Mediterranean: Israel, Greece and Cyprus, BESA Center Perspectives Paper No. 329, 16 February.

Menkiszak, M. 2016. The Russian-American declaration on Syria: A success for Moscow, *Centre for Eastern Studies*, 24.

Michas, T. 2002. *Unholy Alliance. Greece and Milosovic' Serbia*. College Station, TX: Texas A&M University Press, 1-200.

Midkiff, A. 2012. Shifting dynamics in the Eastern Mediterranean: The developing relationship between Greece and Israel, Perspectives on Business and Economics, v.30, 45-53.

Minagias, C. 2012. Οι Επίσημοι Τουρκικοί Χάρτες Αμφισβήτησης της Ελληνικής Α.Ο.Ζ. [The official Turkish maps which dispute the Greek EEZ], *GeoStrategy*, 28 April, http://www.geostrategy.gr/pdf/20120428%20Official%20Turkish%20Maps.pdf.

The Military Balance, Chapter Four: Europe. IISS - International Institute for Strategic Studies, NY: Francis & Taylor, 2015, 57-158.

MIT Energy Institute. 2013. Interim report for the study: Monetization pathways for Cyprus. Economics for Project Development Options, 1-87, http://energy.mit.edu/wp-content/uploads/2013/10/MITEI-RP-2013-001.pdf.

Morgenthau, H. 1993. *Politics among Nations: The Struggle for Power and Peace*. New York, NY: McGraw-Hill Inc.

Moussali A. 2003. *The Islamic Quest for Democracy, Pluralism and Human Rights*, University Press of Florida.

Nastos, P. 2013. Greek-Israeli-Cyprus military and security relations: A preview, *Research Institute for European and American Studies*, 15 December, 407-427, http://www.rieas.gr/research-areas/2014-07-30-08-58-27/greek-israel-studies/2077-greek-israelicyprus-military-and-security-relations-a-preview.

North Sea Continental Shelf Cases (Federal Republic of Germany v. Denmark; Federal Republic of Germany v. The Netherlands), ICJ Rep. 1969, 3.

Ntokos. T. 2011. "Ένταση στην Ανατολική Μεσόγειο: Το Γεωπολιτικό 'Τετράγωνο' Ελλάδας-Κύπρου-Ισραήλ-Τουρκίας" [Tension in the Eastern Mediterranean: The geopolitical 'rectangle' of Greece-Cyprus-Israel-Turkey], ELIAMEP, Working Paper No. 23, 1-11, http://www.eliamep.gr/wp-content/uploads/2011/10/23_2011__WORKING_PAPER___Thanos_Dokos.pdf.

Ofrat, G. 1990. *Turning a Back on the Sea: Images of the Place in Israeli Art Literature*. Tel Aviv, Amanut Israel (Hebrew).

Oğurlu, E. 2012. Rising tensions in the Eastern Mediterranean: Implications for Turkish Foreign Policy, *Instituto Affari Internazionali Working Papers* 12/04, March 2012, 1-15, http://www.iai.it/sites/default/files/iaiwp1204.pdf.

O'Rurke, R. 2016. Maritime Territorial and Exclusive Economic Zone (EEZ) Disputes Involving China: Issues for Congress, Report Prepared for Members and Committees of U.S Congress, Congressional Research Service, 27 April.

Organization for Economic Cooperation and Development (OECD), 2011 ed. 2. Environmental Outlook to 2050: Climate Change Chapter. http://www.oecd.org/env/cc/49082173.pdf.

Pearce, D. and R. Edwards, Energy policy in a price-regulated developing economy: A study of Egypt, *Journal of Economic Studies*, 1984, v.11, n.1, 3–26.

Pelto, E., Vahtra, P. and K. Liuhto. 2003. *Cyprus Investment Flows to Central and Eastern Europe - Russia's Direct and Indirect Investments via Cyprus to CEE*, Turun Kauppakorkeakoulu: Turku School of Economics and Business Administration, 11-16.

Peters, S. 2004. Coercive western energy security strategies: 'resource wars' as a new threat to global security, *Geopolitics*, 2004, v.9, n.1, 187-212.

Phidias, P. 2002. *The Role of Cyprus in Inward Investment in Russia, Central and Eastern Europe*. Cyprus: Pricewaterhouse Coopers.

Pisiotis, A. 2001. Greece and Turkey in the Concentric Circles of Russian Post-Cold War Foreign Policy; Geopolitics, Oil and Religion, in C. Yiallourides and P. Tsakonas, eds., *Greece and Turkey after the end of the Cold War*. Athens: Caratzas Publisher, 409-422.

Proedrou, F. 2012. Re-conceptualizing the energy and security complex in the Eastern Mediterranean, *Cyprus Review*, v.24, n.2, 15-28.

Ratner, M. 2016. Natural Gas Discoveries in the Eastern Mediterranean. Congressional Research Service. 15 August, 13, https://fas.org/sgp/crs/mideast/R44591.pdf.

Rosen, M., ed. 2008. *Homelands and Diasporas: Greeks, Jews and their Migrations*. London, I. B. Tauris, 35-81.

Rustad, S. A. and H. Malmin Binningsbø. 2012. A Price Worth Fighting for? Natural Resources and Conflict Recurrence, *Journal of Peace Research*, v.49, n.4, 531–546.

Schofield, C. F. and M.A. Pratt. 2000. Cooperation in the absence of maritime boundary agreements: The purpose and value of joint development, in *The Aegean Sea* 2000, Proceedings of International Symposium on the Aegean Sea (Bodrum, Turkey, 5-7 May, 2000), 152-164.

Schweller, R. 1994. Bandwagoning for profit: bringing the revisionist state back in, *International Security*, v.19, n. 1 (Summer), 72-107.

Schweitzer, Y. and Goldstein-Ferber, S. 2005. *Al-Qaeda and Internationalization of Suicide Terrorism*, Tel Aviv: JCSS.

Schweitzer, Y. and Oreg, A. 2014. *Al-Qaeda's Odyssey to the Global Jihad*, , Tel Aviv, INSS.

Sener, A. 2006. Turkish-Russian relations after the Cold War 1992-2002, *Turkish Studies*, v.7, n.3, September, 337-364.

Sherr, J. 2015. The new East-West discord, Russian objectives, Western Interests, *Clingendael Institute Report*, December, 1-76, https://www.clingendael.nl/publicatie/new-east-west-discord-russian-objectives-western-interests.

Shlykov, P. 2015. Russian Foreign Policy in the Eastern Mediterranean since 1991, in S. Litsas and A. Tziampiris, eds., *The Eastern Mediterranean in Transition. Multipolarity, Politics and Power*, Farnham-Surrey: Ashgate, 31-32.

Siddi, M. 2015. The EU-Russia gas relationship. New projects, new disputes? *The Finnish Institute of International Affairs Briefing Journal* v. 183.

Siman, B. 2016. Russia seizing initiative in Eastern Med., Geopolitical Intelligence Services.

Simon, L. 2016. Sea power and US forward presence in the Middle East: Retrenchment in perspective, *Geopolitics*, v.21, n.1, 115-147.

Sözen, A., Christou, A. Lordos, A. and E. Kaymak. 2015. Solving the Cyprus Problem: Hopes and Fears. Cyprus: Interpeace /Cyprus 2015 Initiative, v. 85.

Stavris, G. 2012. The new energy triangle of Cyprus-Greece-Israel: casting a net for Turkey?, *Turkish Policy Quarterly*, v.11, n.2, 87–102.

Stergiou, A. 2007. Soviet policy toward Cyprus, *Cyprus Review*, v.19, n.2, fall, 83-106.

Stergiou, A. 2012. Russian policy in the eastern Mediterranean and the implications for EU external action, European Union's Institute for Security Studies (ISS)-online-publications-opinions, http://www.iss.europa.eu/publications/detail/article/russian-policy-in-the-eastern-mediterranean-and-the-implications-for-eu-external-action/.

Stergiou, A. 2013. Geopolitics: Greece, Cyprus and Israel change the military balance in the Mediterranean, *Geopolitical Information Service-GIS*.

Stergiou, A. 2014. The Exceptional Case of the British Military Bases on Cyprus, *Middle Eastern Studies*, v. 51, n. 2, 285-300.

Stergiou, A. 2015. The Communist party of Cyprus and the Soviet policy in the Eastern Mediterranean, *Modern Greek Studies Yearbook*, University of Minnesota, v.30-31, 2014-2015, 199-222. I found this pagination at their website.

Stergiou, A. 2016. Turkey-Cyprus-Israel relations and the Cyprus conflict, *Journal of Balkan and Near Eastern Studies, Turkey-Cyprus-Israel relations and the Cyprus Conflict*, v.18, n.4, 375-392.

Strachota, K. and M. Chudziak. 2016. Turkey and the EU: The play for a security zone in Syria. *Centre for Eastern Studies Analyses*, 10 February.

Sun, D. 2009. Brothers indeed: Syria-Iran quasi-alliance revisited, *Journal of Middle Eastern and Islamic Studies* (in Asia), v.3, n.2, 67-80.

Tagliapetra, S. 2013. Towards a new Eastern Mediterranean corridor? Natural gas developments. Between market opportunities and geopolitical risks, *Fondazione Eni Enrico Mattei Papers*, v. 23.

Tank, P. 2015. Cyprus: a note on security guarantees and threat perceptions, *The Turkish Yearbook of International Relations*, XXXV, 169–176.

Tekin, A. and P.A. Williams. 2011. *Geo-Politics of the Euro-Asia energy nexus. The European Union, Russia and Turkey*, Basingstoke, Hampshire: Palgrave Macmillan, 1-230.

Tessler, M. April 2002. "Islam and Democracy in the Middle East", *Comparative Policies*, ,pp. 337-354.

Trenin, D. 2015. Putin's Syria gambit aims at something bigger than Syria. Carnegie Analysis, 13 October.

Tsakiris, T. 2010. Greek-Russian Relations, in G. Valinakis, ed., *Greece's Foreign and European Policy 1990-2010*. Athens: Sideris, 2010, (In Greek), 147-172.

Tsardanidis C. and Y. Nicolaou. 1998. Cyprus Foreign and Security Policy: Options and Challenges, in S. Stavridis, T. Veremis, T. Couloumbis and N. Waites, eds., *The Foreign Policies of the European Union's Mediterranean States and Applicant Countries in the 1990s*, Basingsstoke, Hampshire: University of Reading European and International Studies, 171-194.

Tziampiris, A. 2013. Greek Foreign Policy in the Shadow of the Debt Crisis: Continuity and New Directions, in P. Sklias and N. Tzifakis eds., *Greece's Horizons. Reflecting on the Country's Assets and Capabilities*. Athens: Konstantinos Karamanlis Institute for Democracy, 1-259.

Tziarras, Z. 2013. Economic crisis in Cyprus: repercussions, Turkey and the Turkish-Cypriots, *e-International Relations*, 3 January, http://www.e-ir.info/2013/01/03/economic-crisis-in-cyprus-repercussions-turkey-and-the-turkish-cypriots/.

Tziarras, Z. 2015. The new geopolitical landscape in the Eastern Mediterranean: The Israeli perception, *Eastern Mediterranean Geopolitical Review*, v.1, 32-43.

Tziarras, Z. 2016. Turkey – the 'new Iran': Revolution and foreign policy, Academy for Strategic Analyses, Working Paper No. 52, July, http://www.acastran.org/%CE%BA%CE%B5%CE%B9%CE%BC%CE%B5%CE%BD%CE%B1htt ps://www.academia.edu/27282972/Turkey_-_the_new_Iran_Revolution_and_Foreign_Policy.

Tziarras, T. 2016. Israel-Cyprus-Greece: a 'comfortable' quasi-alliance, Mediterranean Politics, January, v.21, iss.3, 402-427. http://www.tandfonline.com/doi/abs/10.1 080/13629395.2015.1131450?journalCode=fmed20,

Tzifakis, N. 2002. Securitization and Desecuritization Dynamics in South-Eastern Europe (1992-1997), Lancaster University: Doctoral Dissertation, 4-29, 290-304.

United Nations, ed. 1987. Report of the World Commission on Environment and Development: Our Common Future, http://www.un-documents.net/wced-ocf.htm.

United Nations Development Program-UNDP, ed. 2012. Reconfiguring Global Governance-Effectiveness, Inclusiveness, and China's Global Role, http://www.undp.org/content/dam/china/docs/Publications/UNDP-CH_Global_Governance_Report_2013_EN.pdf.

US Energy Information Administration, Eastern Mediterranean Region, Full Report, August 15, 2013.

US Energy Information Administration-EIA, ed. International Energy Outlook, Chapter 2: Petroleum and other liquid fuels, 2016, http://www.eia.gov/forecasts/ieo/liquid_fuels.cfm.

United States Geological Survey S(USGS). Undiscovered oil and gas of the Nile Delta Basin, Eastern Mediterrane-an. Fact Sheet 2010-3027. February 2010.

United States Geological Survey (USGS). Assessment of undiscovered oil and gas resources of the Levant Basin Province, Eastern Mediterranean. Fact Sheet 2010-3014, March 2010.

United States Geological Survey (USGS). 2010. *Assessment of undiscovered oil and gas resources of the Nile Delta Basin Province, Eastern Mediterranean, Fact Sheet 2010-3027*, May 2010.

United States Geological Survey (USGS). *Undiscovered oil and gas of the Nile Delta Basin, Eastern Mediterrane-an. Fact Sheet 2010-3027*. February 2010.

Vogler, S. and E. V. Thompson. 2015. Gas discoveries in the Eastern Mediterranean: Implications for regional maritime security, The German Marshall Fund of the United States Policy Brief, March 2015.

Waever, O. 1995. Securitization-Desecuritization, in Lipschutz, R. ed., *On Security*. New York: Columbia University Press, 1-233.

Wæver, O. 1999. Securitizing Sectors? Reply to Eriksson, *Cooperation and Conflict*, v.34, n.3, 334-340.

Walt, S. 1987. *The Origins of Alliances*. Ithaca and London: Cornell University Press.

Waltz, K. 2010. *Theory of International Politics*. Long Grove, IL: Waveland Press Inc., 1-251.

Weil, P. 1989. The Law of Maritime Delimitation- Reflections, Cambridge University Press.

Whetten, L. 1971. *The Soviet Presence in the Eastern Mediterranean*. Washington: National Strategy Information Center, 1-50.

Yanik, L. K. 2007. Allies or Partners? An Appraisal of Turkey's Ties to Russia, 1991-2007, *East European Quarterly*, v.41, n.3, 349-367.

Zemach, S. 2015. Eastern Mediterranean Development 1: Levant Basin presents narrowing resource opportunities, Oil and Gas Journal, 4 June, http://www.ogj.com/articles/print/volume-113/issue-4/exploration-development/east-mediterranean-development-1-levant-basin-presents-narrowing-resource-opportunities.html.

Zenonas T. 2016. Israel-Cyprus-Greece: a 'comfortable' quasi-alliance, *Mediterranean Politics*, January, v.21, iss.3, 402-427, http://www.tandfonline.com/doi/abs/10.1080/13629395.2015.1131450?journalCode=fmed20.

Zhukov, Y. M. 2012. Trouble in the eastern Mediterranean: The coming dash for gas, *Foreign Affairs*, 20 March, https://www.foreignaffairs.com/articles/cyprus/2013-03-20/trouble-eastern-mediterranean-sea.

Zisser, E. 2003. The Mediterranean Idea in Syria and Lebanon: Between Territorial Nationalism and Pan-Arabism, *Mediterranean Historical Review*, v.18, n.1, June, 76-90.

Zisser, E. 2014. *Syria – Protest, Revolution & Civil War* (Hebrew), Tel Aviv: Tel Aviv University.

About the Authors

Blondheim, Menahem: Director of the Harry S. Truman Institute for the Advancement of Peace at the Hebrew University of Jerusalem and professor in the departments of history and of communication at HU. He earned his B.A. from Hebrew University and his M.A. and Ph.D. from Harvard University. Among his recent publications are "The Prominence of Weak Economies: Factors and Trends in Global News Coverage of Economic Crisis, 2009-2012"; "Just Spell US Right: America's News Prominence and Soft Power" (both with Elad Segev); and "Reporting Recession in Online-News Worldwide" (with Elad Segev and Maria Angeles Cabrera).

Foscolos, E. Anthony: Professor Emeritus at the Technical University of Crete and Emeritus Research Scientist at the Geological Survey of Canada. He is a mentor in the field of Inorganic and Organic Geochemistry and Organic Petrology at the Department of Mineral Resources Engineering at the Technical University of Crete. Mr. Foscolos has produced in his career 84 scientific publications in peer review journals (citation Index 338). He participated in 41 International and National Conferences with presentations and posters and has authored 14 Technical Reports for the Public Petroleum Corporation of Greece (DEP-EKY), the Public Power Corporation of Greece, S.A. (DEH), the Institute of Mineral Exploration, Greece (IGME) and the United Nations.

Kamenopoulos, Sotiris: Holds a Doctorate from the Technical University of Crete, Greece, School of Mineral Resources Engineering. He is a Professional Engineer (Production & Management Engineering, Technical University of Crete, Greece). The main focus of his PhD research is on the sustainable development of mineral resource mining projects and especially of Rare Earth Elements.

Karbuz, Sohbet. Dr. Karbuz currently works at Mediterranean Observatory for Energy (OME). Before joining the OME in 2004, he was with the International Energy Agency in Paris for seven years. Previously, he worked as research associate and manager at several institutions in Austria, Germany and

Turkey. He received his Bachelor of Science and Masters of Science degrees in industrial engineering from Istanbul Technical University, his PhD degree in econometrics and operations research from the Technical University of Vienna and Postgraduate Diploma in economics from the Institute for Advanced Studies in Vienna. His main areas of interests are oil and natural gas markets, geopolitics of energy, energy security, energy modeling and scenario analysis.

Maoz, Moshe: Prof. Emeritus, Islamic and Middle Eastern studies, Hebrew University in Jerusalem. He holds Bachelor of Science and Master degrees from the Hebrew University and Ph.D. from Oxford University in Islamic and Middle Eastern History. He has published 20 books and 65 articles on various aspects of Middle Eastern and Islamic history, politics and society, notably Syria, religious and ethnic communities, Arab-Israel and Muslim-Jewish relations and the Palestinian problem.

Nachmani, Amikam: Professor at the Department of Political Studies, Bar Ilan University, Israel, and the *Patterson Chair for Mediterranean Studies* there. He holds a Ph.D. from Oxford University. His research and publications cover subjects such as culture and society of the East-Mediterranean (Greece, Turkey and Cyprus in particular), water shortage, civil wars, gender and nationalism, rape and war, ethnicity, the role of the military in Mediterranean and Middle-Eastern countries. Nachmani's publications include eleven books and close to eighty articles and book chapters in English, Greek and Hebrew. His latest publications include "Middle Eastern Intellectual Correspondence: Jacob Talmon and Arnold Toynbee Revisited," Israel Affairs, Vol. 20/3, July 2014, pp. 370 – 398; "Israel, Turkey and Greece: Dramatic Changes in the Eastern Mediterranean," in Colin Shindler (Ed.), *Israel and the World Powers. Diplomatic Alliances and International Relations beyond the Middle East*, London, I.B. Tauris, 2014, Chapter 11, pp. 264 – 288;

Stergiou, Andreas: Historian and Political Scientist, Assistant Professor in the Department of Economics, University of Thessaly (Volos-Greece). He has studied in Greece, Germany and the United States. He was Visiting Research Fellow at the Truman Institute for the Advancement of Peace of the Hebrew University in 2013 and Research Affiliate 2014-2015 (academic year) at the same Institute as well as at the *Institute of World Economy and International Relations of the Russian Academy of Sciences (IMEMO)* in Moscow in September 2015. He has published in Modern European History and Politics in French, English, Greek, German and Portuguese.

Tziarras, Zenonas: Associate Lecturer in Security & Diplomacy Studies at the University of Central Lancashire Cyprus. He holds a doctorate in Politics and International Studies from the University of Warwick, UK. He specializes in International Relations, Turkish foreign policy, Security Studies and the international politics of the Middle East and Eastern Mediterranean. Among other things, he has taught Greek-Turkish Relations as well as Strategic & War Studies at the University of Cyprus. His latest book (co-authored with Nikos Moudouros) is titled, *Turkey in the Eastern Mediterranean: Ideological Aspects of Foreign Policy* [In Greek].

Ulusoy, Kıvanç: Professor of Political Science at the Istanbul University. He was previously a Fulbright Fellow at the Harvard Kennedy School (2012-2013), a Jean Monnet Fellow at the Robert Schuman Centre for Advanced Studies at the European University Institute in Florence (2003 2004) and a fellow at the Madrid Diplomatic School (1996-1997). His areas of research include regime change and democratization, Turkish politics and Turkey-EU relations. Some of his recent publications are "The Changing Challenge of Europeanization to Politics and Governance in Turkey," International Political Science Review, Vol. 30, No. 3, (November 2009); "Elections and Regime Change in Turkey: Tenacious Rise of Political Islam", M. Hamad and K. al-Anani (eds) *Elections and Democratization in the Middle East: The Tenacious Search for Freedom, Justice and Dignity*, (New York: Palgrave Macmillan, 2014); Cyprus Conflict: Turkey's Strategic Dilemma", *Journal of Balkan and Near Eastern Studies*, 2016, 18 (4): 393-406.

Rauf, Versan: Professor of Public International Law at Istanbul University since 2001. He holds a B.A. from the Law Faculty at the Istanbul University and LL.B, and Ph.D. in International Law from the Cambridge University. He was Research Fellow at the Max Planck Institute for Comparative Public Law and International Law and Judge Ad-Hoc at the European Court of Human Rights.

www.ingramcontent.com/pod-product-compliance
Lightning Source LLC
Chambersburg PA
CBHW042055290426
44111CB00001B/15